Becoming Orgasmic

Becoming Orgasmic

A SEXUAL AND PERSONAL GROWTH PROGRAM FOR WOMEN

Revised and Expanded Edition

JULIA R. HEIMAN, Ph.D.
JOSEPH LoPICCOLO, Ph.D.

Drawings by David Palladini

PRENTICE HALL PRESS • NEW YORK

Published in 1988 by Prentice Hall Press
A Division of Simon & Schuster, Inc.
Gulf+Western Building
One Gulf+Western Plaza
New York, NY 10023

PRENTICE HALL PRESS is a registered trademark of Simon & Schuster, Inc.

Originally published in 1976 by Prentice-Hall, Inc.
Technical and anatomical illustrations by Leonard Preston

Library of Congress Cataloging-in-Publication Data

Heiman, Julia.
Becoming orgasmic.

Bibliography: p.
Includes index.
1. Sex instruction for women. 2. Orgasm, Female.
3. Sex (Psychology) 4. Women—Psychology. I. LoPiccolo,
Joseph. II. Title. [DNLM: 1. Orgasm—popular works.
2. Sex Manuals. 3. Women—popular works. HQ 46 H467b]
HQ46.H43 1987   613.9′6   87-19139
ISBN 0-13-072711-3

Manufactured in the United States of America

Contents

The G-spot and you.
Strengthening your vaginal muscles.

———— &c ————
Contents
vii

Genital-size concerns.
Advantages and disadvantages of different positions
    for intercourse.
Coital orgasm—is it worth it?
New approaches to try if coital orgasm is important.

Acknowledgments

Many people have contributed to this book. Carl Thoreson, editor of a self-management series of books, and Lynne Lumsden, our first editor, were both very helpful. Coauthor Leslie LoPiccolo and illustrator Leonard Preston were central to the development and warmth of the first edition. PJ Dempsey, our current editor, and David Palladini, our new illustrator, were valuable contributors to the new perspective created in this revised edition. Jan Woodford provided critical and polished typed drafts. The illustrations showing the male and female sexual response cycles are adapted from *Human Sexual Response*, by William H. Masters, M.D., and Virginia E. Johnson, 1966, with the permission of Little, Brown and Company, Boston.

Finally, we would like to thank the many women with whom we have worked using this program. While the program has benefited them, they have also taught us a great deal.

Introduction

If the tone of this book is confident, it is because the program it describes has demonstrated its effectiveness with many different women over the past seventeen years. Many of the procedures described in this book were first developed by Joseph LoPiccolo at the University of Oregon in 1969. Of course, no therapy procedure is ever generated out of thin air. Several other therapists had previously done work that contributed much to this program. In particular, therapy procedures developed by such early behavioral and cognitive therapists as Arnold Lazarus, Joseph Wolpe, and Albert Ellis formed a general theoretical background for this program. The knowledge of human sexuality contributed by such sex researchers as Albert Kinsey, Donald Hastings, William Masters, and Virginia Johnson was also a crucial element in creating this program.

In the years since 1969, we have developed and refined this program in a number of settings and with a number of students and colleagues. At the University of Oregon, W. Charles Lobitz, then a graduate student and now a respected colleague, greatly aided the development of the program. In 1974, Joseph LoPiccolo moved to the Department of Psychiatry at the State University of New York, Stony Brook. At Stony Brook, Julia R. Heiman, who was already engaged in research on female sexuality, joined the program and added her unique skills and abilities. The chairman of the psychiatry department, Dr. Stanley F. Yolles, was very supportive of our development of a sex therapy center in the department and encouraged our work in the area in a number of ways. As all things must end, we both eventually moved on—Julia Heiman to the University of Washington in Seattle and Joseph LoPiccolo to become chairman of the department of psychology at the University of Missouri. Over the years, then, we have had the opportunity to work with hundreds of women in different parts of the country, using this program.

By 1975 it was clear that the program worked. Individual or couple sex therapy, however, was reaching only a small percentage of the women who could potentially benefit from a program such as ours. It became apparent that an easily understood self-help version of this program would be useful for those women who could benefit from such help without the need for formal therapy. Sharing personal reactions gained from women who had participated in the therapy program over the past several years seemed to be of particular importance. Ideas began to take form, and the result was the first edition of this book, written by Julia R. Heiman, Leslie LoPiccolo, and Joseph LoPiccolo in 1976. Around the same time, we also created a film (also titled *Becoming Orgasmic*) showing a couple progressing through the program. At Stony Brook, Patricia J. Morokoff, a graduate student in psychology, collaborated with us on a research project on the self-help use of this program. In this study, one group of women basically treated themselves, using this book. Another group of women used the book but also received fifteen weekly psychotherapy sessions with one of our staff. To our surprise (and delight), the self-treatment group was just as successful in reaching orgasm as the psychotherapy group. In both groups about 90 percent of the women were able to learn to have orgasm in masturbation. Around 80 percent of the women learned to have orgasm with their male partners, and about 35 percent of the women learned to have orgasm during intercourse. In addition, over 95 percent became more satisfied overall with their sexual relationships. These figures are quite impressive compared to other treatment studies, and to studies of the sexuality of healthy, well adjusted women. Put most simply, the program described in this book works.

In the years since the original edition of this book was published, we have learned much more about female sexuality and its problems. Some of this knowledge has come through academic research, both our own and that done by others. Additional knowledge has come from our experience in working with women. This new edition incorporates our new knowledge and also extends the focus of this book. Some of the major changes we have made in this edition include:

- A broader focus than just reaching orgasm
- A new section on problems of lack of sexual desire and suggestions for dealing with this problem
- New sections on aging, menopause, pregnancy, contraception, hormones, and other physical issues in female sexuality
- A new section on the aftermath of rape or incest and suggestions for overcoming any traumatic effects suffered as a result

- Three new techniques for reaching orgasm during intercourse
- A review of new ideas about female sexuality, such as the "G-spot" controversy
- More focus on relationships and emotional conflict and how these issues influence sexuality

1
Getting Involved

Where are you at this particular time in your life? You may be single, married, separated, divorced, or widowed. You may have several children or none at all. You may or may not be involved in a sexual relationship with someone. You may be under thirty, over sixty, or somewhere in between. There may be many difficulties in your life right now, or things may be pretty satisfying.

All of us, wherever we are in our lives, have emotional needs for closeness, intimacy, affection, and sexual gratification. While for most of us our emotional needs are more important than sexual gratification, even the strongest of emotional relationships can be disrupted by sexual problems. For many women, inability to become fully aroused and inability to experience orgasm are major sources of personal frustration and relationship distress. This book is designed to help you address these problems.

As you begin to look through this book you will probably have mixed feelings. Perhaps you are wondering if this book really is for you. You may be worried about whether or not you will get everything you want from it. On the other hand, you may feel unsure about exactly what you do want for yourself sexually or whether you are putting too much emphasis on sex as a problem. You may feel enthusiastic—or very hesitant—about beginning. Perhaps you are tempted to find a magic formula for changing. One thing we are fairly certain of is that you probably feel you want something different for yourself. You want to grow and explore your potentials, and you see the enhancement of your sexuality as part of this exploration.

That's why we refer to this book as a sexual and personal growth program. Specifically, this program is designed to help women who have not yet experienced or who have difficulty experiencing orgasm. We have developed the contents of the book from successfully treating, in sex therapy, numerous women with a variety of problems, fears, and potentials.

Orgasm is certainly a satisfying aspect of sexual growth. And

1

yet, as you proceed through the following chapters, you will find that orgasms are not an isolated part of your sexuality. Orgasmic response depends on many things. Of course, it depends on sexual arousal, but feeling sexual can be influenced by your ability to feel comfortable with yourself, with your ideas about sex, and with your ideas about men and women. Thus, growing sexually has a lot to do with general personal growth. This book offers you a framework for learning more about your sexual feelings, changing those that *you* choose to change, and deciding how you want your sexuality to continue to develop and fit into the rest of your life.

Perhaps you've already read books and magazine articles on sexuality, and you've tried to make changes. You may have even attempted to put into practice certain ideas of your own that you thought would help.

It's important to remind yourself that as recently as twenty-five years ago, orgasms were not considered to be very important to women's sexual enjoyment, though they were considered to be directly linked to more general personality qualities. Thus, a nonorgasmic woman was likely to be labeled "frigid," implying a pervasive problem—something quite deeply wrong and automatically requiring extensive therapy. Then, beginning around the 1960s, these views were challenged and a new standard appeared, this time fostering a supersexual image: Orgasm is a *must.* As a result, in order to feel sexually adequate, many women began to feel pressured to be instantly, regularly, or even multiply orgasmic.

Women we've seen in sex therapy often come to us feeling like failures because the sexual techniques they'd tried didn't work for them. Perhaps you've felt at times that if you could just do things the *right* way, you'd be orgasmic. It's natural to feel this way at times, to put pressure on yourself—to try harder. However, doing this makes orgasm practically impossible. Rather than looking forward to and enjoying sex, you may find yourself wanting to avoid it or getting it over with as soon as possible. There may have been times when you've faked an orgasm in order to protect your self-image and your partner's opinion of you.

We hope that reading this book will help you take the pressure off yourself. We have tried to make this experience more than just a conglomeration of techniques. Sexual growth is not a series of steps or techniques toward a goal. It is a process that involves all of you. It involves your attitudes, thoughts, and feelings as well as your body. Learning to become orgasmic or more readily orgasmic is only

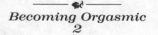

a part of the process of lifelong sexual development. However, it is likely that you have some specific concerns about changes you want to make. We'd like to share with you a few of the questions that women more frequently have.

Will I ever have an orgasm? If you've never experienced orgasm, it's natural for you to worry that you may never have one. One woman in therapy said, "I used to go to parties and look at the other women. I would be sure that I was the only one there who couldn't have an orgasm." Actually, the fact that you may not have had an orgasm yet is not unusual. Currently, about 15 to 20 percent of the cases seen in sex therapy involve women who have never experienced orgasm. An even greater percentage of cases involve women who are orgasmic but who experience difficulty reaching orgasm some of the time or are unable to have orgasms with their sexual partners.

Many factors may be influencing why you haven't yet experienced (or rarely experience) orgasm. For instance, your family's religious and moral values may have strongly shaped your own attitudes about sex. Your positive or negative feelings about yourself as a person and as a sexual being may be conflicting with your attempts to feel more sexually satisfied. Your feelings about your present or past relationships with men, both on emotional and sexual levels, are likely to be important. How comfortable you are with your body and how familiar you are with sexual responsiveness and techniques may also influence whether or not, and how often, you are orgasmic. And there are also other possibilities, many of which we will discuss in the following chapters. It is possible to deal with those attitudes and feelings that are making it hard for you to experience orgasm. You can learn things about yourself and your sexuality that will make orgasm possible.

What will it mean to be orgasmic? Change usually involves some uncertainty, and you may be concerned about the changes that becoming orgasmic may make in your life.

Many women have concerns of this sort, which often reflect mixed feelings about being a sexual woman. Movies and books typically present female sexuality in ways that have an unappealing edge: the message that the sexy woman is at best not worthy of respect and at worst evil and dangerous.

Also, our parents, who serve as models in so many areas, often hide their own sexuality from us. (Do you remember being surprised

when you realized that your parents had intercourse?) Unfortunately, then, women often grow up with very few models for female sexuality whom they respect and want to be like.

So it's not surprising that you may feel some conflict about wanting to change sexually. Most women share some of these feelings. Right now, it is important for you to trust yourself enough to begin to explore who you are and where you might want to change. Becoming orgasmic will *not* make you into a different person in terms of your basic sexual values and moral beliefs. What becoming orgasmic *will* do is facilitate a more rewarding expression of your basic sexual and emotional feelings and needs.

Will becoming orgasmic improve my relationships with men (or with my partner or husband)? If your relationship is a good one, you will probably find that becoming orgasmic will give you a more complete sense of pleasure and satisfaction from sex. However, becoming more sexually responsive or orgasmic will probably not improve other serious conflicts in the relationship. Sometimes it's difficult to gauge the degree to which problems in the sexual area affect a couple's other problems. One way to begin sorting this out is to ask yourself: If sex were no problem, would there still be other serious conflicts in our relationship?

Also, try thinking about your reasons for wanting to become orgasmic. Do you want to learn to enjoy your body and its responses for *yourself* or for the pleasure it can give your partner? You stand a much better chance of reaching your personal goals if you are attempting to grow because of your care for *yourself* first and your care for someone else later. Learning to understand and have some influence over your body enables you to begin to enjoy sex for the sensory and emotional experiences it can provide you. This involves taking responsibility for your own sexuality, something we will talk about in more depth later on.

GUIDELINES FOR USING THIS BOOK

This book was designed so that you can use it in the way that is best for you. The first part of the book (chapters 2–8) deals with exercises and learning experiences you can do on your own. The second part (chapters 9–13) deals with how to improve your sexual relationship with your partner. Each chapter builds on the information and exer-

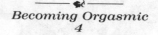

cises in the preceding chapters. For this reason it's best that you begin with chapter 1 and progress through the chapters, trying the exercises in the order they are suggested. Some of the exercises are optional, and at certain points you will be able to skip ahead or go back to previous exercises so that you can progress in the way that is most meaningful to you. If you are already orgasmic, we still suggest you read through *all* the chapters and try the exercises. Changing old patterns, examining your attitudes and feelings, and having some new learning experiences are equally important for you. The material in the chapters will help you do this.

We've included lots of information about sex, particularly about female sexuality, as well as comments that women have made, and common thoughts, fears, or experiences. Often we give you some questions to think about—questions that have been helpful to others. These are questions that we found are important to ask the women we have seen and are now seeing in sex therapy. We hope that they will help you get as much as possible out of each chapter. Doing the various exercises is important, but your personal reactions to the experiences are especially meaningful for your growth. Sexuality involves your thoughts and feelings as well as your body, and change comes from exploring new ways to think and feel as well as new things to do with your body.

Each exercise requires that you have some time to yourself— time when you can be assured of privacy and are free of any responsibilities (at least temporarily). A good idea is to set aside an hour or so for each exercise when you can be sure you will be undisturbed by business, children, friends, the phone, or your partner. If you have children, you might want to take advantage of times when they are in school or in bed. Exchanging baby sitting with a friend or neighbor on a regular basis has worked for some women. If you have a partner or spouse, ask his help in making these individual sessions possible.

Take your time, and read each section through before doing the exercises described. Become familiar enough with what you will be doing so you don't have to keep referring to the book as you do a particular activity. Try to think about the questions at the end of the suggested activities while your reactions are fresh in your mind.

We suggest the amount of time you should spend on each exercise and also the number of times to try each during the week. You may find you need more or less time than we suggest. That's fine. What's important is to find a comfortable rate of progress. At the beginning, plan on around four to nine weeks for chapters 2–8 and three to six weeks for chapters 9–13. Try to have at least three individual sessions a week when you try the exercises in the book and practice what you've learned. You may find that unforeseen circumstances interfere at times. That happens. Try as much as you can to keep up some sort of schedule for this program. This is important because of the nature of what you'll be learning and exploring. Each new experience builds on previous ones and makes learning easier. Also, at times you may be tempted to give in to the part of you that resists further change. You will find that having a schedule for progress gives you a little push to help overcome these natural fears about changing.

You are not every woman. You are yourself. You will have your own unique process of sexual growth. Some of the exercises we describe may benefit you a great deal, some may not, and others may initially sound simplistic and even silly. Laugh about them, but try them, too—we've seen women make unexpected discoveries.

Some suggestions may sound easy—for example, taking a personal sexual history. Yet you may find that you postpone trying it or, when you do try it, that you feel somewhat irritable and want to stop. On those exercises with which you may find it too uncomfortable to proceed, we will be giving you specific ideas about what you can do. Two general guidelines that you will find helpful when confronted with an impasse are: First, accept your response, do not judge it. Your negative response is an honest one and is there for a reason; to blame yourself is a waste of energy and self-defeating. Second, get acquainted with, rather than avoid, the negative feelings that are behind your negative reaction. You may need to name the feeling (is it anger? fear? shame?) first and then examine it (where in your experience does it come from? what memories or fantasies are tied to it?).

The shift we want to encourage within you is away from the critic who chants, "What's wrong with you, how have you failed this time?" and toward the curious explorer who asks, "That's interesting, what's going on here?"

We've mentioned that anticipating change can be frightening because it means interrupting comfortable, predictable (although often unsatisfying) patterns and risking potential disappointment as well as potential satisfaction. Change is also irregular. If you have ever tried to change other areas of your life—by dieting, learning how to dance, learning how to talk in front of a group of people, teaching yourself to be better at ice-skating, swimming, or tennis—you have probably found that improvement occurs with stops and starts. To prevent giving up during the difficult moments, it is important not to expect huge changes all at once. Growth, whether physical or emotional, is a series of small and uneven steps, so it's important to enjoy each small change, experience it fully, and resist the temptation to devalue the change and yourself by worrying about how much further you have to go. It's very important to acknowledge whatever gains you make and to take credit for them.

Relax. Give yourself time. The exercises, questions, and learning experiences we've included in this book are not tests of your ability that you can either pass or fail. Rather, they give you a chance to learn about yourself in ways that can not only enrich the sensual-sexual aspect of your life but other areas of your life as well.

Before you go on and actually begin the program, we'd like to recommend strongly that you have a gynecological exam if you haven't had one in the last year. This type of exam (also called a *pelvic*) should reveal certain physical problems that, if they are present, may be interfering with your enjoyment of sex. It is currently recommended by most doctors that women have such a checkup every one to two years. This is important for your general health as well. At this time, a Pap smear (a test for early detection of cervical cancer) is routinely done. A breast examination is also given, though we (and most physicians) recommend that you do this yourself each month after your period. Chapter 9 provides several self-help guidelines that explain how to do a breast exam if you do not already know.

IF YOU HAVE A SEXUAL PARTNER . . .

Because a sexual relationship involves two people, the sexual responsiveness of your partner can influence your own responsiveness. (Given the focus of our clinical experience and research, we will discuss only the issues pertaining to heterosexual couples.)

If your partner has difficulties getting or maintaining an erection, or ejaculates before you have sufficient time to get aroused, this can directly influence whether or not you are orgasmic. If these problems are a common part of your sexual experiences together, you should consider getting some additional sex therapy in order to work on them (see chapter 14). However, you can progress through the first part of this book (chapters 1–8) on your own.

If male functioning is not a problem, you are probably wondering about how to integrate the learning experiences you will be having on your own into your sexual relationship with your partner. There are several ways in which others have done this that we'd like to offer you.

Both of you should think and talk about these alternatives and make a decision about which ones you feel would work for you.

First, a general way in which some couples have shared this growth experience is that the male partner read through and tried some of the exercises on his own. For example, exercises on body exploration, thinking about feelings and attitudes, and self-pleasuring could be done by him, too. Often men are surprised to find that they have something to gain from such exploration.

In our sex therapy work with couples in the last few years, we have routinely asked the male partners to participate in the program in this way. While this active participation by the partner does seem to be helpful in many cases, it is not crucial. If your partner is not interested in participating actively, don't insist on it. A good discussion with him about the issues involved in your sexual growth, and his support of this growth, are the most important aspects of his participation. Going through a process similar to what his partner is going through often enables a man to be more understanding and supportive of her. Some men, however, have trouble being sympathetic, since to them it doesn't seem difficult to have orgasms. Whether or not your partner makes an effort to understand your attempts to change, we would like to caution him not to interfere, not to be critical, and not to try to direct or advise you himself. Some reassurance from him will make changes easier, but his help is not essential for you to make some progress on your own. Later, when you try these sexual activities together, his cooperation will be vital.

In terms of your sexual activities together, one possibility is for you to continue having sex with your partner as you've done in the past, while you individually progress through the growth program. This usually works best for couples whose sex life is enjoyable for both of them and who have no major sexual problems except for the woman's difficulty in experiencing orgasm. For some couples, though, feelings of frustration and pressure to have orgasm have disrupted or replaced feelings of pleasure in sex. When this happens, one or both partners may find sex unpleasant and try to avoid it or get it over with as soon as possible. These feelings are understandable. However, continuing unpleasant sexual activity while you are involved in learning to become orgasmic can interfere with your progress. This makes sense if you think about any new way of feeling or behaving. At these times, in order to feel motivated and encouraged to keep changing, you need a chance to have many good, positive experiences, with no constant reminders of unpleasant old habits.

Try to evaluate how the continuation of sexual activity with your partner will affect your ability to make progress sexually through this growth program. Ask yourself about the quality of your sexual experiences together. Are they mostly positive and enjoyable, or are they negative and unpleasant for you? Will you feel pressured to have an orgasm or to give your partner an orgasm during lovemaking sessions? Are you tempted to continue sex with your partner because you're worried about how he would feel about not having sex (including intercourse) for a while?

Both of you need to consider your feelings about this latter possibility. Discontinuing old sexual patterns that have been harmful or unpleasant is the second alternative that has worked for some couples. In most sex therapy clinics, couples are usually asked to refrain from intercourse for a while so that new sexual attitudes and experiences can be explored. "Banning" such sexual activities as intercourse does not have to mean you can't be physical with your partner. Rather, through a series of sensual massage experiences, you can begin to rediscover the enjoyment of sexual expression or feelings without pressure to have intercourse. We shall describe the kinds of sensual activities that you can do a little later in this chapter. For now, we would just like you to consider this as a possibility.

Leaving intercourse out of sex can be a new experience. For many couples, making love has always meant intercourse and, at least for the male, orgasm. Not expecting or demanding this allows you to explore a fuller range of sensual pleasures that can be neglected in the "rush" to go on to intercourse and orgasm. This pattern can be destructive to your sexual enjoyment because you become focused on where you are going rather than on the pleasure of each moment. It's not surprising that couples who have been in a sexual relationship more than a few years often complain that sex between them was better earlier in their relationship. The fact that some of the novelty may have worn off is usually only part of the difference. There is also a tendency for couples to stop doing some of the enjoyable sexual things they used to do together. In the beginning of their relationship, many couples spend more time on sexual play than on intercourse. Once married, when "real" sex is okay, making love can easily become a pattern of hurried foreplay, quick intercourse, and ejaculation. The pleasures of touching, kissing, caressing, and fondling each other somehow get forgotten. Restricting or refraining from intercourse is one way to allow yourselves time to rediscover each other through the sensual experiences.

Yet the idea of not having intercourse, or of not having your male partner have an orgasm in your sexual activities together, may seem impossible right now. The difficulties most couples encounter are in trying to deal with the man's feelings of sexual frustration and the woman's feelings of guilt. Over time, many women who are seldom or never orgasmic find that they do enjoy feeling close and participating in their partner's pleasure during intercourse. By not having intercourse, especially for several weeks, you may feel bad about not responding in this way. Think about your own feelings, and talk with your partner to find out his feelings and attitudes. During your sensual experiences together, we stress the importance of not trying to get sexually aroused. At times, however, your partner may become aroused, want to go on to intercourse, and find it frustrating not to be able to do so.

There are several things you can do if this situation occurs. Some men are able to adjust to the idea of no intercourse. They know that it's temporary, and they understand that in the long run it will be the most beneficial way for their partner to make her own sexual progress and for their sexual life together to improve. Other men find that they feel less frustrated if they have a physical outlet, such as masturbation. Since couples often have conflicting feelings about masturbation, we'd like to spend a few minutes talking about it. Although much of the discussion applies to both partners, for now we are concentrating on the male, since in later chapters we will discuss further issues related to women.

Almost all males and a majority of females masturbate at some time during their lives. Typically, males masturbate more frequently during their teens and prior to marriage, but a fairly large percentage of men continue to masturbate after marriage. Although we are all familiar with the tales of the ill effects of masturbation, we now know that masturbation is a normal and healthy pattern of sexual expression. In fact, research has shown masturbation to be beneficial to adequate sexual functioning, especially among women (more on this later). Unfortunately, most men and women grow up feeling very guilty and ashamed that they masturbate. It was something that was hidden from parents and usually from friends, too, for fear that it would be punished or ridiculed by others. If you, and here we are speaking to the male partner, still have some negative feelings about masturbation, it is not surprising. Or if you have been masturbating and don't feel bad about it but find it difficult to mention to your partner, that's not unusual either. Sharing your thoughts about masturbation may be easier after you finish this chapter, since we will give you a framework of ideas to think over. For now, what we are most interested in having you consider are the *benefits* of masturba-

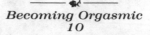

tion for you while your partner is progressing through her own sexual learning experiences.

1. The freedom to masturbate when you feel the desire to do so will allow you to enjoy your pleasuring sessions with your partner without feeling physically frustrated and emotionally resentful.

2. Your willingness to find some sexual pleasure and release by masturbating will tend to take pressure off your partner. She will not have to feel guilty about not having intercourse, since you are trying to cooperate in improving her chances of making changes. If you want to help her change, it is only going to be possible if you take a share in reducing any pressures she feels. Worries about pleasing you will keep your partner from focusing on and really enjoying her own pleasurable feelings. Being able to do this is crucial for a woman who is learning to become orgasmic.

3. Not having to focus on arousal and orgasm takes pressure off you also. Rather than trying to "give" your partner an orgasm and have one yourself, you are free simply to enjoy what you're feeling. We suspect that you will discover some new information about your sexuality, too. We have seen many men surprise themselves in learning that a sensual experience without intercourse or orgasm can be very satisfying and enjoyable.

Sometimes one partner interprets the other's masturbation as a rejection or as an indication that their sexual relationship is a failure. If you, the woman, feel this way, it will make it hard for you to help your partner deal with his sexual needs and feelings. You may give a mixed message to your partner: He should not have to feel frustrated by not having intercourse, but at the same time, you are leaving him no alternative ways to achieve physical pleasure. In trying to work out this conflict, it will be important for you to talk over your own feelings with your partner. In turn, he could make an effort to reassure you that masturbating is a positive expression of his sexuality rather than a negative reflection on your relationship. How do you both feel about this? You both may have to rethink some of your own attitudes about different patterns of sexuality. Whatever you work out, keep in mind that a solution should maximize satisfaction and freedom to learn new patterns for both of you. That will probably involve some compromises and understanding on both sides.

Remember, too, that the male partner does not *have* to masturbate, particularly if he doesn't want to, in order to decrease physical arousal. Instead, he may be able to adjust temporarily and without frustration to moments of sexual tension. We have seen this happen with men who are able to accept the situation (since it is temporary) and who simultaneously derive a great deal of pleasure from their *sensual* experiences with their partners.

There is a third option for sexual activity while the woman is progressing through this program, but again, it is one that needs to be discussed fully between the two of you. This third option is for the woman to give sexual gratification to the man, without (temporarily) the requirement that she also be aroused and gratified sexually. This option works best when the man finds solitary masturbation unsatisfying and the woman genuinely enjoys bringing the man to orgasm, provided she is not also pressured to become aroused and orgasmic herself. If this pattern describes your relationship, your couple sessions might involve mutual kissing, caressing, and body massage and the woman then caressing the man's genitals to orgasm. While this pattern can work to reduce pressure for intercourse from the male, it can interfere with the woman's progress unless she finds the experience of providing orgasm for the man to be a pleasurable form of giving. Certainly, if she feels coerced to provide this gratification for him, growth in her ability to enjoy sex for herself will be disrupted.

Here are three alternative patterns you might decide on as you proceed:

1. Continue sexual experiences as before. This option should be chosen only if the sexual experiences are comfortable and pleasurable for *both* partners.
2. Discontinue intercourse temporarily, or any activity that is uncomfortable or unpleasant for either partner.
3. Discontinue intercourse, any unpleasant activities, and the pressure for the woman to be aroused and orgasmic. Under this option, however, the woman continues to give pleasure sexually to the man.

A fourth pattern combines these three. In other words, if what you do together sexually is not unpleasant for either of you but is generally enjoyable, you may choose to continue this during the first part (chapters 2–8) of this growth program. That will involve anywhere from one to nine weeks or so. When you are ready to begin the part of the book that involves both of you, you should then refrain from intercourse and follow the sequence of exercises described in chapters 9–13. You will also be able to include some of the sensual massage experiences.

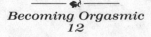

An important consideration when including intercourse in your sexual experiences together is whether or not to use a contraceptive. This, of course, is a personal decision, one that should take into account your feelings as well as current medical knowledge about the effectiveness and the potential drawbacks and dangers of the different forms of contraception (see *The New Our Bodies Ourselves* in the bibliography).

If you are premenopausal and don't use contraception, there is a possibility that fears of becoming pregnant will interfere with your enjoyment of sex. If you feel this may be true for you, you need to reevaluate your feelings about contraception, unless strong personal or religious beliefs prevent you from considering it. If you do use contraception, it is best to use a method that you feel comfortable with and that best meets your physical needs.

SENSUAL MASSAGE

Both of you are probably missing a lot of the good feelings that touching different parts of your body can provide. The massage exercises we describe are called *sensual* because they encourage you to appreciate more than just sexual or genital feelings. There is no real difference between "sensual" and "sexual," of course, but we would like you to attune yourselves to feelings other than genital ones and mutually pleasurable activities other than sexual ones, such as intercourse or oral-genital sex. We will not elaborate on any particular massage techniques, but we have listed in the bibliography some massage books that couples in sex therapy have used with good results. What we want to outline for you are the general principles of a sensuous massage, with specific hints to help you experience as much satisfaction as possible. Feel free to expand on whatever you learn here.

1. First, set a mood for your massage. You can make the atmosphere as relaxed or romantic as is agreeable to both of you. Make sure the room temperature is comfortable for being nude together and that the light is not too glaring—candles or dimmed lights are especially nice. Put on relaxing music if you like.

2. Choose a time of day when you can have privacy and uninterrupted time together (thirty minutes to one hour, if possible). You

may want to do this just before you go to sleep, but watch out for fatigue—it can make you edgy and decrease your ability to enjoy this experience.

3. Try to spend a little time together before you begin. You may want to talk or have a glass of wine. Or try sharing a shower or bath together first.

4. The main purpose of this experience is to increase your pleasure and awareness of your partner's response to physical—but not necessarily genital—stimulation. You will be taking turns caressing, stroking, and rubbing different areas of each other's bodies. Although you may find yourself becoming aroused, this is not the goal, and you shouldn't *try* for arousal. The first few times you do this, we would like you to massage any areas *except* the genitals and the woman's breasts. Explore the toes, feet, thighs, tummy, arms, face, hair, and buttocks. Do this *slowly*—allow at least ten to fifteen minutes for each of you. Remember, this is supposed to be sensuous, not a rubdown, so try light touches as well as strong kneading touches. Use your palms, fingertips, or fingernails; pieces of material or fur; or your lips or hair.

Do not massage each other simultaneously—it's impossible to experience a massage as intensely as you might if each person takes turns.

5. As you take turns, it's important to *talk to each other* about what feels good and what doesn't. The person being massaged should try to say what he or she is feeling, such as, "Good, harder, easy, use your nails more, go slower, mmm," or, "Yes, that's great," fairly often in order for the person massaging to be able to give the most pleasurable stimulation. The person massaging might say, "How's this?" or "Does it feel better here?" if he or she is unsure about the other's feelings. It's extremely important to communicate your likes and dislikes in a clear way. Communication allows you to give and receive pleasure in personal, more meaningful ways. Everyone has different needs and pleasures, and they change as people change. By letting each other know what feels good, you help make each massage (and later each sexual experience) less routine, more spontaneous, and more intimate.

6. On the third or fourth session together, you can include breast massage, but continue to explore different strokes and touches that each of you likes.

7. Gradually, by the sixth or seventh massage, or whenever you both feel comfortable about it, add each other's genitals into your massaging. (You may want to wait until you are at chapter 9.) Again,

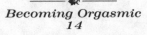

the idea is just to give yourselves pleasure, not arouse each other. When it comes time to include genitals in massage, it is often tempting to zero in on those areas and forget about the rest of the body. This can build anxiety and reduce the total pleasure of the experience. So, when you do begin to explore the touching of genitals, try including them as just another source of pleasure and spend a proportionate amount of your massage time there.

8.   While you are being massaged, try to focus on the feelings at the place where you are being touched: Let your attention remain on those feelings. If your thoughts wander, bring them back to your physical feelings, and follow your partner's touch with your mind. This will help you get more pleasure and relaxation out of the massage. Remember, when you are being massaged, you have no responsibilities except to communicate clearly—verbally or nonverbally—what feels good and what would feel better.

9.   If you find that these sensual massage sessions are not going well (or if they are and you just want to try something different), try changing the focus of your sessions. Instead of focusing on giving your partner pleasure, try massaging in ways that give *you* the most pleasure. The only restriction is that you do not do anything that is painful or in any way distressing to your partner. The partner who is being pleasured is to relax and focus on his or her feelings rather than to guide or direct the massage. Often, people who were anxious or upset while focusing on their partners' pleasure are able to relax and enjoy massaging in this demand-free way.

All of the above suggestions have been useful for other couples. In addition, some couples like to try massaging with different lubricants (oils or lotions, for example) in order to change the friction and texture of the massage. Oils tend to intensify the touches you experience and make your skin feel warmer; lotions tend to make the skin feel cool and are sticky after they dry. Powder is another possibility, and any of the above in some perfumed fragrance can be nice. The genitals are extremely sensitive, so don't use anything except a sterile lubricating gel when massaging them. K-Y and Astroglide are two such lubricants and are available over-the-counter in most drugstores. Explore and find out what's good for *you*.

Keep in mind that if you are in a bad mood, very tired, very distracted, or angry with your partner, it will influence how completely you are able to enjoy sensual massaging. Sometimes you will be able to overcome whatever is bothering you by letting the enjoyment of the moment take over; at other times you may not be able to let go of what's bothering you. If you find that a sensual massage experience isn't pleasurable or is making you feel bad, stop and try to discuss with your partner what is interfering. This gives you a chance to share feelings and to begin to deal with any difficulties.

2
Getting to Know Yourself

Why is it that so many women have problems with sexual responsiveness? As we work with more and more women, we find ourselves pondering this question. No one really knows exactly why some women have no difficulty experiencing orgasm while others do, but we have developed a better understanding of some general factors that might be significant. We'd like to discuss them briefly in the hope that some of our ideas may help you to begin thinking about your own sexual development and to put your own sexuality into perspective.

Certainly, experiences we gather as we grow up influence our feelings and attitudes about sex and our bodies. From the moment we are born, we begin to learn about our bodies. By the time we are adults, we have learned to recognize and have some control over hunger, pain, and fatigue; but often we may have very little knowledge or understanding of, or sense of control over, our sexual functioning. Why? As children, we are usually encouraged to explore and experiment with what we can do with our bodies. We are encouraged in all sorts of ways to learn to use our bodies. For the very young child, for instance, such learning might take the form of a "name game," in which the parent names a part of the body and the child points to it. Success in such games is usually followed by lots of attention and approval. Yet, even in this context of fun and private learning, the genitals are usually not mentioned. A child can interpret this omission in several ways: Perhaps the genitals are unimportant; perhaps they are too bad or dirty to talk about. Exclusion of the genitals as natural parts of the body can begin the process of isolating sexuality from the rest of a person's life experience. Sometimes, however, this message is much clearer. As recently as twenty years ago, books on child rearing encouraged parents to ignore or distract their children when they were found playing with, touching, or fondling their genitals, as this was thought to be harmful.

Many of us probably had learning experiences that suggested that there was something different about our bodies "down there."

Most of us were not encouraged to recognize or explore our genitals, and certainly we were not encouraged to talk about or be proud of them. In fact, many women don't know exactly where the vagina is until after they have begun to menstruate (perhaps you remember trying to figure out how to insert a tampon from a diagram) or after they have had intercourse. Similarly, the clitoris is kept "secret"—until recently most health books used in schools labeled the vagina but made no mention of the clitoris.

Your early experiences with menstruation can also influence your feelings about your body and your sexuality. Many young girls are totally unprepared, and understandably they find the experience of sudden bleeding a very traumatic one. Other women's parents prepare them minimally, but with an attitude that menstruating is a "curse," dirty, or just a burden women have to bear. Having periods is usually regarded as a bother, and their onset is almost never considered a cause for celebration (the very idea seems foreign). Additionally, most of us received very little information about sex when we learned about menstruation. Some basic information on why menstruation occurs, and possibly a warning that "now you can become pregnant," may have been the extent of our introduction to sexuality.

With this learning history, it's not surprising that many of us grow up feeling less positive about our genitals than about other parts of our bodies, and we therefore feel insecure about our sexuality. For some women, the effects of these early experiences contribute to their lack of sexual responsiveness.

How pleasant various experiences were for you while growing up helped to determine your feelings and attitudes regarding your sexuality. Because your background includes certain features that no other person's does, we can't point out the specific events that might most strongly have influenced you. We hope you can begin to do this on your own by remembering situations that occurred with regard to your parents' attitudes toward sex and affection, your first dating and sexual experiences, any frightening experiences with sex, or in your relationships with men.

A good place to begin this growth program is to think about the events in your life that have influenced your feelings and attitudes toward sex. For this reason, we are including a few questions to ask yourself that will help you get a picture of your personal sex history. You may want to write your responses down so that you can refer to them at some later time. If you have a partner, you may want to share some of your answers with him or share some of your early experiences. He may also want to take his own sex history and share this

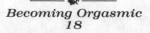

information with you. However you choose to use these questions, they will prove helpful as you begin to put your experiences into perspective. Here are some suggestions for Exercise I: *A Personal Sex History.*

- Take your time on each question. In sex therapy we usually allow up to two hours or so for exploring these types of questions.
- Try to focus on each question as it relates to your feelings or attitudes about yourself or about sex in general.

EXERCISE I: A PERSONAL SEX HISTORY
Part 1: Self-Inquiry

RELIGIOUS INFLUENCES

1. Was religion an active force in your early life (Sunday school, parochial school, and so on)? How important was it to you and your family?
2. In what ways did your religious upbringing influence your attitudes toward sex?
3. How do your religious beliefs *currently* influence your attitude about sex?

AS YOU WERE GROWING UP

1. Were you allowed to ask questions about or to discuss sexual topics?
2. Was physical affection shown between your parents? How were your parents affectionate toward each other?
3. Were your parents verbally or physically affectionate with you?
4. What was the attitude toward nudity (or modesty) in your home?
5. What do you think your parents' attitudes toward sex were:
   a. With each other?
   b. Toward your own developing sexuality?
   c. Regarding the differences between male and female family members?
6. What was your family's attitude toward homosexuality?
7. What influence did your siblings or friends have on what you thought about sex at this time?
   a. Was it ever discussed with friends or siblings?
   b. Was it the subject of jokes and embarrassment?
   c. Was it considered "dirty"?

8. Do you recall playing any games with sexual content as a child (such as "doctor")?
9. At what age do you recall first having genital feelings? Were they pleasurable or exciting?
10. At what age did you first experiment with masturbation (or any other solitary activity that produced genital feelings of pleasure)?
   a. How and where did you do this? How often?
   b. How did you feel about doing this?
   c. Were you ever discovered at this?
   d. In what ways did you explore your own sexuality?
11. Do you remember any upsetting experience having to do with sex that occurred during your childhood?
12. When did you first learn about conception and childbirth?
   a. How did you learn?
   b. How did you react to this?
13. At what age did you start to menstruate?
   a. Had menstruation been explained to you in advance? How and by whom?
   b. Was the subject discussed among your friends? What term(s) did you use to refer to it?
   c. What were your feelings in anticipation of menstruation?
   d. How did you feel after it began?
      1) How do you recall it influencing your life-style?
      2) In what ways did you feel differently about yourself and your body?
   e. What kind of menstrual difficulties, if any, have you had?
14. In terms of closeness and respect, how did you feel toward your mother? Your father?

DATING

1. At what age did you start to date?
   a. In groups?
   b. On single dates?
2. What did you most want out of dating? Popularity? Security? Affection? Sex? Companionship?

TOUCHING (PETTING)

1. What kinds of petting did you engage in?
2. Where did this sexual touching usually occur? Under what circumstances?

3. Was there any genital touching or manipulation involved?
4. How did you respond sexually to this behavior?
5. How did you feel about engaging in this activity? What did you enjoy and not enjoy about them?
6. How would your parents have reacted if they had known? What were their attitudes about petting or other nongenital sexual contact?

INTERCOURSE

1. Did you ever engage in nonmarital intercourse? If so, what was it like the first time?
2. When and where did intercourse usually occur?
3. How did you respond sexually? (Were you aroused? Orgasmic? Did your partner have any problems with erection or premature ejaculation?)
4. Did your parents ever discuss intercourse with you? Contraception?
5. What feelings usually accompanied intercourse?
6. Were you ever suspected or caught?
7. Have you ever had any problems with sexually transmitted diseases such as chlamydia, gonorrhea, or syphilis?
8. What form of contraception do you use, if any? Whose responsibility is this? Do you have any problems related to the type of contraception you're using?
9. Have you ever experienced pain during intercourse? Frequent vaginal infections? Frequent urethral infections?
10. Have you ever had difficulty with penetration? Is the penis unable to enter the vagina because of the tightness of the vaginal muscles?

OTHER EXPERIENCES

1. Did you ever have any sexual fantasies accompany masturbation, petting, or intercourse? If so, are there common themes or images?
2. Do you remember any sexual encounters with a person of the same sex? Have you ever had sexual feelings for women? If so, how did you react to these feelings?
3. Have you ever been tempted to have an affair? Has it happened to you? How did it benefit or harm you or your relationship?
4. Do you remember ever seeing a person expose himself or masturbate in public? How did you react?
5. Did you ever have any unpleasant experiences involving undue physical intimacy with strangers, family members, or friends?

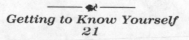

Getting to Know Yourself
21

PREMARITAL BEHAVIOR WITH SPOUSE

1. What were some of the sexual activities you engaged in with your spouse before marriage?
2. Describe the quality of these sexual experiences. How did you respond sexually? Were you aroused, orgasmic, uncomfortable, angry, tense, or afraid?

CURRENT ATTITUDES AND BELIEFS

1. What is your attitude toward sex in general? What specific activities do you find enjoyable? Do you ever feel inhibited, embarrassed, or guilty about any aspects of sex?
2. If your sex life is satisfactory, what does it say to you about the quality of your relationship in general? What if sex is not satisfactory? Where did these beliefs come from?
3. Do you feel positive, negative, or neutral about:
   a. Your genitals?
   b. Masturbation?
   c. Oral-genital sex?
   d. Foreplay?
   e. Intercourse?
   f. Orgasms through means other than intercourse?
   g. Erotic literature?
   h. Pornographic movies?
   i. Sexual fantasies?
4. As you think back over your personal sex history, what would you change if you could? Why would you or wouldn't you?

Part 2: Self-Reflection

You need not come to any conclusions by reflecting on your answers to these questions. They basically afford a brief sketch of what may have been important influences during your life. What you have or have not experienced is less important than how you felt and continue to feel about the experiences. For example, if your parents were not affectionate toward you, did this bother you a great deal or did you just accept it? Whatever strong feelings you gathered in your childhood, adolescence, and early dating may still be with you, influencing how you feel about yourself, other people, relationships, and sex.

In other words, our past experiences are very important in shaping our sensitivities and strengths. However, a major influence determining the impact of past experiences is how we interpret them, what we decide they mean, and to what degree we believe that they are good, bad, or indifferent. For example, a woman may believe during her growing-up years that her mother is cold and unaffectionate and her father is warm and spontaneous. Then, at some point in her twenties, she takes another look at her family and realizes she saw only part of the story: Her father was rarely home, he often drank, he was not so warm and spontaneous with his son, and he could not be counted on to be reliable, while her mother was always there, dependable, distant, but equally fair to each of the children. What changed? Nothing except the daughter's thoughts and beliefs. We all are able to revise some aspects of our personal history—not what happened but our reactions to what happened. You will have several opportunities to do this as you continue this program.

It should not surprise you, then, that there is no particular set of experiences that determines who will and who won't be orgasmic. There is not one type of woman who never or seldom has orgasms. However, there are several kinds of experiences that many women we see have in common. Mentioning them here will give you an idea of how various experiences influence sexual responsiveness.

Many women we have seen come from strict religious backgrounds or from parents with very restrictive morals about sex. Sometimes this means that sex is regarded as dirty, that it is not to be discussed, and that it should never occur outside marriage. Sexual thoughts and activities may have been punished or labeled "sinful." Because of this, some strictly religious women try hard to avoid doing or even thinking anything sexual; other religious women are sexual but are tense while they are having sex and feel very guilty afterward. Many of these conflicts, of course, do not suddenly stop after marriage. It's difficult to let yourself enjoy sex and be responsive if you have experienced years of feeling that chastity was best and sex was not something "nice" women enjoyed. If religious values are an important part of your life, you may be comforted to know that many religious women have no sexual complaints. In fact, in a national survey of 100,000 women, those who were more religious reported greater sexual satisfaction. So religious beliefs themselves do not need to interfere with sexual satisfaction.

For some women, sexual responsiveness is influenced by the nature of their relationship with their partner and his sexual response. For instance, some women would like their mates to be more affectionate in nonsexual ways but find it difficult to tell them so. An equally common problem is that many women would like more foreplay be-

fore intercourse or would like intercourse to last longer. Couples sometimes have difficulty talking about this, and attempts to change sexual patterns often result in disagreements and hurt feelings, something we will discuss more in later chapters.

RESEARCH QUESTIONS AND SURPRISES

No one really knows why some people from a particular background develop sexual difficulties while others from a very similar background do not. We talk about religious factors, as have other therapists including Masters and Johnson, because many of the women we see talk about religion. However, a survey of 100,000 readers of *Redbook* magazine contradicts the notion of religiosity putting a damper on sexual satisfaction. Religious women were only slightly more reluctant than nonreligious women to masturbate and to try oral sex. And religious wives were more orgasmic, equal in intercourse frequency, and happier and more satisfied with their sex lives than the study's nonreligious wives. Keep in mind that a *Redbook* reader is not necessarily representative of you, of women in general, or of religious women who may feel too inhibited to fill out a questionnaire. The same goes for satisfied women who are not religious. The *Redbook* results do tell us that for some women—perhaps for many—it is possible to combine strong religious feelings and sexual happiness. (Tavris, C., and Sadd, S. *The Redbook Report on Female Sexuality.* NY: Delacorte Press, 1975.)

Another study, in the *New England Journal of Medicine*, by Frank, Anderson, and Rubenstein, also contains a bit of a surprise. In this study, 100 happily married couples were asked about their sexual relationships. The results showed that, even in happy marriages, sexual problems are surprisingly common. While 40 percent of these women reported their sexual relationship was "very satisfying," another 58 percent rated their sex life as only "moderately satisfying" or "not very satisfying." Overall, 48 percent of the women reported they sometimes had difficulty in getting sexually aroused; 46 percent reported intermittent difficulties in reaching orgasm; and 15 percent were completely unable to have an orgasm. This 15 percent is about the same as was found in the famous Kinsey reports, based on several thousand women. Clearly, in our culture, in which women are often raised to have rather negative feelings about sex, many women suffer from an inhibition of their natural sexual responsiveness. (Frank, E., Anderson, C., and Rubenstein, D. "Frequency of sexual dysfunction in normal couples." *New England Journal of Medicine*, 1978, *299*, 111–115.)

A number of women that we see in therapy report a history of unpleasant or deficient first experiences with sex: pain, embarrassment, fear of pregnancy, fear of being caught—all contributed to their tension and detracted from their personal pleasure. For some women their first experience was rather brutal. One of our clients mentioned how, at eighteen, she had a boyfriend who had pursued her for months, claiming he loved her and wanted to make love to her. This continued for almost a year; she felt she was in love with him, and so she did have sex with him. Immediately afterward, he called her a slut, walked away, and never spoke to her again. Fortunately, this kind of experience is rare.

You may be one of the 15 to 35 percent of American women who have been raped as adults or molested as children. Did an adult or older person initiate sexual activities with you when you were a child? Were you ever forced as a child to have sexual activity against your will under some kind of threat of harm or injury? Either of these instances is considered sexual abuse because one person, the child, is involved without having the knowledge necessary to give completely free consent—in other words, their rights are abused. So, if as a child you were touched by an adult (or a person old enough to know how to behave) in a sexual way—stroked on the genitals, asked to touch the other's genitals, or exposed to the other's sexual arousal—it can be considered abusive and coercive even if that person was a loved one and even if you did not find it unpleasant at the time.

Some women with histories of sex abuse react in a variety of ways, depending on what happened and how long ago it happened. Other women have no apparent long-term negative consequences. Often a woman's ability to have orgasms is not impaired, but the conditions under which she is easily orgasmic may be restricted. Childhood sexual coercion is also likely to affect a woman's general attitudes toward sex and her interpersonal sexuality. Links between feeling sensual and feeling close to someone, between sex and trust, and between sex and emotional commitment are weakened or changed in an unexpected way. Sex may be used to buy love and never enjoyed for itself. Or sexual partners may be restricted to those who are not emotionally intimate: casual acquaintances or unavailable or married men. Women who are sexually abused after childhood, through rape, for example, can experience similar consequences. However, some women who have been raped as adults or molested as children have a type of chronic posttraumatic stress reaction, in which sex with their partners reactivates fear and unpleasant memories. These women are often unable to tolerate, let alone become aroused by, sexual contact with their partners. These issues and how to manage various reactions to them will be discussed in greater depth in chapter 12.

At this point, if sexual force has been part of your history (or, as some women have told us, you think it has but you are not sure), it has probably affected what sex means to you. In this program we will offer you insights to support your sense of control over your sexuality and your body. Your special assignment is to move at exactly the pace that is comfortable for you.

As you think about your past and current experiences, keep several things in mind. One is that you are not born with certain feelings or a certain way of expressing yourself sexually; you learn these through a variety of experiences over your lifetime. That is what growth is all about, and that is why you can learn to develop new feelings and new ways to respond sexually. This brings up a second point: Even if you feel you know exactly why you have trouble sexually, just knowing what's wrong will not necessarily result in change. It may help you understand who you are, provide you with some reassurance about yourself, and motivate you to do something about it, but changing is an active process. We have tried to make the exercises that follow meaningful in helping you to get away from old ideas and patterns of response and to begin the process of exploring new dimensions of your sexuality.

ASSUMED REALITIES: MYTHS AND MISCONCEPTIONS ABOUT FEMALE SEXUALITY

Below we've listed a number of ideas that women and men often believe to be the truth about sex. These ideas are myths; they do not actually fit real people. Nevertheless, these myths are hard to give up. They almost have a life of their own, appearing suddenly at the most inconvenient times. Perhaps they remain in our thoughts because, in subtle and not so subtle ways, our culture (which includes our parents, ourselves, and our children) helps to keep them alive. Why? On the one hand, our culture is still rather suspicious of and worried about sexual satisfaction. Thus, as you read through the "myths," you can see a lot of sex-negative messages. Such limited and constrained views of sex do not allow anyone to feel very adequate. On the other hand, if good sex is so narrowly defined and difficult to find, it must be very rare—and thus people's desire for "something better" is stimulated.

Think over these myths and add more that you have heard from friends or the media.

Myth 1: Sex is only for those under thirty.

Another side of the story: It's well established that women's sexual responsiveness increases with age, doesn't peak until their mid-30s, and continues throughout life with only slightly reduced interest and functioning

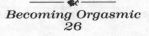

except for illness. Psychologically, much of the culture, women included, believes that sex is for the young and beautiful and thus at some point gives in to the idea.

Myth 2: Normal (real, feminine, or sexual) women have an orgasm every time they have sex.

Another side of the story: Even for women who can have orgasms easily, orgasm doesn't occur every time—70 to 80 percent of the time is the average for the most orgasmic group.

Myth 3: All women can have multiple orgasms.

Another side of the story: The best research estimate is that 15 to 25 percent of women are multiply orgasmic. There is no relationship between sexual satisfaction or sexual adjustment and multiple orgasm.

Myth 4: Pregnancy and delivery reduce women's sexual responsiveness.

Another side of the story: Many women note a marked *increase* in responsiveness and orgasm after pregnancy, probably related to physiological changes (such as increased blood supply to the pelvis) that occur during pregnancy.

Myth 5: A woman's sex life ends with menopause.

Another side of the story: Studies show as many women with *increased* sexual responsiveness after menopause. This is probably a result of the reduced fear of pregnancy, no longer having to use contraception, and the end of menstrual distress. Estrogen cream or pills are necessary for some women to prevent vaginal dryness after menopause. Regular sex helps maintain vaginal tissues and lubricating mechanisms.

Myth 6: There are different kinds of orgasms related to a woman's personality. Vaginal orgasms are more feminine and mature than clitoral orgasms.

Another side of the story: An orgasm is an orgasm, not a personality characteristic. Personality type does not have any influence on the type of stimulation preferred, although there may be differences in the intensity or quality of the stimulation depending on a woman's age, relationship, emotional state, or other physical or emotional factors.

Myth 7: A sexually responsive woman can always be "turned on" by her partner.

Another side of the story: Fatigue, distraction, anger, worry, and many other emotions can and will suppress arousal even in highly responsive, orgasmic women as can emotional problems in the relationship with the partner.

Myth 8: Nice (feminine) women aren't aroused by erotica (books, films, and so on).

Another side of the story: All recent research shows very little difference in the ability of men and women to become aroused by sexual pictures, stories, and fantasies. A woman's arousal from erotic materials is not related to her femininity or morality but to her receptiveness to these forms of sexual stimulation.

Myth 9: You are frigid if you don't like the more exotic forms of sex.

Another side of the story: Many very sexual women aren't interested in certain sexual acts, such as oral or anal sex, using sex toys, group sex, swinging, and so on. The type of sexual activity you prefer does not determine your degree of sexuality.

Myth 10: If you can't have an orgasm quickly and easily, there is something wrong with you.

Another side of the story: The threshold for orgasm varies in women as part of their basic biology—just as some women can run faster than others. Some women with no psychological or emotional problems will always need a lot of intense physical stimulation to trigger an orgasm, while other women, no more psychologically or sexually well adjusted, will have orgasms with less stimulation.

Myth 11: Feminine women don't initiate sex or become wild and unrestrained during sex.

Another side of the story: This is a Victorian cultural stereotype. Lots of research shows women do have a spontaneously occurring sex drive and do initiate sex if their partner is responsive to this. Women with more years of education (usually with fewer traditional sex-role stereotypes) initiate more and are less restrained and more expressive during sex.

Myth 12: Double jeopardy: You're frigid if you don't have sexual fantasies, and you're a wanton woman if you do.

Another side of the story: Many, but not all, sexually well-adjusted women have fantasies about men other than their husbands. This is not related to their sexual adjustment or morality.

Myth 13: Contraception is a woman's responsibility, and in any case, it's only an excuse if she says contraceptive issues are inhibiting her sexuality.

Another side of the story: Many sexually well-adjusted women find that existing contraceptive techniques detract from their sexual pleasure. *Both* partners should share in the responsibility. The best solution for couples who are certain that they don't want more children is vasectomy.

EXERCISE II: IMAGES OF YOURSELF

Part 1: Body Images

As you found in Exercise I, most of us have feelings and concerns about our bodies. These concerns often influence how we feel about ourselves in general and how we feel about ourselves sexually. This

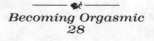

exercise will help you to become more aware of some of these feelings and will suggest some ways to deal with them.

For this exercise, set aside forty-five minutes to an hour when you can have privacy. There are two parts to this exercise, which can be done separately or in one session. This is your time. Try to clear your mind of other responsibilities and worries. Make sure that the room you will be in is comfortable enough for you to be nude. We suggest you begin by taking a relaxing shower or bath. You will need a hand mirror and, if possible, a full-length mirror.

While you are in the shower or bath, stop for a minute; just stand (or lie back) with your eyes closed and let the water run over your body. Let yourself relax. Now try to picture yourself in your mind. Can you see yourself? Open your eyes and look at your hands and arms, down at your breasts, stomach, legs, and feet. What do you see? How do you feel about what you see? Do you like what you see? How would you change what you see if you could? What you say to yourself may sound like this, for example: I have nice arms. My hands are looking older. The skin is more wrinkled, but they look like strong hands. And so on. After a few minutes, relax and finish your shower or bath. After you're dry, take some time (ten to fifteen minutes or more) and look at yourself in a mirror (a large or full-length one if possible). This may or may not be easy for you to do. Looking at ourselves with our eyes (as in the bath or shower) or with our mind's eye (as when you closed your eyes) is often easier than looking in a mirror. Often we see ourselves at those times in more accepting ways than we do in the harsh reflection of a mirror. You may find you've avoided looking at your whole body in a mirror, or that you've gotten into the habit of taking quick, fleeting glances from the most flattering angle. If so, you may want to keep your towel around you for a while. Give yourself time to relax and feel more comfortable.

When you're ready to begin, start at the top of your head: Look at your hair, the shape of your face, the texture of your skin, your eyes, nose, and ears. What do you see? What would you change if you could? How do these things make you feel about yourself sexually?

Next, move on to your torso. Remove your towel so you can become familiar with this part of your body. Look at your shoulders, arms, hands and fingers, breasts, waist, hips, and pubic hair. Ask yourself again, What do I see? How do I feel about what I see? What would I change? How do these things influence how I feel about myself sexually? When you're done, go on to your legs, feet, and toes and ask yourself the same questions.

If you have a full-length mirror, turn around and look at the back of your body. You may want to try moving around a bit in front of the mirror. After you feel you've spent enough time, take a few minutes and think about this experience.

1. Was doing this a positive (pleasant, interesting) or negative (unpleasant, boring) experience for you?
2. Were there parts of your body that influenced how you felt about yourself sexually? Were these strictly erotic or sexual parts of your body, like your breasts?
3. How do you stress the things about your body that you're proud of? How do you try to hide the things about your body you dislike?
4. What are the things you don't like about your body? Are these things *you* genuinely don't like or have you accepted the judgment or opinion of another person? If so, who are the people whose opinion of your body concerns you? Do they tend to be men or women?
5. Where did you get your ideas of what is attractive—your mother, men, yourself, television, magazines?
6. Have you ever been satisfied with how your body looks? How does or did that influence how you feel about your sexuality?

Most women feel dissatisfied with some part of their body. Sometimes these feelings are constructive, in that they prompt us to do something for ourselves that is important for our health—for example, dieting or exercising if we are overweight or out of shape. Being overweight and out of shape or in poor condition *can* influence how free you feel to move and be active during sex, which of course influences how much you enjoy what you do. We have suggested some books in the bibliography that other women have liked and found helpful in improving the condition of their bodies. If you found this experience unpleasant because you don't like the condition of your body, it will be important for you to work on changing this at some point in your life for the sake of your general health and, to some extent, that of your sexuality.

Often, however, women don't like their bodies for reasons they cannot and possibly should not try to change. Let's talk a little here about some frequent concerns women have about their bodies.

You may feel that your breasts are too large, too small, or unequal in size. Perhaps you have suffered pangs of embarrassment about being the last one or the first one among your friends to develop. Padded bras, bust developers, exercisers, creams, and even surgical procedures have capitalized on and helped to maintain women's concerns about breast size. Actually, the size of your breasts

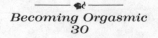

is pretty much determined before you are born, just like your hair color, body build, and height. It doesn't reflect anything about you as a person and doesn't influence how sexually responsive you are; and it's not true that you must be buxom to be sexually appealing. At one time, large breasts were in vogue, but society's version of the ideal female form changes every few years. Not too long ago it was the fashion for women to flatten their breasts with tight corsets and chest cinches in order to look flat-chested. Since our culture's standards of beauty are always changing, it will save you a lot of frustration if you can begin to accept your breast size. (There are exceptions, of course. Some women find very large breasts physically uncomfortable and are relieved to be able to have them surgically reduced.)

Some women have faced breast cancer and have had surgery involving partial or total mastectomy (breast removal). They suffer in several ways: They must face a life-threatening illness, the loss of a body part, and a sense of more general loss—sometimes of femininity, of attractiveness, of wholeness. A period of depression and feeling disfigured may occur, but with support and time, these women can begin to focus on their successful survival rather than on their losses. A different feeling of wholeness results. The several women whom we have seen in therapy who had had mastectomies seemed to have come to better terms with their bodies than those women who had not had to confront a body-changing illness or accident.

Another variation among women is the amount of hair they have on their bodies. All Caucasian women have some, since this is important protection for the skin and particularly the sensitive areas of the body. However, some women have only a little hair or light hair that is not very visible, while others have a great deal of dark, far more visible hair. Non-Caucasian women, especially black and Asian women, often have very little hair over most of their skin. Some women have some hair surrounding the dark area (areola) of their nipples, and the amount of pubic hair a woman has also varies. In some women, the pubic hair extends from the genitals in a line up to or near the navel.

How you feel about this may be important. Whether or not you shave the hair off your legs and underarms, think carefully before you regularly remove hair from other areas of your body, since the skin may become irritated over time. For some reason, less body hair is considered more feminine in Western culture. Yet, many men consider a lot of hair around the pubic area to be attractive. Also, the presence of hair often makes being caressed a more sensual experience. The amount, color, and texture of your body hair is part of you

and is a normal variation among women just as it is among men. Like breast size, your body hair may influence how you feel about your appearance, but it does not affect how responsive you are.

Women often are inhibited about their bodies because they feel ashamed of any scars or stretch marks on their skin. Actually, skin marks are quite common. Often, women have stretch marks around their hips, stomachs, and breasts whether or not they've had children. These are usually most noticeable to the woman herself.

We put weight in the category of things you cannot change as well as that of things you can because some women really lose their perspective on how thin or fat they are. Women with severe weight obsessions—anorexics who starve themselves or bulimics who vomit for weight control—can be thirty pounds underweight and still see themselves as fat. While these severe problems are unusual, milder versions are part of the more weight-conscious woman's daily life. There is always more weight to lose, somewhere, or the possibility that the next meal could put on weight, or that you will lose control and never stop eating. The problem is that women and their bodies become enemies in the battle for thinness—and women who make their bodies their enemies have trouble appreciating the body's pleasure-giving capacities, such as sex.

Perhaps doing Exercise II has gotten you in touch with certain concerns you have about your physical appearance. You probably have others we haven't mentioned here. If you feel these concerns are making it difficult for you to feel good about yourself sexually, you need to examine them carefully. We encourage you to work on those things about yourself that you can change that are potentially dangerous to your health. But for those parts of you that you can't change, perhaps you need to do some rethinking about your standards. Pay particular attention to where your standards are coming from and whose image (what magazine, perfume, designer) you might be buying. Chances are that your ideals have been adopted from television, magazines, and films in which the stereotypical woman is still large-breasted, slim, flawlessly complexioned, stylish, somewhat athletic, and barely twenty-three. This image is as fictitious as an afternoon soap opera. If you feel pressured to be more perfect in order to please your sexual partner, remember that he, too, has been influenced by the same fabrication of what's beautiful. Given the rather narrow definition of feminine beauty in our culture, it's a real challenge to learn to accept who you are and what you look like. We hope that being more aware of what influences your ideas of appearance will help you to begin to focus on what you see as your positive

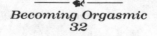

qualities and not to let the things you don't like prevent you from feeling that you are a worthwhile person. But remember, too, that you don't have to be completely satisfied with yourself in order to grow sexually. As one woman who was halfway through our program said, "It's nice to know that even though my body's not perfect, it can still give me pleasure."

Part 2: Genital Images

How are you feeling now? If you feel like continuing, and you have another fifteen minutes or so left to your hour, do so. If you feel rushed or tired or you would like a chance to reflect some more on the first part of this exercise, then stop for now and do this next time.

If you have decided to continue, take a few minutes to relax. You may want just to lie down for a few minutes with your eyes closed. Or you may want to try controlling your breathing as a way to help you relax.

Lie down. Inhale through your nose slowly to the count of five.

Feel your entire chest expand and fill with air. Then part your lips and exhale completely, pushing all the air from your lungs. Try this a few times with your hand on your stomach so that you can feel the air filling and leaving your body. Or you may want to raise your arms slowly from the side (not in front of you) over your head as you inhale and lower them as you exhale. This will help your chest expand fully.

When you feel relaxed, prop your back against something such as a wall, a headboard, or several pillows. Using a hand mirror, we'd like you to look at your genitals. We've included one drawing to help you identify the different parts of your genital area and several other sketches to give you an idea of different genital proportions. Don't worry if you don't look exactly like the drawings. Genital appearance, like facial appearance, varies tremendously among women.

Begin with the bone and mound of hair that cover your genitals. This is called the *mons*. Feel the curved bone of the mons through your *pubic hair*. This hair serves to protect this very sensitive area of your body from irritation by clothes and perspiration. Your pubic hair may be thick or sparse, and its texture and color will also be uniquely your own. Now move your fingers down the center of your *outer lips,* or *labia majora,* which are also covered with pubic hair. These lips help protect the *inner lips,* or *labia minora.*

Find your inner lips. These may be large or small. In some women they are completely hidden by the labia majora. In other women these inner lips are more prominent and hang down between the labia majora. These variations are normal. The color and texture of the inner lips will also vary. Yours may be basically pink or tend more toward the browns. The inner lips usually meet at the top of the *clitoral shaft,* although in some women they do not. Find your clitoral shaft. At the top of the shaft are the *clitoral hood* and the *clitoris.* The clitoral hood is a fold of skin that covers a small round organ—the clitoris. The hood helps protect the clitoris, which is extremely sensitive, much as the foreskin protects the penis in an uncircumcised man. Pull back the clitoral hood and look at your clitoris. In some women the clitoris seems to adhere to the hood so that the hood cannot be pulled back very much. This does not seem to be related to sexual responsiveness, and it is not necessary to detach the hood surgically. The size of the clitoris and its distance from the vagina varies from woman to woman. The clitoris is extremely sensitive to sexual stimulation. Years ago it was thought that the vagina provided the main source of sexual stimulation for women. Today we know that although the whole body contributes to sexual stimulation, the clitoris

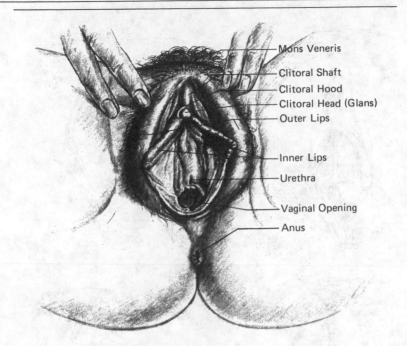

- Mons Veneris
- Clitoral Shaft
- Clitoral Hood
- Clitoral Head (Glans)
- Outer Lips
- Inner Lips
- Urethra
- Vaginal Opening
- Anus

is the most important source of sexual pleasure for most women. The vagina produces a different type of stimulation, more sensitive to pressure, that women find pleasurable.

When you looked at your labia minora, or inner lips, did you notice whether they are connected to the clitoral hood? During intercourse, the movement of the penis in the vagina will cause these inner lips to move. If the inner lips are connected to the clitoral hood this will cause the skin surrounding the clitoris to move and stimulate the clitoris. If the inner lips are not connected to the clitoral hood, it is possible for clitoral stimulation to come from direct contact with the movement of the penis or from the man's pelvic bone in certain intercourse positions.

Sometimes, women who have not already experienced orgasm consider altering or removing their clitoral hood with the idea that this will make them orgasmic. This type of operation is not useful and may create problems rather than solve them.

Now spread your inner lips and look at the area around your vagina. Locate your *urethra,* the small opening through which urine passes. This is above your vaginal opening. Take a good look at your *vagina.* Notice the shape of the opening, its color and texture. As you're looking at your vagina, try clenching or contracting the muscle around it. This is called the *pubococcygeous muscle.* If you are con-

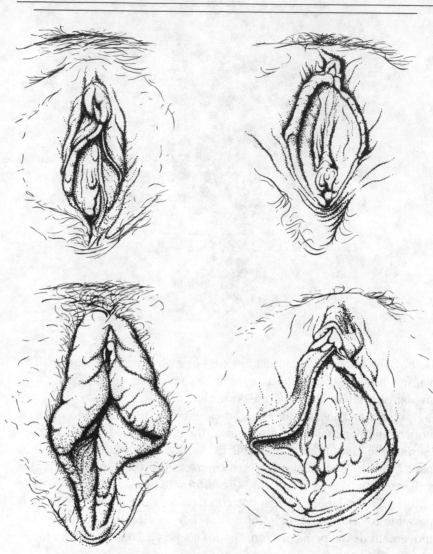

FOUR VARIATIONS OF THE VAGINA

tracting the right muscle, you will probably be able to see some movement just inside the vaginal opening. Don't worry if you don't see anything. We will be talking more about this important muscle in the next chapter.

The area between the bottom of the vaginal opening and the *anus* is called the *perineum*. Often, this is where stitches are placed after childbirth. The *anus* is also surrounded by powerful muscles. Like other openings into the body, such as the ears, mouth, and vagina, the anus is often sensitive to erotic pleasure.

When you've completed your exploration, take a few minutes to

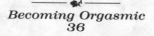

relax. Close your eyes and breathe deeply a few times. Inhale slowly and exhale. Rest for a minute, and tune into any feelings you have from what you have just experienced:

1. How did you feel as you were looking at your genitals?
2. What did you like and dislike about what you saw?
3. Were you surprised by anything you discovered about your genital area?

It would be natural if you felt somewhat uncomfortable or embarrassed as you did this. Many women have never looked closely at their genitals or have looked at them only when they had to: after the delivery of a baby or when experiencing genital discomfort or pain. This seems amazing if you think about how often you have looked at other areas of your body. Perhaps the idea of really looking has never occurred to you, or you may have gotten the message as you were growing up that "nice girls don't do that." So don't be concerned if you feel somewhat uncomfortable doing this. You will begin to feel more comfortable with this important part of your body as you become more familiar with it.

Try repeating this exercise again in a few days. Also, take advantage of those times when you have a natural opportunity to look at yourself—for example, while bathing or dressing or undressing.

First, let's talk about some of the things you may have discovered about yourself. Some women are surprised to learn that the urethra, which passes urine from our bodies, is separate from the vagina. Even though it is, you probably noticed that the two openings are close to each other. Because of this, the urethra is stimulated during sexual arousal due to increased blood flow and vaginal tension, and during intercourse by the movement of the penis in the vagina. For this reason, women often experience a desire to urinate during or just after sexual stimulation. Urinating after intercourse is sometimes a good idea because vaginal infections can spread to the urethra and bladder or vice versa. Burning, itching sensations, or painful urination should always be checked by your doctor.

Women are often surprised by the shape and size of their vaginal opening. This is probably because the vagina is often described in books and drawings (as well as in jokes or slang terms) as a kind of open hole. As you can see, it is actually more of a "potential" space, although the opening may be a little larger in women who have given birth to several children.

When the vagina is in an aroused state, its walls almost touch each other. The vaginal muscles are very flexible, however, and easily

open to accommodate a man's penis. Arousal causes an increased flow of blood to the genitals, and the diameter and length of the vagina increases. For these reasons, it's not necessary for you to be concerned about the actual size of your vagina or the size of a man's penis, since various sizes tend to accommodate each other (more on this in chapter 11). However, keeping your vaginal muscles healthy and strong is important, and we've included some exercises for this in the next chapter.

Perhaps you noticed some moisture or secretion as you explored your genitals. This is natural, since there is always some lubrication in the vagina, although the normal amount varies from woman to woman. This lubrication is secreted by the walls of the vagina and helps protect it from irritation and infection. It's a good idea for you to learn what normal healthy secretion or lubrication looks like for you. Certain oral contraceptives will increase or decrease the amount of lubrication you have, as will age or certain illnesses. Also, vaginal infections can often be detected by noticeable changes in the amount, consistency, color, or smell of your secretions. Any such change, or itching or irritation of the genitals, should be immediately checked by your doctor.

When the vagina is healthy (when there are no infections), most lubrication has a faint, not unpleasant smell. Regular washing of your *external* genitals with soap and water is all that you really need to do in order to keep your genitals clean. Commercial deodorant sprays for your external genitals are not necessary and have been found to irritate the delicate skin of many women. Your natural vaginal odor is probably mild and not noticeable to others except perhaps during sex. At those times, the natural smell of clean, healthy genitals can be a source of pleasurable erotic stimulation for your partner.

Douching or cleansing the vagina with water or other solutions, or the insertion of vaginal suppositories for this purpose, is also a practice that doctors have found unnecessary. Douching was practiced at one time as a form of contraception, but (largely because it is not effective) it is rarely recommended for this purpose today. Most often, douching is recommended by physicians in order to treat vaginal infections with solutions that need to be applied inside the vagina. Douching regularly with commercial products as a way to cleanse yourself or to deal with concerns about genital odor is likely to do more harm than good. Strong douche solutions tend to interfere with your body's natural lubricating protection against infection.

Women are often surprised that their genitals did not seem ugly

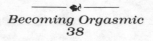

or look unpleasant to them. They report being curious about the different colors and the delicate look of their skin. Sometimes, however, women do find this experience upsetting (particularly if they've never looked closely at themselves before).

Perhaps you found you were unable even to complete the exercise. That's okay. You need to spend a little more time getting comfortable. Start by looking at the drawings of women's genitals on page 36. See if you can notice the differences between them. Next, see if one picture makes you less uncomfortable than the others. What is it about this picture that makes you less uncomfortable? Then, see if one of the pictures reminds you of your own genitals. What about it is similar to your genitals?

If you are still feeling uncomfortable, go back over your sexual history, and try to identify the sources of these feelings. Are they holdovers from a childhood experience in which you were told this area of your body was bad? Do these feelings relate to childhood sex play, masturbation, or the onset of menstruation? If any of these possibilities applies to you, think about the differences between yourself *now,* an adult woman, and the child you were.

After becoming more comfortable with the pictures, try another session in which you look at your genitals. You may be surprised to find it a little easier. If not, we suggest you skip ahead to chapter 3 and practice the exercises for relaxation. After you feel you are able to relax effectively, try another session of looking at your genitals.

If you were able to look at your genitals but found it upsetting, try to give yourself credit for having done this exercise at all. And even though you may not feel the way you'd like to yet, at least you've made a start. Here are some suggestions that will help you to feel more positive about your genitals over a period of time:

1. As we suggested earlier, do this exercise again and take advantage of other opportunities to look at your genitals.
2. Try describing your genitals in words. What seemed unpleasant for you? One woman in sex therapy described her genitals as "ugly and wrinkled . . . sort of an old dried prune." With this kind of image in her mind, it was not surprising that it was hard for her to feel anything but negative about her genitals. Try writing down your description. Look at the words you've chosen and the image that they create in your mind. Now try creating another image that is somewhat more positive. For example, try looking at your genitals and comparing their shape to parts of a flower, or a shell, or a design.

Thinking about this part of you in this way may seem strange now, but we have seen many women learn to appreciate their genitals as beautiful parts of themselves.

3. Try reading and doing some of the exercises for relaxation (chapter 3) before your next "looking" session. Being relaxed may make it easier for you to begin to feel more comfortable.

4. If you still experience a great deal of difficulty, you may want to move ahead to the next chapter. We will continue throughout this book to deal with your feelings about yourself, your body, and the experiences you have had. So don't feel you must change drastically right now. Remember, change can be a slow process, and it's important to feel good about yourself for the things you can do *now*.

3
Exploration Through Touch

I n the last chapter you began to learn more about yourself by examining your past and the ways in which it has influenced your attitudes toward sex. Also, you began looking more closely at your body and exploring yourself visually.

In this chapter you're going to continue this exploration in two ways—by expanding your experience through your sense of touch and through exercises designed to increase your awareness of sensations in your body.

Touch plays an important role in our ability to enjoy sensual feelings. Touch allows us to experience what we cannot see or hear— the textures and temperatures of our environment. What differences are there in touching a real orchid, a plastic orchid, and a colored photograph of an orchid? Suppose you hear a kitten purring; what difference does it make when you actually hold it while it purrs? Our sense of touch and our ability to perceive sensations can provide both information and pleasure about ourselves. As you do the exercises in this chapter, try thinking of your body as a new world to be explored, full of different textures and shapes.

To do the first exercise, choose a time when you feel good (not worried or pressured) and can spend thirty minutes to an hour by yourself. Have on hand some body lotion, oil, or powder that you like. You may want to start with a relaxing bath or shower. When you're done, stay nude and find a comfortable spot where you can lie or sit in a reclining position, leaning your back against something for support—your bed, some cushions on the floor, or your couch, if you have the living room to yourself. (You may want to spread a towel out under you if you are using an oil or lotion.) Now apply some body lotion, powder, or oil to your arms and legs. Slowly begin exploring your body all over—your arms, hands, feet, legs, breasts, stomach, the insides of your thighs. You may want to close your eyes as you do this, or you may like the idea of looking at yourself in a mirror. See if you can really focus on what you're feeling. Tune out other things. How do your hands feel going over each part of your body? Let your hands experiment with different ways to touch—use your fingertips for a while, and then try the palms of your hands or your wrists.

What do different areas of your body feel like to you? Is one area soft and smooth, another muscular, another rough? Notice sharp, angular places, curves, and fullness. If you like, turn on your stomach and feel your buttocks and the backs of your legs. Change position as often as you like. Spend around ten minutes or so on these parts of your body, and then let your hands slide along the insides of your thighs to your genitals.

Take your time. Let your fingers explore your pubic hair; notice its texture. Is it soft or coarse? Then touch the soft skin of your outer lips and the muscular area between your vagina and anus (the perineum). Move your fingertips into the moist inner lips. Compare the feel of the outside surface to the inner area of the lips. What does the skin here feel like to you? Does it feel like any other parts of your body? Don't try for any particular feelings; just be aware of the shapes and textures.

Then explore your clitoral shaft and see if you can feel your clitoris through the clitoral hood. Pull the hood back and lightly touch your clitoris. Trace the outer edge of your vagina. Let your fingers go inside your vagina to the moist warmth. Do you feel any muscle inside your vagina? Try contracting the ring of vaginal muscles you looked at in the last exercise. Can you feel it contracting around your finger? Explore the walls of your vagina. Is the texture smooth or rough, flat or ridged?

As you are exploring the inside of your vagina, you may wish to attempt to locate something that has been called the *G-spot*. Several researchers have described an area, located about an inch or two inside the vagina and on the anterior (toward your stomach) wall, that feels like a small, slightly raised bump. There is a theory suggesting that this area may be an especially sensitive site within the vagina, and that its stimulation may lead to especially intense orgasms. At this point, since you are just exploring, even if you can locate it, you should not expect to feel any particular pleasurable sensations from the G-spot. Don't be concerned if you cannot locate an area that meets this description. There is a great deal of controversy among sex researchers and sex therapists about the whole notion of the G-spot. We are mentioning it because it has received a lot of attention in women's magazines, television, and the media as a whole.

You may want to go back to touching some of the rest of your body again as a way of ending this exercise. Take a few deep breaths.

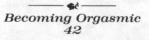

Inhale slowly for three counts. Exhale slowly for three counts. When you are ready, think about the following questions:

1. How did you feel touching your genitals? (Did you feel comfortable, awkward, silly, shy, embarrassed, disgusted?)
2. How did you feel touching the other parts of your body? Describe these feelings.
3. Did you learn anything new about yourself?

Perhaps you felt comfortable doing this exercise or touching certain parts of your body, or you may have been uncomfortable through all or part of this exercise. These feelings are natural. Usually we touch ourselves for functional reasons: dressing, washing, scratching, or tending to a cut or bruise. It may be difficult for you to feel that it's all right to touch your body, especially your genitals, for the purpose of learning about yourself. Repeating this exercise a second time can help allay these uncomfortable feelings. You may feel less awkward and embarrassed and your body will seem more familiar to you.

If you still feel awkward touching your own genitals, it may help to go back to chapter 2 and try to identify the events in your own sexual history that have led you to feel uncomfortable with this part of your body. Often, some of these uncomfortable feelings are residues of childhood experiences. Were you told by your parents that "nice girls don't touch themselves down there"? Reexamining the basis for your awkward feelings and thinking about whether you still agree with the childhood messages you were given about your genitals may help you to become more comfortable.

Learning to relax will help you feel more comfortable now as well as throughout this growth program.

THE G-SPOT

In the last few years, there has been a great deal of writing and discussion about an area in the vagina that has come to be known as the *G-spot*, named after the gynecologist who discovered it, Ernst Graffenburg. This theory has been most thoroughly explored in a book called *The G-Spot*, by Alice Ladas, John Perry, and Beverly Whipple, published in 1983.

The G-spot is described as a lump that can be felt on the wall of the vagina toward the stomach, about an inch or two inside the opening. During sexual arousal the G-spot seems to swell up and become larger, much as the clitoris and labia do. The theory suggests that this spot is possibly the female equiva-

lent of the male prostate. That is, during development of the fetus, both male and female embryos start with an undifferentiated genital bulb that eventually develops into either the male or female structures. However, since both male and female start with the same genital bulb, it seems quite possible that at least some women do have some partial development of a prostatelike gland. It is theorized that during sexual arousal, this gland enlarges from increased blood flow and from filling up with the same sort of fluid that causes vaginal lubrication. The G-spot theory also suggests that for some women, orgasm can result in a "female ejaculation" with a spurting discharge of this fluid from the female's urethra.

Early work on the G-spot reported that some, though probably not all, women definitely did have this "female prostate," and would have ejaculation during orgasm. Since this fluid comes from the urethra, researchers were quick to stress that these women were not urinating, they were ejaculating. There has been great concern that a woman's enjoyment of sex and her ability to become aroused and orgasmic would be inhibited by the thought that this fluid was urine.

Currently there are no conclusions on the validity of the G-spot theory. Some studies have indicated that there is prostatic tissue in women, and some biochemical results show that because of secretions (enzymes) present in this female ejaculate, it is prostatic fluid and not urine. However, other studies have found that the ejaculate fluid *is* urine and does not contain prostatic secretions.

While definitive answers cannot be given at this point, it seems likely that there are several different types of female ejaculation. Certainly our knowledge of embryologic development makes the theory that some women do have a kind of female prostate entirely possible, and indeed likely. During orgasm these women could be expected to have a discharge of fluid from this site that is not urine and that would indeed be similar to male ejaculate fluid. However, there are at least three other possibilities.

One is that even without development of a female prostate, some women will have an ejaculation from the urethra that is not urine. There are other glands along the female urethra that, during sexual arousal, fill up with fluid. This is the same fluid that creates vaginal lubrication, and is caused by the increased blood pressure in the blood vessels of the pelvis that occurs during sexual arousal. During the contractions of orgasm, this fluid is expelled from the glands along the female urinary tract and would appear as an ejaculation.

A second possibility is that a few women may have a spurting discharge of a small amount of urine when they have orgasm. Even after emptying the bladder, some urine typically remains. During very strong orgasmic contractions, the muscles that surround the vagina and the neck of the bladder may squeeze out a little of this residual urine. Many people don't realize that urine is sterile, if a person is healthy. Having a small amount of sterile liquid appear at orgasm certainly does not have to be a major problem and need not inhibit sexual enjoyment. For women who have this pattern, we simply suggest that

they put a towel on the bed, and after making love, toss the towel in the washing machine.

The third possibility is that for women who have a lot of vaginal lubrication, contraction of the muscles around the vagina during orgasm will cause some of this vaginal lubricant fluid to spurt out. It's rather difficult for women or their partners to identify whether the fluid comes from the urethra or the vagina.

Whether the ejaculate fluid that a small percentage of women produce at orgasm is urine, prostatic fluid, fluid from glands along the urethra, or vaginal lubrication really does not need to be an issue that inhibits a woman's sexuality. In fact, some couples experience this response as part of the "sexiness" of orgasm. The only time a woman needs to be concerned is if she has other symptoms: if she is unable to empty her bladder when she wishes to or leaks urine when she coughs, stands up suddenly, or engages in other muscular activities. If so, she should see her physician for an evaluation. However, in a woman who has no other problems with urinary control, some discharge of fluid during orgasm does not necessarily indicate a problem. In fact, such women often have very strong pelvic muscles and experience very intense orgasmic contractions, which "milk" or squeeze out a little fluid at orgasm.

Another controversy concerns the notion that the G-spot is especially sensitive and will lead to greater sexual pleasure if it is directly stimulated. Some theorists have even suggested that stimulation of this area may be very effective in helping women to reach orgasm during intercourse. Again, at the time of this writing, all these questions are unresolved.

Certainly many women report that one area or another in the vagina feels better than any others. It has been our experience, however, that exactly where this area is varies from woman to woman. For some women it is along the first inch or so of the front wall of the vagina. However, this may simply be because the clitoris and the nerves that are involved in clitoral stimulation lie along this wall, rather than because of the existence of a G-spot.

The controversy about the G-spot does have a lesson to teach. Popular media and magazines presented the G-spot theory as if it were an established scientific fact, and we have counseled women who were concerned because they didn't seem to have a G-spot. As we've discussed, there are a number of possible explanations for both the question of female ejaculation and the question of particular areas in the vagina feeling better than others. As you grow and discover your own sexuality, it is important to discover what is reality for you, not what is presumed "fact" by the media.

EXERCISES FOR RELAXATION

You may feel that you know quite well how to relax. Most people, however, do have times when tension takes over, when their minds and their bodies are "uptight." At these times it is particularly diffi-

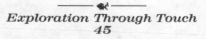

Exploration Through Touch

45

cult to let yourself experience pleasant feelings. The following pages include some exercises that will help you learn to recognize tension in your body and to relax. They are useful for another reason—by using them, you can develop a better ability to focus on and appreciate sensations of all types throughout your body.

If you felt comfortable during the exercises in chapters 2 and 3 (Looking at Yourself and Exploration Through Touch), do the Deep Muscle Relaxation exercise three to five times a week for two weeks, or until you feel you can relax yourself fairly easily. The Muscle Control exercise is optional for you.

If you felt uncomfortable during the exercises in chapters 2 and 3, do the Deep Muscle Relaxation exercise once or twice a day for two weeks. As soon as you feel ready, you may want to repeat the exercises in chapters 2 and 3 that made you uncomfortable or that you were unable to do. This time you should feel more relaxed and enjoy your session. If you have difficulty doing the Deep Muscle Relaxation exercise, go on to Exercise 2, Muscle Control. Practice it, and when you feel ready, go back and try the Deep Muscle Relaxation exercise. When you can do this comfortably, you may want to repeat those exercises that were difficult for you. You should feel more relaxed and at ease this time.

Exercise 1: Deep Muscle Relaxation

This is an effective technique that will give you a way to relax whenever you feel the need. You shouldn't expect to be able to do it perfectly the first few times. Think of this exercise as a skill that needs to be practiced.

First, make sure you have fifteen to thirty minutes to spend without interruption. You may want to begin by taking a warm bath or shower, turning on some soft background music, or doing whatever you've learned helps you relax. If you are dressed, make sure your clothes are loosened. Take off your shoes and your glasses or contact lenses, if you wear them.

Choose a place that is relatively quiet and will help you to concentrate only on yourself. Create an environment for yourself in which you feel comfortable; some things you might think about besides music are lighting and room temperature.

You'll want to find a place to sit or lie that will leave your body

as supported and tension-free as possible (a bed, couch, reclining chair, or cushions arranged with some support for your back and head).

Now let your arms and hands hang or rest in a loose, relaxed manner. Lean your head back against its support. Close your eyes. Try to relax deeply. Make your body heavy. Begin by tensing your forehead into a deep frown. Feel the tension in your forehead, the pull on your scalp, the sensation of pressure. Now relax these muscles. Feel your forehead become smooth, your scalp relax. Concentrate on the feeling of relaxation.

Now tense the muscles around your eyes and nose by closing your eyes as tightly as possible. You don't have to tense your muscles so much that they cramp. Just tighten up enough to feel the tension so that you can notice the difference when you relax. Feel the tension in your eyebrows and the bridge of your nose. Focus on the tension. Now relax. Feel the tension flowing from around your eyes and your nose, each part becoming quiet and smooth. Enjoy this feeling of relaxation. Try tensing your lips and jaws by clenching your teeth together. Feel the pressure on your gums. Hold the tension. Focus on the tension. Now relax. Flow with the relaxation. Notice the different sensations accompanying relaxation. Enjoy the feeling of relaxation that is becoming more and more evident in your head and face.

Now press the back of your head against its support. Study the sensations of tension and strain in your neck. Now relax. Let your head hang limp and loose for a moment. Let it feel heavy and loose and relaxed; then tense again, and note the difference. Now relax. Feel the muscles in your neck become smooth and quiet. Now tense the front of your neck by pushing your chin into your chest. Feel the tension in your neck and throat. Focus on the tension. Notice the sensations. Now relax and breathe deeply. Let yourself enjoy the feeling of becoming more and more relaxed. Your forehead and eyes, nose and jaws, cheeks and neck should feel smooth and quiet. Now, in the same way, tense and relax the following body parts:

1. Hands, by clenching them
2. Wrists and forearms, by extending them and bending the hands back at the wrists
3. Shoulders, by shrugging them
4. Chest, by taking a deep breath and holding it, then exhaling
5. Back, by arching the back up and away from the support surface
6. Stomach, by sucking it in and forming it into a tight knot

7. Hips and buttocks, by pressing buttocks together tightly
8. Thighs, by clenching them
9. Lower legs, by pointing the toes and curling toes downward

When you are done, stay in touch with your feelings for a few minutes. When you are ready to get up, take a few deep breaths, open your eyes, and get up slowly. Stretch your whole body.

• Were you able to distinguish any particular areas of tension that you were not aware of before? Describe them.
• Did you experience difficulty relaxing a specific muscle group? If so, concentrate on the area during your next practice session.

If you had problems, perhaps you were tensing your whole body rather than one specific group of muscles at a time. If you think this may be so, go to the next exercise and practice it. When you can do the Muscle Control exercise successfully, try this exercise again.

If you felt sleepy and found it hard to continue, make sure you are not doing this exercise when you are tired or just before going to bed. If you used your bed or bedroom, try repeating this exercise in another part of the house or apartment.

If you couldn't concentrate and your mind wandered or your thoughts interfered, you need practice on focusing your attention. Try to clear your mind of distracting thoughts. If this is too difficult, you may want to postpone your sessions for another time. Another exercise, Body Awareness, will also help you learn to shut out distracting thoughts.

Exercise 2: Muscle Control

These techniques increase your control of specific muscles. When you learn any physical skill, you train certain muscle groups to perform. Often, how well you do depends on keeping other muscles relaxed. This allows you to make the most of your energy.

1. In order to gain control of the different muscles of your body, you need to be able to identify them and tell them apart. Lie on your back with pillows under your head and knees. Now begin tensing your body, one part at a time. Begin with your feet. Contract your feet, then your calves, thighs, buttocks, fingers, hands, arms, shoulders, neck, and face. Concentrate on the sensation of tension in each body

part. Now relax each muscle group, one part at a time. Do this sequence three times.

2.   The next step is to learn to contract one muscle while relaxing all other muscles. Lie down as before. Contract and tense your right arm, but keep the rest of your body relaxed. Hold this for a count of 10. Relax your arm. Do the following sequence, concentrating on tensing *only* those muscles listed and keeping the rest of your body loose and relaxed:

- Contract right arm
- Contract left arm
- Contract right leg
- Contract left leg
- Contract right arm *and* right leg
- Contract left arm *and* left leg
- Contract both arms
- Contract both legs

Remember, keep the rest of your body relaxed! Now go on and try these:

- Contract right arm and left leg
- Contract right leg and left arm

This exercise is even easier to master with someone helping you. After trying it the first time by yourself, you may want to do it with your partner or a friend. His or her job is to tell you which muscle groups to tense and to check to make sure the rest of your body is relaxed. This can be done by lifting the untensed leg or arm slightly and seeing how loose and relaxed it feels. However, you can master this on your own if you choose to.

Practice this for a few days. If you had trouble with Deep Muscle Relaxation, try it again. You will probably have better control over your muscles now and should be able to tense particular muscle groups while keeping the rest of your body relaxed. If you did both exercises, you probably noticed some differences. Which did you like better? How did each make you feel? Do you feel that either worked well for you?

Some people find that muscle relaxation exercises seem to make them more tense rather than more relaxed. If this was true for you, try the Body Awareness exercise below. Read the procedure first, and then close your eyes and visualize the various scenes. You may want

to write a one- or two-word description of each and to refer to it if you need to. Or you might record the procedure on tape and play it back while you go through the scenes. Another possibility is to ask another person to read them to you as you are relaxing.

Begin by making yourself comfortable. As you consider each scene, let yourself become totally immersed. Try to concentrate for several seconds (five to ten, perhaps) on each particular image.

Exercise 3: Body Awareness

- Close your eyes. Be aware of the point at which the back of your head comes into contact with the chair.
- Imagine the space between your eyes.
- Be aware how close your breath comes to the back of your eyes every time you inhale.
- Imagine that you are looking at something that is very far away.
- Be aware of the points at which your arms are in contact with the chair. At which points do your arms lose contact with the chair?
- Is either your left or right foot resting on the floor; if either or both of them are, can you feel the floor beneath your foot?
- Imagine a beautiful flower suspended a few feet in front of you. Close the lids of your inner eye so that you no longer see the flower.
- Be aware of the space within your mouth. What is the position of your tongue within your mouth?
- Imagine a slight breeze against your cheek.
- Is one of your arms heavier than the other?
- Is there a tingling or feeling of numbness in one of your hands?
- Is one of your arms more relaxed than the other?
- Can you notice any change in the temperature of your body?
- Is your left arm warmer than your right?
- Can you imagine you are a rag doll?
- Be aware of your left forearm. Can you feel any tightness in it?
- Imagine something very pleasant.
- Can you feel yourself floating as if on a cloud? Or are you feeling much too heavy for that?
- Do your arms feel very heavy, as if they were stuck in molasses?
- Imagine once again that you are looking at something that is very far away.

- Is there a heaviness coming into your legs?
- Imagine yourself floating in warm water.
- Feel the weight of your body in the chair.
- Allow yourself to drift along lazily.
- Imagine another beautiful flower. What color is it? Close the lids of your inner eye so that you no longer see the flower.
- Is one of your arms heavier than the other, and one of your legs heavier than the other?
- Open your eyes.

How did you feel about doing this? Were you able to visualize the scenes? Did you become more relaxed? Whichever relaxation procedure works best for you, practice it regularly until you can quickly and easily relax after a while. You will find that you do not need to go through the entire procedure, but that just a few minutes of relaxing particular areas of your body or visualizing certain scenes will be enough.

Vaginal Exercises (Kegels)

In the last chapter, you tried to contract your vaginal muscles. Again, these amazing muscles are the pubococcygeal muscles. These muscles are important to your health, and they also play a part in increasing vaginal sensations.

Your genital muscles need exercise just as your other muscles do. In 1952 some exercises for women who were experiencing urinary incontinence and related problems were developed by Dr. Arnold Kegel. It was found that in these women the pubococcygeus muscles were out of shape and could not function properly. Exercising these muscles eliminated the medical problems and, to everyone's surprise, also seemed to increase these women's potential for genital sensation and orgasm. This is probably partly due to the fact that blood flow increases to muscles that are exercised, and that increased blood flow is related to the ease of arousal and orgasm. Learning these exercises will help you keep these muscles functioning while also increasing your feelings of genital pleasure.

In recent years there has been a good deal more research on and clinical experience with the use of the Kegel exercises. It has become well established that increasing strength in these muscles will, for most women, lead to an increased ability to have orgasm and to experiencing more intense orgasms. As you build strength in a mus-

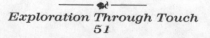

cle, you increase the blood supply to the muscle. One side effect of the Kegel exercises, then, is to increase blood flow to the pelvis, which leads to higher levels of arousal and more intense orgasm. It also seems likely that as a woman does these exercises, she increases her sensitivity and ability to feel different sensations in her genitals. You may notice that your ability to perceive feelings in your genitals changes, in part from focusing on this part of your body while exercising it.

However, as is often the case as we learn more, things are not quite as clear or simple as we first thought. Several studies have demonstrated that not all women who do not have orgasms have weak Kegel muscles. Therefore, do not be surprised, as you try the vaginal exercises, if you find you already have very strong muscles and good control over them. While this is not common, there are women who do have very good strength and control in these muscles but who nevertheless have difficulty with orgasm. Kegel and his followers have also suggested that strength in these muscles was particularly helpful in learning to have orgasm during intercourse itself, as the woman should have an increased ability to feel the penis in her vagina. More recent research has not entirely supported this idea. Although strength in this muscle does seem to be important for having orgasm, it does not seem to be related specifically to the ability to have orgasm during intercourse. We will have more to say about the issue of orgasms during intercourse in chapter 11.

Our experience is that women benefit from developing a sense of connection and control with respect to their genitals. We therefore encourage you to do these exercises even if your musculature is well developed.

Remember, these exercises will require some concentration at first, but they will become routine after a short time. When you first try these exercises, start by contracting this muscle while urinating. See if you can stop and start your urine midflow. Make sure your legs are fairly well apart so you'll be sure you're using the correct set of muscles. After you've done this a couple of times, finish emptying your bladder. You *should not* continue to do Kegel exercises while you urinate because this procedure sometimes does not allow the bladder to empty as completely as it should, which could lead to infection. The reason we suggested you *try* Kegels during urination is so that you will be sure you are tensing the correct muscles.

Now that you've located the muscles, try doing your exercises while standing, sitting, or lying down. They can be done anywhere, anytime. No one but you will know. A good idea is to set aside a certain time each day to practice. Check occasionally by resting your hand on your abdomen as you do the contractions, to make sure you are not using your abdominal muscles too. When you have learned to do them easily, you can do them almost anytime—while you're driving, brushing your teeth, or whatever.

At first these muscles may be weak and you may not feel them contracting or tightening. If you're not sure anything is happening, insert one of your fingers into your vagina. If you're exercising correctly, you should be able to feel your muscles contracting. Don't be concerned if you can't, however. After you've practiced these exercises for a while you will be able to feel the contractions.

Vaginal Exercises (Kegels)

1. Contract the muscles, hold for a count of three, then relax. Breathe regularly.
2. Contract the muscles while inhaling, pulling them upward with the intake of breath. This may be harder to do because you may find your stomach muscles contracting as well. With time you will learn to do this one without contracting the stomach muscles.
3. Contract and relax the muscles as quickly as possible while breathing regularly.
4. Bear down on the muscles as if pushing something out of the vagina or trying to urinate in a hurry. You may find yourself holding your breath, but try to breathe regularly.

You may notice a warm or full feeling in your genitals as you do these exercises. The important thing is not to try to make yourself feel a particular way. Just relax, and focus on what you *are* feeling. Remember, the purpose of these exercises is to help you build a healthier body and to tune you into feelings and sensations in your genitals—whether they be pleasant, unpleasant, or neutral. This awareness is the first step in gaining understanding of, and some control over, your body and its responses.

How Often Should You Practice?

Find a convenient time every day to practice. These exercises become easier to do with time, and they take only a few minutes a day. During the first week, do each exercise ten times, twice a day.

Continue to do these exercises at least once a day for the remainder of the growth program. Actually, continuing on a regular basis throughout your life is one way of maintaining healthy vaginal and urinary muscles.

When you feel comfortable with what you've done in this chapter (anywhere from a few days to a few weeks), go on to chapter 4.

4
Touching for Pleasure: Discovery

W hat do you think of when you hear the word *pleasure?* Perhaps you think of something physical—a massage, a dip in a cool swimming pool on a hot day—or something that involves your feelings—the anticipation of an upcoming vacation, the company of a good friend, or the satisfaction of doing something well.

Pleasure is a mixture of physical sensations and emotions: savoring a delicious meal, playing tennis, or taking a walk on a beautiful day. Sensual and sexual pleasure also result from an interaction between physical sensations and your thoughts, feelings, and attitudes.

The particular combination of ingredients that evokes pleasure in you is uniquely your own. You learn what these are through a wide range of experiences and exploration over the course of your life. As we explained earlier, it is not unusual for women to grow up with little knowledge of their body's capacity for sensual, sexual pleasure. Without this knowledge, you may find yourself frustrated and at a loss to express your sexual preferences during lovemaking. Knowing how to give pleasure to your body and accept pleasure from it can help you to get what you want sexually.

What reactions do you have when you think about exploring your body for areas and ways of touching that will feel pleasurable? For many women this is a new idea or one they've been taught to ignore or inhibit. You may think of your body as something that should give pleasure to someone else, and the idea that you can enjoy your body for yourself may somehow seem unnatural or wrong. Thinking back to your goals in this program may be helpful at this point. Sexual growth and the development of more enjoyable sexual expression with or without a partner start with self-knowledge.

So let's take a few minutes and look at what you've accomplished so far. You've now spent some time thinking about the attitudes and feelings you have about sex. You've looked at your body and explored its contours and textures. You've probably already become more comfortable and aware of your body. Becoming familiar with special places on your body and knowing how to touch them in order to provide sensual or sexual pleasure is a natural next step. Learning these unique things about yourself will help make it possible for you to achieve sexual fulfillment and satisfaction on your own or with a partner. You will be able to share this information with your partner (as discussed in chapters 9 and 10), which will enhance the quality of sexual experiences for you both.

Also, research has shown that for many women, the easiest and strongest orgasms occur during self-pleasuring, or masturbation. For women who have not yet experienced orgasm, masturbation often provides the kind of stimulation most likely to lead to feelings of arousal and orgasm.

Since masturbation is a good way to experience frequent orgasms, it gives the orgasmic response a chance to become well established. Blood flow to the genitals increases as your body learns this new skill. This means that orgasm is more and more likely to occur. Also, the more orgasms you have, the more comfortable you will feel about trusting yourself and letting your feelings flow.

There is another, less obvious value in trying masturbation. It emphasizes a very important and very basic fact: *Your body belongs first of all to you.* Unless you can develop some kind of sense that your body is your territory (which you can choose to give as a gift, share, or keep to yourself), you cannot freely give it in a sexual interaction with another person. It will seem that the other person already owns it, and when that occurs you are less likely to feel you have the right to say yes or no to sex, less likely to help guide the sexual interaction, less likely to try sexual activities that interest you, and even less likely to know what you want sexually. In fact, if your body belongs to your partner, so will your pleasure, your pain, your arousal, and eventually your orgasms. That's a lot of power and responsibility to place with another person, and it is a setup for both your and your partner's disappointment. So, in a way, masturbation is only a method for claiming your body and its responses as your own, as part of you.

Yet, knowing all the "facts" and all the advantages to be gained does not necessarily make it easy for women to overcome feelings about masturbation that have been ingrained since childhood. Often these feelings and attitudes are the result of misinformation and myths about the supposed harms of masturbation. Perhaps you've been taught that masturbation is immature—something that one does as a child but shouldn't do as an adult or after marriage. Actually, masturbation is something that many mature people engage in from time to time, married or not. Rather than being "abnormal," masturbation is just another frequent and natural expression of sexuality. Most men and women masturbate at some time during their lives. Contrary to old beliefs, masturbation does not cause psychological or physical harm. Rather, it provides a healthy release for sexual tension, and it can be a good opportunity to learn about (and keep in touch with) your sexuality.

People often express the concern that masturbating will reduce their desire for sex with their partner. There is no psychological evidence for this belief, since most people would prefer to share sex with someone they feel sexual toward than to masturbate alone. There is also no physiological basis for this belief, since achieving orgasm through masturbation is no more "draining" than an orgasm achieved through intercourse or some other activity with a partner. In fact, studies have shown that masturbation can have a positive influence on sexual relationships with a partner. It has been found that women who are orgasmic through any means before marriage, including masturbation, often have less difficulty experiencing orgasm with their partners after marriage. Women who have no orgasmic experience have more difficulty becoming orgasmic with their partners.

Finally, women sometimes express the fear that they will become dependent on masturbation—that they will want to masturbate too much or to experience orgasm only in this way. In our experience seeing women in therapy, there is no such thing as "too much" sex. Sexual pleasure is self-limiting. Women are usually able to use what they learn through masturbation to enrich the quality of their sexual relationships with their partners. (Ways to do this are discussed in chapters 9–11.) Because they are more aware of their bodies and their own sexual responsiveness, these women usually become orgasmic through other forms of stimulation, such as manual caressing by their partners and oral-genital sex.

Try putting your concerns aside temporarily so that you can continue the exploration and growth process you began in chapter 2. Often, with time and practice, an activity that is initially difficult and uncomfortable becomes easier and more a part of your routine. Also remember that you do not have to love masturbation. Self-pleasuring may be something you only do in the context of this exploration and sexual growth program. Or you may choose to continue masturbation after you have completed this program. This is for you to decide. These exercises are only vehicles that can help you get to where *you* want to be sexually.

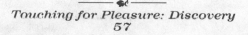

Touching for Pleasure: Discovery
57

DISCOVERING PLEASURE

Begin by reserving thirty minutes to an hour for yourself. Relax in a way you enjoy and that you've found works well for you—perhaps a bath or relaxation exercises. Create a relaxing atmosphere with pleasing lighting, incense, or other small details that make a difference to you. *Be good to yourself;* feel free to be as fussy about the trimmings for your own session as you would be if a lover were joining you.

Use some body lotion, oil, or powder as you touch yourself. Warming the lotion or oil is easy to do by setting the bottle in hot water; this gives a nice sensation as you smooth it on your body. You might start with your arms and hands and move down to the rest of your body, or start with your feet and legs if you prefer. Focus your attention on the feel of your hand on your body. Massage and touch yourself in different ways. Try to help your body feel good—don't try for arousal. Let your hand touch your breasts, abdomen, inner thighs. Try some of the different strokes and ways of touching you began to explore in the last chapter. Be gentle with yourself, and try to tune into any feelings of pleasure your body is giving you. Closing your eyes may help you to focus your attention.

Let your hand find your labia and clitoral shaft. Stroke your lips lightly, run your finger alongside the clitoris and up over the shaft. Massage the clitoris lightly between two fingers, or try a circular motion. You may want to explore with one or both of your hands at the same time. Or use one hand on one part of your body and your other hand on another. Vary your strokes and rhythm and move to new areas. Try strong pressure as well as light touching. Explore different parts of your body for pleasurable feelings—try your arms and the insides of your legs as well as your breasts and clitoris. Touch just inside your vagina to see how this feels. Focus on feelings—stay with areas that feel good or better than others. Share your body with yourself. When you feel ready to end this session, try lightly massaging any areas of tension until you feel relaxed and good all over. Close your eyes, and take some deep, full breaths, inhaling through your nose, exhaling through your mouth.

How did you feel about this experience? Were you more or less comfortable than you expected?

Women react in different ways to the exercise above. You may have felt curious, afraid, guilty, repulsed, excited, or nervous. Perhaps you were aware of several feelings. Sometimes these are the result of watching yourself, almost as if you were a spectator observ-

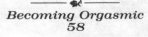

ing from a distance. You may have thought about how awkward or silly you looked doing this, or how other people would respond if they knew what you were doing.

This tendency to fall into the spectator role is a natural result of feelings of anxiety or embarrassment, and it often occurs at the beginning of any process of change. Refocusing your attention back on your body and what it is feeling will help you deal with the tendency to be a spectator. In the next chapter you will learn more specific ways to improve your ability to become totally involved in your self-pleasuring.

Were you expecting (or putting pressure on yourself) to feel arousal?

It's very easy to become caught up in seeking arousal. However, this usually does not work. Chasing sexual arousal makes you an observer of your responses rather than a participant in your pleasure. You may find yourself worrying about how well you're doing and putting pressure on yourself to try harder. This interferes with whatever pleasure you might experience.

For now, try to relax and let yourself experience whatever it is your body is feeling. If you aren't aware of any pleasurable feelings right now, that's all right. It may take you a while to learn to label the different feelings you may be experiencing. Do try to focus on any areas that feel different from others, and to notice your reaction to different ways of touching yourself. Instead of noticing pleasure, let yourself notice differences in pressure and sensitivity.

If you were extremely upset or repulsed by this activity, you need to go more slowly. Keep in mind the reasons why it's important for you to have this knowledge about yourself, and your original reasons for wanting to embark on this program for sexual growth.

Return to this exercise when you want to attempt it again. Relax first by doing one or more of the relaxation exercises from chapter 3. Spend only a few minutes in self-pleasuring at first, and gradually increase the time as you begin to feel more comfortable.

If you have repeated strong negative feelings during your sessions, take the time to examine them. Negative feelings—anger, revulsion, and fear, for example—are there for a reason. Perhaps they are trying to protect you from painful old memories or experiences that are somehow triggered by these sessions. To manage the overwhelming and invasive qualities of these feelings, try the following. First name the feeling (work with only one feeling at a time). Then locate the feeling. Where in your body do you feel the negative feeling? In your mouth? Your throat? Your stomach? Focus on it in its location. Could you draw a picture of it? Try to do so, either mentally or on paper. Draw it exactly, to the inch. It will change in size, and possibly in shape, as you focus on it in its location in your body. Gradually, if you keep focusing on it, it will decrease in size and weaken in intensity. If you continue to have difficulties at this stage, you may want to try some "cognitive restructuring."

COGNITIVE RESTRUCTURING TECHNIQUES

One system of therapy, called *cognitive therapy*, can help you if you are still experiencing negative emotions about exploring your body. What follow are some techniques for promoting your growth and development in this area:

1.   As you identify the negative emotions, be sure you have them labeled correctly. For example, is it really revulsion or disgust that you feel? Perhaps the feeling can more accurately be described as guilt or shame. This step is important, since as a general feeling like "disgust" is hard to change, while a more specific feeling like "guilt about a particular event" can be reexamined and more easily changed.

2.   Let yourself think about where your emotions come from. How have you come to feel negative emotions about something as natural as looking at and touching your own body? Often, these feelings arise out of past events, a sort of "cultural conditioning" from specific experiences in childhood or adolescence. Many women were directly told—by parents, teachers, or religious figures—that their bodies were "not nice." Normal childhood curiosity about genitals can terrify parents into shaming or punishing their children for touching their own genitals or playing childhood body games.

3.   Reexamine the basis for your negative feelings. Do you rationally and intellectually still believe that it is wrong to look at and touch your own body? Or are these feelings irrational, gut-level residues of negative experiences? What are your beliefs and values about your sexuality *now*, as an adult, as opposed to what you uncritically accepted as a child?

4.   Develop a set of "coping statements" to help you overcome irrational negative emotions. A "coping statement" is a sentence that you can write out and go over a few times each day, to work through your negative emotions. Here are some examples:

- "There's nothing wrong or unnatural about learning to enjoy my body."
- "I'm not a child anymore. I can make up my own mind about what's right and wrong for me."
- "The experiences I had were very powerful for the child I was *then. Now* I'm an adult. I can let these things belong more to the past than the present. I can choose not to be controlled by them anymore."
- "I'm not willing to let them (whoever) continue to interfere with my sexual and emotional life. I've let them decide for a long time. Now *I'm* ready to decide for myself."
- "I like looking at my face (or hair, or eyes, or so on). The rest of my body is no different. It's all me, and I can appreciate all of it."
- "I already enjoy the feelings I get from my body when I move (dance, run, play tennis, swim, and so on). Feeling body pleasure in this new way is really not too different."
- "My breasts and genitals are aspects that make me a woman, and they are parts of me that can give me a lot of pleasure. They are also the parts of me that bring pleasure to my partner. My body's pleasure is part of a love relationship."
- "The women I respect and admire value their bodies and the pleasure they can bring to themselves and their lover through their bodies."
- "The things I learned about my body as a child no longer apply. Now that I'm a grown woman, I can have different feelings."

Try to develop a set of at least ten coping statements that fit for you and address the important issues in your own negative feelings. Go over these and think about them several times.

5. Practice "self-efficacy" statements and "mastery imagery." Develop a set of ten "self-efficacy" statements. Similar to coping statements, these are sentences that stress the strengths and resources you have in your overcoming of negative emotions. Some examples:

- "I *can* do it. I'm making progress."
- "I've taken the first step, and that's the hardest. Now it's just a matter of time."
- "Lots of other women have dealt with these feelings, and I can, too."
- "The part of me that's negative is gradually fading, and the part of me that wants to grow and change is getting stronger."

"Mastery imagery" involves daydreaming, or fantasy. Try closing your eyes, visualizing yourself being able to look at, touch your body, and enjoy the experience. Really try to "see" these images, as if you were watching a movie of yourself. When you can successfully imagine and visualize yourself doing the self-exploration with pleasure, try to role-play or act this out in reality. That is, try to act as if you had already successfully overcome any remaining negative feelings. Repeat the self-exploration exercises as if you were an actress making a movie about sexual growth. Often, when people act "as if" they were not frightened and anxious, they discover that the anxiety and fear does indeed go away. By acting as if you were able to enjoy self-exploration, you may find that you really *are* enjoying it.

SOME ADDITIONAL SUGGESTIONS

To make each session a real exploration, try varying some of the following:

Where you have your session. If you have privacy in rooms other than your bedroom, you might try these areas. One woman who followed this program enjoyed doing her touching for the first few sessions while in a warm bath.

Your position. You may want to sit up or lie on your stomach or side. You may also enjoy the feel of a pillow under different parts of your body.

Some women enjoy the feelings that come from pressing their legs together tightly. Occasionally, a woman will be orgasmic using this type of stimulation. The problem with this seems to be that it is often difficult for these women to become orgasmic through partner stimulation. This makes sense, since there is no way a partner can pleasure you in this way; and intercourse particularly may interfere with the pattern of thigh pressure. For this reason, we won't encourage exploration of this type of stimulation right now. At some later time, when you are orgasmic in other ways, you may want to include this. However, you should be able to experience feelings of pleasure in your genitals in ways other than through thigh pressure.

If you have been using thigh-pressure stimulation and find it difficult to get pleasure from other forms of touching, there are sev-

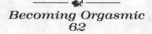

eral things you can try. Since thigh pressure provides a lot of indirect stimulation from tensing certain muscles, you might concentrate on providing pressure to your mons area with several fingers or the entire palm of your hand, rather than stimulating the clitoris and vaginal area directly. At the same time, *without* clenching your legs together, you can tense your buttocks and leg muscles. Practicing this should provide you with pleasurable feelings and also allow you to increase the variety of ways to be stimulated. It will probably take a while to learn to enjoy this, so be patient if the first few attempts are not as satisfying as your old method.

Use some kind of gentle lubricant. Secretions from your vagina or saliva may be enjoyable and add to your sensitivity. However, be cautious of anything with perfume or other strong ingredients. The skin of your genitals is extremely sensitive, and alcohol or other additives in lotions or oils may irritate or cause a burning sensation. Instead, try the water-soluble gels such as K-Y (or Astroglide, Lubrin, Trans-Lube). These are available in drugstores, and you do not need a prescription to buy them. These are the *only* things (except saliva or your natural vaginal secretions) that should be used while you're exploring the *inside* of your vagina. They will not irritate you or interfere with your body's natural lubrication. It is *not* a good idea to use baby oil or petroleum jelly, since they are not water soluble and tend to interfere with the vagina's natural protection against infection.

Vary the amount of time you spend. Be flexible within the fifteen to thirty minutes, concentrating on different areas and spending the amount of time that feels comfortable for you.

Try exploring other textures and feelings. For example, try rubbing a rough towel, a piece of velvet, or a silk scarf along your body. Be as inventive and creative as you like. Explore ways to awaken your body—keeping "discovery" an active part of your sessions prevents them from becoming mechanical or a chore.

Vary the time of day. Try mornings, afternoons, and late and early evenings if you can. You may find that your body is more responsive at certain times of the day or of the month. Many women find changes in their sensitivity just before or just after their menstrual flow. As you find out this information about yourself, taking advantage of good times whenever they occur to have a session will help encourage your spontaneity. (This may not be possible very often if you have many responsibilities.)

Try to repeat this exploration two times over the next week. Spend fifteen to thirty minutes each time. When you feel that you have learned about the sensitive and pleasurable areas of your body and ways to touch them, go on to chapter 5. If you feel uncomfortable doing this exercise, or if you are not able to distinguish any pleasurable feelings, give yourself more time. Spend another week or so on this, and then move on to chapter 5.

5
Touching for Pleasure: Focusing

In the last chapter you learned how touching and pleasure are connected. At this point you may feel that you've made a good start in learning about the places on your body that are most likely to feel good and what kinds of touches are most appealing. Or you may feel that you have not found out anything new and that, no matter what you do, your body just will not signal pleasure when you touch it. Change does not happen all at once—sometimes it is a slow, gradual process. Changes have usually already begun before we even notice them—for example, losing or gaining weight begins before we see and feel the difference in pounds. *Your* changing has its own unique patterns. The key to fostering change is to respect and appreciate whatever gains you make and to try to understand and be patient with those that seem temporarily to elude you. Remember, changes begin to take place even before you are aware of them.

This chapter will offer you a chance to expand your ability to give yourself pleasure. We will be discussing ways in which you might decrease distracting thoughts during your self-pleasuring sessions, and we will give you aids for getting into the mood to have a session. For instance, we will talk about some body exercises you can do to feel physically looser and more agile, and also to become more comfortable with tension and movement during sex. We will also discuss some exercises that some women have found helpful for increasing their ability to focus on sensual-sexual sensations.

Continuing to experiment with your self-pleasuring sessions will help you begin to feel more comfortable about letting yourself touch your genitals for pleasure. This touching will let you develop a clearer understanding of how various kinds of stimulation affect you at different times. Of course, you will not learn all of this the first time you try. Your body may respond a little differently each time, but it always provides you with information about what does or doesn't feel good. Give yourself at least three or four sessions in order to become comfortable and learn several ways of stimulating yourself.

When you do find that you are having difficulty getting in the mood for your self-pleasuring sessions, you may be a little discouraged. But having trouble at this stage is a useful and meaningful reaction. You are learning important information—from those times when you can't seem to get anywhere, try to learn something about *why* it's difficult. Has something upsetting happened earlier in the day? Do you feel pressed for time? Do your thoughts wander? As you attempt to identify at what point your progress seems to slow down, we will be offering suggestions regarding several of the more frequent trouble spots.

Some women have commented that they are not really sure if they are experiencing pleasure, particularly when they are touching their genitals. "It's different," one woman said, "but I'm not sure if it's pleasurable or neutral." Another woman commented, "I just feel a sort of nervousness when I touch there [her clitoris]." If these are new feelings for you, you may find it difficult to label them at first. Whatever sensations you detect, explore them (as long as they are not painful) and let them continue, no matter how small the difference or the pleasure may be for you. Give yourself plenty of time and a number of different occasions to develop the kinds of stimulation that you like. If you do feel pleasure or sexual arousal for a few seconds and then lose the sensations, don't worry: This is a natural pattern, especially when you are beginning to experience new sexual feelings.

GETTING STARTED

Try having one thirty-minute session now or later on today. Make your usual preparations to assure that you have some time to yourself. Touch and stroke various areas of your body, and then begin to focus on the most pleasurable areas, including your genitals. Then just try to continue letting pleasurable feeling flow with whatever touches seem to work.

After you finish, think over the following questions:

What were the most difficult parts of this step? Try to identify what went well and what seemed to cause you trouble. Common areas of difficulty include: *(a)* Getting into the mood for a session. Are you allowing yourself uninterrupted time during the day when you are not fatigued or pressed to do other things? *(b)* Do you find your mind wandering, and is it hard to concentrate on yourself? *(c)* Do you find

that it is difficult to feel very sensual about stimulating your genitals—perhaps it seems a little mechanical and no one type of stroke feels better than any other? You may be expecting too much progress too fast. Try being more patient with yourself and seeing if you can come up with some ways of your own to make the experience more sensual.

It is also possible that you are still having some negative feelings about the whole idea of masturbation, and this could hinder you from letting yourself experience pleasure in this way. Learning to deal with your reservations about masturbation also takes time. Does it continue to seem unnatural? Are you afraid you will like it more than other kinds of sexual activity as you continue to do it? Try to remind yourself that masturbation is not the goal of your sexual growth; it is just one of the techniques that provides you with safe opportunities to learn about your body and its mysteries of sensitivity and pleasure. Perhaps at the end of this program you will never masturbate again; perhaps you will masturbate frequently. *It* will not decide, *you* will. And even though we focus on sex as if it is a separate category of life, it is not. Your sexuality is part of your expression as a person, and therefore it is unlikely suddenly to take over and dominate every other aspect of your life.

Whatever reservations you have about masturbating, they are real and important, and you don't have to get rid of them completely in order to continue your self-pleasuring explorations. Instead, we suggest that for now you think about a few of the positive things you can gain from learning to masturbate—for instance, feeling relaxed, feeling pleasure, becoming more sensual. Focus only on the potential gains.

What kinds of stimulation were most effective in giving you pleasure? When do you notice the most sensitivity or feeling—during what kinds of pressure, strokes, rhythms—and where on your genitals does stimulation feel best? Good feelings often ebb and flow, so if you notice an area feeling numb or uncomfortable, try a different kind of touch or another part of your body.

Do you find yourself concerned about whether you will experience sexual arousal? This is one of the most tempting, and least helpful, concerns during self-stimulation. When you find yourself mentally "watching" your own responses, try to stop those thoughts and refocus on the feelings inside your body. Let your mind's attention center completely on the precise places where your body and hand are in contact, letting other thoughts or sensations drift out of your awareness.

Not all of your sessions will be the same. Sometimes you will feel that nothing is happening; at other times you will feel you have made progress. This is a natural growth process that everyone experiences, so don't put pressure on yourself if things seem to go slowly for you. It's important not to compare sessions. Just try to treat each session as one more opportunity to learn about yourself. This isn't always easy, especially if you feel you are not making any progress. If you do have a difficult or unrewarding session, try the following: *(a)* Think about little details of your session and try to pick out a few "small" things that went a bit better than they have in the past—it may be simply feeling a little more comfortable touching yourself or enjoying a different kind of stimulation you hadn't noticed before. Give yourself credit for any aspects of your sessions that are showing even slight improvement. *(b)* Think about what you can learn from a disappointing session. Think about what made it disappointing. Were your expectations too high? Did you try too hard? Did you have trouble concentrating or getting into the mood? Were you upset about something else when you began? Identifying some possible sources of interference is a beginning; doing something about them will come with time and patience.

WAYS TO FOCUS ON AND ENJOY SELF-PLEASURING

The following suggestions are included to help you become more involved in your sessions—both mentally and physically—to feel more in tune with your body. First, we will talk about some sensual "loosening" exercises. Then we will discuss sensate focus as a way to tune into your physical sensations mentally. And finally, we will talk a little about erotic literature and fantasy.

"Loosening" Exercises

The following exercises will benefit you in several ways. To begin with, you will be using the muscles that are involved in sexual activities, so the exercises should help you strengthen those muscles and get adjusted to the kind of physical tension that accompanies sexual

arousal. Also, some of the exercises allow you to practice certain movements that occur during sexual activities. Feeling free to move during sex can be very important in helping you let go and enjoy sexual feelings—both emotionally and physically. In addition, exercises generally help people feel better about themselves. For instance, some people just feel more "alive"—maybe this would mean that you will feel more agile or a bit more energetic as you continue to practice them. Exercise also gives a psychological boost: You may feel more in control of your body. If you see these aspects of exercise as important, incorporate those listed here into your exercise program. (We recommend some excellent exercise books for this in the bibliography.)

The following stretching exercises are designed to help you move more freely and feel more relaxed. We all have muscles that are tight. In some cases these muscles may reflect real feelings of tension. In other cases, these muscles have just never been used or stretched. Some of these exercises are common yoga positions; others are used in such programs as bioenergetics.

It would be best if you wore loose-fitting clothing, or no clothing at all if you prefer. For some of the exercises, you may find it helpful to set up a large mirror against a wall or chair to see how your body moves. However, don't keep your eyes on the mirror throughout the exercises. Your attention should be focused on how the movements feel, not how they look. You may feel awkward doing these exercises at first—try not to worry about doing them perfectly. The most important thing is to try them several times and to concentrate on your physical feelings during and after the exercises. Use your own judgment about how many you do or how hard you try. Modify any that seem too strenuous, and gradually work into the more difficult versions. If you have had any physical problems, such as back pain, be particularly careful to avoid those exercises that would strain troublesome muscles. If you are concerned, consult your doctor before trying these exercises.

Breathing in and out. Our breathing patterns change with our emotional state. For most of the early part of your sessions, you try to maintain a full, even pattern of breathing in order to help your body stay relaxed. Start now—let your mouth remain slightly open. As you take breath into your body, let your lungs and stomach fill out. Then exhale—all the way. Pause for a natural amount of time. Then begin again. Periodically, check yourself to make sure you are not holding your breath. Holding your breath or breathing shallowly can be a sign of tension or of trying too hard, which can make it difficult for you to focus fully and enjoy physical feelings.

Chest exercises. To help free this area of tension, lie down on your back. As you take a very deep breath, raise your arms up, then over your head in a high arch. As you exhale, put your arms back down. Repeat this five times, breathing in (hands over head), breathing out (lowering arms). Then reverse the pairs: Breathe out as you raise your arms, breathe in as you lower them. Repeat five times. Finally, go back to the original pairing. How do you feel? What do you notice about your body?

You may feel some slight tingling in your hands and face. That's what you are supposed to feel. Allow this feeling to happen—it is similar to the tingling that can occur after orgasm. Tingling is often present after exercise; but we usually ignore it. What we want to work on is tuning into this tingling feeling, just as you will later be tuning into your feelings of sexual arousal.

Neck tension. Put your fingers behind your neck and feel for any tension in the muscles along the ridge at the base of your skull. This area and your forehead work together to cause you discomfort—sometimes to cause headaches.

To relieve this tension, you will need a small, firm ball. Lie down on the floor, place the ball at the back of your neck, and relax your head's weight on the ball. Roll your head around to work the ball back and forth across those areas that feel tense. Relax completely. Continue your breathing.

For your forehead, do the "spectacles stroke." Take your thumb or forefingers and stroke across your eyebrows past your temples above your ears. Trace a pattern with your fingers following where glasses would be worn. Do this ten times.

The rocking pelvis. This is a multipurpose exercise. As you do it you may recognize it as an intercourse thrust, or as a movement you use during your pleasuring sessions. It can be done while you are lying or sitting down, and it is designed to help you loosen your lower back area. The exercise combines deep breathing with pelvic movements. Some women have also found it useful in reducing menstrual cramping.

Lie on your back. As you breathe in, rock your pelvis backward

by arching the small of your back; as you breathe out, let your pelvis rotate forward. Try this very slowly, holding your pelvis cocked and then relaxing it. It may help to have your hands on your hips as you are practicing the motion. Try it for five minutes—don't hurry, and remember to coordinate your breathing with your pelvic movements.

The bouncing pelvis. To make you more aware of your pelvic feelings, lie on your back with your knees up. Raise your hips and bounce your pelvis. Try this on your stomach, too; you may want to use your hands to raise your body a little. It helps to brace your feet against the wall while you bounce.

The pelvic lift. This common yoga exercise gives you a chance to practice pelvic movements further.

Lie on your back, legs bent, knees in the air. As you take a breath, cock your pelvis backward by arching the small of your back. Then, as you expel your air, raise your pelvis slightly, one vertebra at a time, beginning at your tailbone, until it is off the floor. Continue this until you are resting on your shoulders and feet. Come back down gently and slowly. Repeat this sequence ten times. Take your time with this. If you feel pain or discomfort, stop.

How do you feel about these exercises? If you couldn't do some of them, don't feel discouraged. Give yourself time. These exercises feel awkward to most women at first. Some may have been too difficult for you to perform, others too easy. Spend a moment now and think about how you felt *during* these exercises. Did you feel good? Were you emotionally uncomfortable about any of the movements? This may be because active movements during sex may be a new experience for you, and perhaps because you are unsure about how active and expressive you want to be.

If you found these exercises useful, if they made your body feel good, do them whenever it suits you. Their purpose is to get you in touch with any uncomfortable or negative feelings you may have about intercourse. For instance, you may have been reminded that certain positions during intercourse have made sex uncomfortable or unpleasant for you. Try to see these exercises as one way that will allow you to change the old patterns that have been unsatisfying for you in the past. They are a way of trying out expressive movements that can prepare you, mentally and physically, before you are actually involved in sexual activity.

Sensate Focus

Sensate focus is designed to give you practice in attending to your inner body sensations. It will help you to deal with distracting thoughts and can also be used to help you relax and feel more in the mood for a session.

First, lie down in a comfortable, private room that is free of distractions. Close your eyes and focus on sounds in the room. Try hard to pick out different sounds. Do this for a few minutes before you go on.

What were some of the sounds you were able to focus on? Perhaps you noticed the sound of cars going by, the refrigerator humming, or your own breathing. When you began to concentrate on these sounds, you were probably less aware of other sensations, such as the feeling in your hands. This is because your awareness is like a spot light. Focusing on one particular thing makes it clearer, while other things tend to fade into the background. As you go through this exercise, practice focusing on particular parts of your body. You may want to have someone with whom you feel comfortable read the steps to you. If the procedure is taped or read, make sure it is done slowly so that you have time to practice the focusing.

Sensate focus exercise. Close your eyes and relax. Are you comfortable? See if you can get more comfortable by changing your position slightly. Now become aware of your breathing. Feel the air move into your nose or mouth and down your throat into your lungs. Notice all the details of how your chest and belly move as air flows in and out of your lungs. If you notice your attention wandering to other thoughts, refocus your attention on your breathing.

Start at your feet. Concentrate on the sensations in your toes and arches. Wiggle your toes and feet. Do they feel warm, cool, tense, loose, tingling, heavy, light? Move up to your ankles, calves, knees. Do this slowly, giving each part of your body a minute of your full inner-centered attention.

Now focus on your genitals. Are you aware of any sensations in your labia, clitoris, or vagina? Contract your vaginal muscles. Focus on the sensations this produces in your genitals.

Move to your hands. Are they tense or relaxed? Concentrate on the places where your hands and arms make contact with the floor or bed.

Move on to your shoulders, neck, and head. Try focusing your awareness on each part separately. Are you aware of any feelings of

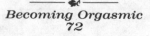

heaviness or tenseness. Does your scalp feel tight or relaxed? What smells are you aware of?

Now become aware of your breathing again. Focus on it for a few minutes. Take a few deep breaths and just enjoy the sensation of relaxing.

When you are finished, think about the following questions: (1) How did you feel after this exercise—relaxed, sleepy, calm, alert? (2) Did you find that your mind wandered to other things and that you had to keep bringing your thoughts back to your body? (3) Was it more difficult to focus on your genitals than on other parts of your body?

You should try this on several different occasions *before* your masturbation sessions. A number of women have found that this exercise can be a good preliminary step toward getting in the mood for a session. Concentrating on the feelings in your body and shutting out the outside world for a few minutes is an important beginning for you to be able to become involved with self-pleasuring.

Erotic Literature

The previous two sections discussed ways that can help you focus on sensual and sexual feelings in your body. Reading or viewing erotic materials may also help you get into the mood for a session and enhance your feelings of sexual pleasure.

Part of sexual growth is exploring different forms of sensual-sexual expression. Erotic themes are expressed in many ways—music, art, literature, and photography. The word *erotic* means that something sexual is suggested or depicted in the content, which in turn is likely to evoke sexual feelings in the person who is viewing or reading the material. We see erotica as a useful way to aid sexual arousal and help you to clarify for yourself what does and does not turn you on.

Like many women, you may find yourself turned on at times by erotic stories or erotic pictures in magazines. How do you feel when this happens?

It would not be surprising if your feelings were mixed. One reason is that it has long been believed that romance, not sex, was the fire of women's sexual arousal. Putting it another way, women were expected to be turned off, repulsed, by sexually explicit materials, preferring instead tales of deep mutual feelings and being in love. In fact, this may be true for some women (as can be seen from some of the selections in the next section). However, research since 1970 has clearly shown that women can become very sexually aroused by explicitly sexual stories, films, and fantasies.

For instance, when women hear a tape that describes two people making love, they usually become aroused regardless of the presence or absence of romantic ideas in the scene. This does not mean that romantic themes (such as a committed relationship, emotional passion, and statements of mutual deep feeling and love) are not also appealing to women. It does mean that strictly erotic themes that simply describe two people who are enjoying having sex together are sexually arousing for women, just as they are for men. So if you have been turned on in the past by sexy scenes in movies or books, or if you have tried not to let yourself be aroused because you think women shouldn't be aroused, keep in mind that there is nothing wrong with you. It makes sense that you would empathize with the feelings of the characters. While maturing, you may have picked up feelings of guilt, embarrassment, and shame about erotic materials out of a fear of being thought unfeminine or too sexual. You may even have tried to avoid any exposure to erotica. Or you may have seen a few selections on sexual themes that you felt were unpleasant or distasteful (there are plenty of sleazy selections available) and, as a result, decided that all erotica is terrible.

Not all types of erotic content are universally appealing, so don't expect yourself to become automatically aroused at the first sight of a naked body. It's fine to be selective in your tastes. However, try to view the use of erotica as an occasional enhancer of sexual pleasure, and accept that using it in this way is normal and healthy. Keeping an open mind and a sense of self-exploration will help you change some of your old attitudes and discover a little more about your own sexuality.

Although it may surprise you, it can take a while to recognize your own arousal to erotica. Women are often taught to ignore or at least not to admit to their sexual feelings. In fact research has shown that some women seem to be totally unaware of their body's sexual responses. Other women may mislabel sexual arousal as either neutral feelings of genital throbbing or uncomfortable feelings of body tension. One woman going through sex therapy interpreted her nipple erection as a sign that she was cold (rather than aroused) even though it was eighty-degree summer weather.

When you read or watch erotica, a variety of factors may decrease your awareness of physical arousal. First, your attention is usually less on your body than on the material you are observing, so you simply don't notice arousal until the feelings are strong. Second, you may not know what to expect to feel—women described all kinds of sensations, usually including some type of pressure, throbbing, pulsing, or warmth in the genital area. Third, as mentioned before, other feelings—worry, embarrassment, guilt—may be strong enough to mask your feelings of sexual arousal and either slow down your physical arousal or make your mind ignore the physical arousal even though it's there. You may need to remind yourself that you will not be harmed by reading or seeing erotica. Using it at this point is merely one way to help get your mind focused on sexual thoughts and images—as this will be an increasingly important contribution to your physical, sexual feelings.

We have included here a list of some books and magazines that we compiled by asking women what sort of reading has aroused them sexually. Although we call these works "erotic," not all of them are explicitly sexual. Some, such as *The French Lieutenant's Woman* and *Tender Is the Night*, are nonexplicit, suggestive, or romantic selections; while others, such as *The Godfather*, include aggression and violence as well as sex. Certain of these selections will appeal to you, and others won't. Similarly, some of the pictures in the magazines may be enjoyable, others will be neutral, and others will be unpleasant for you. The majority of erotic books, films, and magazines are directed at male customers, so you will probably have to hunt around a while to find something that appeals to you. Many of these books are advertised in magazines, or are easily found in bookstores and even in some supermarkets. Others may have to be ordered for you or purchased in an "adult" bookstore. If you feel comfortable about going into one, you may want to consider it. If not, there are lots of choices available through other sources.

BOOKS

Boys and Girls Together, William Goldman
Candy, Maxwell Kenton
The Carpetbaggers, Harold Robbins
Couples, John Updike
Diary of Anaïs Nin, Anaïs Nin
Doctor Zhivago, Boris Pasternak
Fanny Hill, John Cleland
Flowers of Evil, Charles Baudelaire
Forbidden Flowers, Nancy Friday
The Fountainhead, Ayn Rand
The Four-Gated City, Doris Lessing
The Fox, D. H. Lawrence
The French Lieutenant's Woman, John Fowles

The Godfather, Mario Puzo
The Group, Mary McCarthy
The Happy Hooker, Xaviera Hollander
The Joy of Sex, Alex Comfort
The Kama Sutra, Vatsayana
Lady Chatterley's Lover, D. H. Lawrence
Little Birds, Anaïs Nin
Love Poems, Anne Sexton
Madame Bovary, Gustave Flaubert
More Joy, Alex Comfort
My Life and Loves, Frank Harris
My Secret Garden, Nancy Friday
Myra Breckinridge, Gore Vidal
The Pearl, Anonymous
The Perfumed Garden of the Sheikh Nefzaoui, Anonymous
Peyton Place, Grace Metalious
Romeo and Juliet, William Shakespeare
The Sensuous Couple, Robert Chartham
The Sensuous Woman, "J"
Sons and Lovers, D. H. Lawrence
The Story of O, Pauline Reage
Tender is the Night, F. Scott Fitzgerald
Tropic of Cancer, Henry Miller
Valley of the Dolls, Jacqueline Susann
The Virgin and the Gypsy, D. H. Lawrence
Women in Love, D. H. Lawrence

MAGAZINES

Oui
Penthouse
Penthouse Forum
Playboy
Playgirl
Viva

Your sessions. Try spending thirty to forty-five minutes on your pleasuring sessions at least three times a week. Use erotic literature or look through a magazine that has pictures that are sexually interesting to you. You can begin stimulating yourself as you read or look, or wait until you either feel some good feelings (for instance throbbing or tingling) in your genitals or just feel like touching yourself. If you find what you are looking at is distracting from your pleasure, put it down and focus all your attention on your physical sensations.

You might also read a passage earlier in the day and find that you

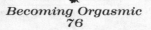

do not get turned on until you think about it later. At that time, find a place where you can have privacy and try stimulating yourself.

Again, erotica is an enhancer. Try using it a few times, and if you enjoy it, continue as often as you like. You may be concerned that you will come to like or depend on this too much. Try seeing this as something special you are doing for yourself right now. In the course of learning what arouses you, you may want to read from an erotic book or look at erotic pictures more frequently than you will later. That's fine. This is still an exploration of feelings and experiences.

Fantasy

Something else that can help you focus on your body and its sensations is fantasy. At times you may find your body is not responding to stimulation because your mind is elsewhere. As we said before, sexual pleasure means involving your body *and* your mind. Fantasy is one way to do this.

All of us have fantasized at times. We may be sitting and reading or in the middle of working, when all of a sudden we realize that our mind has wandered off and we are daydreaming. Dreams and daydreams are forms of fantasy. The difference is that when we are dreaming we have little conscious control over the content of our dreams, but when we daydream we have the pleasurable opportunity to create or re-create a scene consciously.

How do you feel when you fantasize about something sexual? Is it something you find easy or difficult to do, or is it something you have never deliberately tried? Some women find it easier to fantasize than others, but it is something you can teach yourself to do. Like becoming comfortable with sexual feelings, it means becoming comfortable enough with sexual thoughts to let go. This means you must feel basically good about yourself and be willing to trust yourself.

Sometimes, we may be afraid of *what* we fantasize. What will it mean if we fantasize about someone other than our spouse or partner, or if we fantasize about something that we wouldn't really enjoy or act out in real life? You may feel (or perhaps you have been taught) that to think about doing something is as bad as doing it. If you have these fears, it will help you to cope with them if you realize that sexual fantasy is a normal, natural activity. Fantasizing about something does not mean that you will actually do it. In fact, the beauty of fantasy is that it allows you the freedom to experiment with sexual variety beyond the limits of reality.

If your fantasies involve doing something sexual with another woman, this does not automatically mean that you secretly prefer women as sexual partners. Or if your fantasy themes include orgies, or the idea of another person forcing you to do something sexual (while you are tied up, for example), it does not mean that there is something wrong with you. Such fantasies are quite common among women, and enjoying them does not mean that you are immature or perverted or that you would necessarily act them out if a real opportunity presented itself. Rather, fantasies are a way of reexperiencing pleasurable or exciting situations, behaviors, and experiences; expressing creativity; and satisfying natural desires for variety, novelty, and excitement.

We'd like you to get a copy of *My Secret Garden* or *Forbidden Flowers* by Nancy Friday. These are collections of women's fantasies. You will probably experience lots of different reactions as you read them. Some fantasies will surprise you, some will make you laugh, some will turn you on, and some will definitely turn you off. What we would like you to get from reading these books is a feeling for the

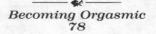

tremendous range of fantasies. We hope that doing so will make you feel more comfortable about exploring your own fantasies and about seeing how they develop and change over time.

Because these are women's fantasies, they have a special meaning for you. If you have a male partner, you may want to have him read the books, but don't be surprised if his reactions are different from your own. Sharing can be a good experience if you don't judge, evaluate, or impose expectations on each other (more on this in chapters 9 and 10). On the other hand, you may not feel like sharing your fantasies or reactions to these fantasies with your partner. That's all right, too. You can have your own "secret garden."

For the rest of the program, we'd like you to try to develop and use fantasy each time you have a self-pleasuring session. After you've relaxed and made yourself comfortable, mull over some ideas that might be appealing fantasies.

If you currently have a sexual partner, you might try imagining him in a fantasy. Close your eyes and pretend that he is touching your body as you touch yourself. Imagine that he is caressing all of the favorite places on your body and that he is willing to pleasure you in any way you want. Let your imagination go.

Or you might like fantasizing about an actual occasion on which you made love with someone. Let your mind take you back—linger over the sexually pleasant things you and he did. It may help to recall as many details as possible: where you were, how you got undressed, what you said to each other, how his skin and hair felt, how you both moved, and so forth.

There are several very common fantasy themes that women enjoy. One theme is that of being forced to have sex with someone. The idea of force may be expressed in many ways. Sometimes the force theme does not include any cooperation on the woman's part; for instance, some women imagine that they are being raped. The force theme can also incorporate some cooperation on the woman's part. An example of this would be a scene in which a woman is sitting in a restaurant: A man approaches her, they are attracted to each other, they talk, they walk to a place where they are alone, and the man becomes sexually forceful while the woman expresses restrained but reciprocated passion.

Why is the idea of force appealing to a lot of women? No one really knows, but there are a number of possibilities. One is that women are given conflicting messages about being sexual. They are generally taught the importance of being sexually attractive, but they

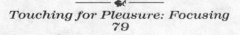

are also taught that they should, at some point, say no. In other words, women should look sexual but not really *be* sexual. Fantasy provides a good solution to this dilemma; the woman who is forced into sex has very little if any choice and responsibility for what happens. Being forced helps eliminate feelings of guilt about being sexual and aggressive.

Another speculation regarding the popularity of the force theme is that being "taken" sexually assumes that the woman is desirable. The cultural message for both male and female sexuality is that being desirable and sexually irresistible are very important. Force might indirectly imply that the female is so utterly sexually appealing that the man cannot control himself. (Of course, being irresistible does not have to mean that force must be involved—you may imagine yourself tantalizing or stimulating several men in a situation in which *you* are in control of what happens.)

Another common theme incorporates more "romantic" elements into a sexual scene. Often women imagine themselves having a clandestine affair with an important or well-known person. The fantasized person might be someone you know or someone you have seen on the stage or in films. Imagining that you are making love with someone you have seen in the movies may be particularly easy, since so many movies include some sexual activity.

Another theme that many women find arousing is that of being aggressive. You may find that you like to imagine yourself in control of a sexual encounter, selecting a partner of your choice, initiating sexual activity with him, turning him on, teasing him to the point of orgasm several times before you let him climax, having him moaning for more, being able to have him do anything you want him to do. You can expand this to several different men, each of whom you control according to your sexual desires. Aggression in fantasy allows women a chance to express what is not culturally approved of: the initiation and direction (or even domination) of a sexual encounter.

In your own attempts at developing fantasies, you might start by recalling a film scene that you particularly liked and add your own preferences. Or, if it suits you better, you might begin your self-pleasuring session by reading about someone else's fantasy from *My Secret Garden,* by reading parts of an erotic story, or perhaps by looking at some pictures that you find sexually appealing. As you get more into the fantasy and can picture it clearly, begin touching yourself. At some point you can put the book down and continue the fantasy on your own.

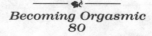

Putting Erotica and Fantasy in Context

At this point in your personal exploration of sexual feelings, we hope you are able to sample the world of erotica and fantasy. But since women occasionally have problems related to the erotic material they need to become aroused, we will discuss some common questions that they have had.

Isn't erotica pornography, and isn't pornography about dirty sex, bad women, and perverted men? Pornography has become a legal term and therefore changes depending on alterations in the legal system. *Erotica* covers more love-sex and literary-artistic materials, while *pornography* covers more hard-core, sex-for-sex's-sake media. In fact, the two words have often been used interchangeably, since they both include explicit sexual descriptions that are expected to increase the observer's sexual arousal or desire. We use *erotica* because most of the women we have known have used the word and have preferred the type of materials that fall under the meaning conveyed by *erotica.*

All pornography is about sex. A portion of pornography (like most other fiction) is also about human degradation, hostility toward women, and destructiveness and humiliation. You may want to avoid these materials, as they will inevitably support any negative feelings you may have about yourself as a sexual person.

There are erotic materials that are sexy without being violent, hostile, or degrading to women.

Can someone use erotica too much? Of course, the problem is how to define too much. If one uses erotica to the extent that it interferes with the rest of one's life (missing work, school, or chances for mutual interpersonal sexual contact), that's very likely too much. We've never seen this happen to the hundreds of women we have worked with on their sexual growth.

What kinds of problems might develop for women who use erotica or certain fantasy themes? One woman we saw was quite disturbed by the fact that the only way she could get aroused with her husband was to read a certain passage from *The Story of O* every time she had sex. She was afraid to change this ritual, as it had been going on for over ten years and it always worked. She felt trapped in

her erotic image and needed help to become more flexible in her imagery and more confident of her sexual responsiveness. In this case, her husband also had to change some of his sexual approaches to her.

Another type of issue that can arise is that a woman is distressed when she realizes that only one image arouses her and that image is intellectually repugnant to her—for example, that she is being humiliated in her fantasy.

This combination of *exclusive* or addicted devotion to one very *destructive* fantasy is a signal that sexual tension has become linked with very negative feelings about sex and about oneself. Further examination of this issue with a therapist trained to understand such conflicts may be of value.

Another issue is how close to home your fantasy object should be. When trying to change sexually with a current sexual partner, some women are able to incorporate their sexual partners into their fantasies. Others are not, at least at the beginning. For these women we often recommend actors, athletes, or other public figures they find attractive. Several studies have found Robert Redford, Paul Newman, and Tom Selleck to be the most frequently reported figures in women's fantasies. While it's very normal to feel some sexual attraction to men other than a current partner who is in your daily life, fantasies about such men have the potential to create conflict or guilty feelings that can inhibit your sexual growth. In other words, you are unlikely to feel guilty about a sexual fantasy involving Robert Redford, but indulging in sexual fantasies about your best friend's husband or your next-door neighbor may make you feel uncomfortable or vulnerable rather than help you to learn more about your sexual responsiveness. Another advantage of using an imaginary lover in your fantasy is that you may feel more free to imagine him—or you—doing things that you wouldn't actually do in "real life." If you find you only have frequent and urgent fantasies about an acquaintance for whom you already have strong feelings of attraction and interest, it may mean that you need to reexamine some general aspects of your current relationship, with your partner or with a therapist.

One final comment on erotica and fantasy "contexts." Romantic and sexual fantasy is almost incessant when one is fairly newly in love. Constantly thinking of one's lover and imagining all sorts of activities together are normal states of mind when you are in the early stages of falling in love.

Suggestions to Expand Your Ability to Fantasize

1.   A fantasy does not have to be some elaborate and involved story. Your fantasy may just be a series of brief images (a particular scene, a look, a face, or a touch) that holds meaning for you.

2.   What turns you on need not be explicitly sexual. It may be more romantic and sensual—such as the thought of someone stroking your face tenderly, someone holding you very close, or being surprised by someone's touch.

3.   Little details can often be important to the creation of a fantasy. Try to discover what elements are important to you. Women who have described what parts of their fantasies are arousing mention the thought of their partner getting very aroused while they are making love; the image of their partner reaching orgasm; the thought that their partner will do anything for any length of time to give them pleasure (such as thirty minutes of oral-genital stimulation or an hour of intercourse); pretending to have sex in a different place—in the woods, underwater, in the snow, on a beach; or imagining spontaneous sex, such as having sex the minute you walk in the door without even taking off any clothes. (You can make this fun by keeping some of your clothes on while stimulating yourself.)

4.   Also, try blending your sensate focus exercises with a fantasy. For instance, as you concentrate on the feelings in your thighs, touch yourself there, and imagine that your fantasy partner's hands are doing the caressing.

After you've tried some of the above a few times, you will probably find it easier and more enjoyable to fantasize during your pleasure sessions.

BEFORE YOU GO ON

Try to have five or six sessions over the next two weeks in which you use fantasy, erotic literature, sensate focus, and loosening exercises. You can try one or two of these focus techniques during each session and begin to get an idea of which ones seem most useful for you.

6
Going Further

At this point in the program you've been masturbating for up to thirty minutes per session. Although you've probably experienced high arousal, you haven't yet been able to have an orgasm. Don't panic! You've learned a lot about your body and how it responds—you just need some more time and exploration. Let's make sure, however, that other problems or feelings aren't interfering.

Do you find it difficult to get in the mood for your sessions? Do you sometimes feel that you would rather not spend this time with yourself? Most women experience these reactions from time to time; but if you find you have them frequently, you need to stop and think about possible causes. Think about the difference between those times when you enjoy feeling sensual or sexual and when you don't. Does the kind of day you had make a difference? This often affects how we interact with others and feel about ourselves. If you've had a hectic day, if you've felt pressured, or had conflicts with others, it's not surprising that you may have trouble focusing on yourself in pleasurable ways. Putting off your session for another day is one possibility. Another is allowing yourself some extra time to unwind. Try to set aside some time in the evening—a time when you can be alone if you want, and a time when you can relax. A bath, a snack, reading, or running through the relaxation exercises—any or all may help you to put the day behind you.

Example: One of our clients, Evelyn, was having great difficulty getting in the mood for her sessions. Evelyn is a thirty-one-year-old married woman with two small children, and she stopped working as a commercial artist when she had the children. Evelyn tried to have her sessions during her children's afternoon nap but often found her mind wandering. At other times she would avoid having a session, preferring to paint or read during the children's nap. In talking with Evelyn, one thing that emerged was that she found it difficult to switch from her nonsexual mother role to thinking about her sexuality and getting in touch with her sexual desire and pleasure. After identifying this issue, Evelyn restructured her sessions. She re-scheduled them to times when she was more aware of herself as a sexual woman than as a mother. For Evelyn, those times might follow an evening out with her husband, shopping for perfume or lingerie, or even playing tennis.

How does the time at which you do your sessions influence their quality? If you are putting your sessions off until the end of the day, you may feel physically or mentally worn out. You may come to feel that your sessions are just one more thing you have to do before you can relax. If you begin your sessions in this frame of mind, nothing you do will give you much pleasure. Instead, you may pressure yourself to hurry up and end the session, and you may feel guilty and blame yourself afterward.

If this seems to be causing you problems, try changing the time at which you have your sessions. Perhaps during the day, if you're home alone, or in the early evening, or any time you can arrange to be free of responsibilities for at least an hour. Mornings can also be nice times for pleasuring yourself, so try to arrange to have a morning or two free to see if this is a better time for you.

Example: Sharon was a twenty-six-year-old married woman with one child. She was working very long hours as a sales manager, and she was also working hard on her sexual growth. Sharon was rigidly scheduling herself for a masturbation session every night and was not feeling much arousal during these sessions. She became angry that, with all her effort, nothing was changing sexually. She slowly came to realize that sexual feelings can't be forced; changing sexual patterns is something that has to occur at a pace that is realistic for the rest of one's life demands. Sharon stopped scheduling sessions for every night, when she was often quite tired, irritable, and stressed. Instead, she began to let sessions occur spontaneously, when she was in the mood. This meant that often she would only have sessions on the weekend, when she was relaxed and rested. At this pace, she began to make real progress in appreciating her body's response and in recognizing her sexual arousal.

Are your best sessions more likely to happen when you feel good about yourself? Feeling positive about yourself probably makes it easier for you to deal with any reservations you may have about taking time for yourself and about masturbating. It's easier to feel that you deserve the time and that you have a right to spend it on yourself.

When you feel bad about yourself, everything tends to look bleak. You may think about all the other things you should be doing, or about why you feel bad about yourself, and old doubts about yourself and sex may intrude.

Unfortunately, most of us, throughout our lives, are involved in struggles to feel better about ourselves. We have a tendency to compare ourselves with others as a way of judging our own worth. The most obvious example of this is the concerns most women have about physical appearance. But there are many other areas in which we can feel that our expectations of ourselves are not being met— for example, in our jobs or in our efforts at being good parents. It may be difficult for you to accept yourself. You may be more critical of yourself than anyone else. Do you have an "inner voice" that is always saying, "Don't do or think this," or "You shouldn't," or "How could you?" Since we all have some parts of ourselves that we would like to change or improve, most of us carry around some of these inner critics. But if you *never* seem to measure up to your expectations, you need to reevaluate them and also to learn how to go about feeling better about yourself. In the bibliography we have listed some books that others have found helpful. If self-criticism is causing you a great deal of concern at this point in your life, that can make it hard for you to really let yourself get involved in your sessions.

Example: Madeline, a forty-seven-year-old woman, was having problems with self-criticism inhibiting her arousal during sessions. This centered around her weight—about twenty-five pounds over her ideal weight at the time. During her sessions, she would find herself focusing on her appearance rather than being able to focus on pleasure and arousal. Several things helped Madeline to work through this problem. She joined a diet and exercise program in her neighborhood; just beginning to work on her weight made a big difference in her self-esteem. More important, she very gradually began to question the idea that she had to be "a perfect 10" to enjoy sex. Madeline had had very critical and demanding parents, and without realizing it had unwittingly adopted their attitude toward herself. She came to realize that she was an attractive, sexual woman who was a little overweight, like many of us, and that her worth as a person was related to things other than her weight. We should mention that it was more difficult for her to let her feelings and ideas about herself change than it was for her to lose weight (she did lose ten pounds, even though she had stopped trying to do so).

Something else that may be interfering with your sessions may be feelings about taking time just for yourself. You may rush through your sessions because you feel guilty that you are being selfish and taking time away from your family or from other responsibilities.

Perhaps you don't feel justified in taking time for yourself because you are far more accustomed to giving time to others. This is true for most women. We are brought up with the idea that being a good person means doing things for other people, and that the satisfaction of our family, spouse, children, and friends is far more important than our own. And yet at times we all feel the need to explore some things that are pleasing to *us*, as part of our desire for fulfillment and self-expression. These things contribute to our growing sense of identity as women and as individuals, which, if not given a chance to develop, are likely to breed feelings of resentment. If you are doing some things for yourself, the time you spend with others is likely to be more enjoyable and rewarding.

What does this mean for you? Your sexual expression is obviously a part of your identity, and you need and deserve the time to develop it. If you don't feel that you can take or that you deserve the time, what sorts of reasons are you giving yourself—are you overly committed to serving other people? Does it just seem uncomfortable? Try rethinking your reasons in light of what your own priorities for growth and change really are. It may be that you have to remind yourself occasionally that you do deserve some time to yourself in order to develop (sexually and otherwise) into the person you want to be.

Perhaps you're uncomfortable about taking time for your individual sessions because you feel that your partner or spouse or children resent this time you spend alone. If your children are old enough to understand the need for privacy, it may help to teach them that *everyone* needs and has the right to time alone. They do not need to know how you are spending this time; you could be reading, resting, taking a relaxing bath, or having a pleasuring session. See if you can arrange some time for yourself during the day a few times a week when your children will respect your need to be alone.

If you feel your spouse or partner is uncomfortable about your individual sessions, try talking this over with him. See if you can understand his fears and concerns and offer some reassurance. These individual sessions are important to both of you, since what you are learning will help improve sex with your partner.

Another concern may be that enjoying masturbation will turn you off to sex with your partner. Actually, masturbation does not decrease the desire for sex with another person. In fact, as we said earlier, women who are orgasmic through masturbation are more likely to be orgasmic with a partner. Learning to enjoy sensual and sexual feelings then will make sex with another person more enjoyable. Most women describe the experience of orgasm during masturbation as different from orgasm while making love with a partner. Each is enjoyable, and each is different. Becoming orgasmic through masturbation can enrich the quality of the sexual relationship you develop with your partner.

Example: Before beginning this program, Kim, a twenty-four-year-old woman, found sex to be unpleasant. She had sex with Robert, whom she loved very much and was living with, only when he was reaching his limit of frustration. Otherwise she refused or didn't respond to his advances. After following this program for a while, she found herself, to her surprise, enjoying her masturbation sessions. At this point, she began to feel guilty: Poor Robert had tolerated her lack of interest in sex, and now she was enjoying and indulging herself while still not feeling interested in sex with him. Kim came to realize that her own sessions were just the first steps in a process of change that would ultimately mean a good sex life for both her and Robert. For the moment, however, she still needed time alone. When she discussed this with Robert, she was surprised to hear him say, "It's okay. I've waited a long time; I can wait a little more." Not all men will react this way. Some men feel isolated from their partner and it worries them. Their sensitivity can be a sign of their involvement and concern, and some support and acknowledgment may be valuable as a woman continues to progress.

How do you currently feel toward your sexual partner? Occasionally, a woman will report that she avoids sessions because, when she has them, she feels invaded by negative and critical feelings toward her sexual partner. If this is happening to you, it could have a number of sources. The most obvious is that differences between you and your partner are not getting resolved—they keep gnawing at your thoughts. It could also mean that your anger toward your partner, or possibly toward some other man you thought you had forgotten, is not being recognized and worked out. Alternatively, it is possible that your negative feelings about sex in general are becoming focused on your partner.

If there is anger and unresolved conflict in your relationship, you may need to spend time changing the relationship (we propose some general guidelines for dealing with conflicts in chapter 9, but they are more specific to sex and are probably not sufficient for serious conflict). However, you do not necessarily have to resolve relationship issues first; you can put those issues in the background of your thoughts while you develop your own sexual feelings. If you think you can't do this, ask yourself why. You may be making the assumption that whatever changes you make sexually, you'll have to share—that in some way you will be forced to be sexual. No one wants to do something, sexual or otherwise, with a sense that they will be expected to act and feel a certain way about it. So it makes sense that this internal pressure interferes with an exploratory attitude toward your sessions. In fact, there are no strings attached to learning to feel more sexual. You don't *have* to do anything with them. For a while that may mean drawing an imaginary line between your sexual feelings alone and your sexual feelings with someone else. Alternatively, you may want to slow the rate of experiences and exercises we suggest, in order to get more comfortable with the difference between feelings that are "yours" and "his."

One woman, Anne, came to therapy only four times. At first, she reported having difficulty finding time for sessions (she worked on a light construction crew). She had lived with her boyfriend, Ron, for three years in a house with another couple. Both worked hard and did not spend a lot of time talking (he was a computer engineering student while working full-time). When they finally did start talking and Anne began to make a little progress, they discovered that they were very different people and had never worked out a way to resolve differences or problems in their relationship. This frightened Anne, and she decided to stop therapy but took this book and said, "I do better if I don't have to discuss it; I just want to go at my own pace." This was probably a wise decision on her part, since coming to therapy imposed indirect pressure for them to change. She also felt that it was too soon for her and Ron to manage all of the other problems in their relationship that remained hidden until they tried to change one area: sex.

How you feel about a session before you start also influences what happens. Are you aware of any particular feelings you have before a session? Do you look forward to it, or do you feel some reluctance—a desire to get it over with? Feeling some reluc-

tance is not unusual at this stage of sexual growth. Earlier in the book, we mentioned that part of you is unsure of what becoming orgasmic will be like and of what changes it will bring. You may be afraid that orgasm is something so powerful that you can't control it, or that in letting go and totally experiencing your sexual feelings, you will be giving some power or control over yourself to someone else.

Since most of us have been taught to remain in control (especially in terms of anything to do with sex), it is hard for us to think about letting any of our strong emotions out. Were you ever told as a child, "Don't cry," "Sit still," "Act like an adult," or "Don't be so childish"? All these reminders gave us the message, "Control yourself!" After so many years of overcontrol, it makes sense that we feel out of touch with our emotions or feelings, come to see them as shameful or dangerous, and so ignore or deny them. Take the fear that many people have of expressing anything negative. If we've been told as children, "Don't say that!" or "That's horrible!" or "How could you say that to your mother [father, sister, brother]?" we begin to perceive our feelings, particularly the negative ones, as powerful weapons.

Women describe this fear in many ways in relation to sex. One woman described the feeling as one of being on the edge of a cliff. If she let herself get any more aroused, she feared she would fall off. Maybe you've felt yourself stopping when you get to a certain point of arousal. Are you aware of almost telling yourself to cool down?

The first step in overcoming these fears is to learn to trust yourself. Perhaps you've noticed that in becoming aroused, there are changes in your body—for example, increased muscle tension, heavier breathing, a desire for continued movement of your hips—that may seem to take over. As orgasm approaches, these changes intensify, as does the desire to continue stimulation. It can feel as if your physical desire is overcoming you. Orgasm does involve uncontrollable physical responses, but not all women show their reactions in the same way. Some women merely sigh and shudder a bit during orgasm, other women moan or cry out and throw their bodies around, and still other women let their bodies become rigid with sexual tension. Even for a particular woman, expressiveness varies from orgasm to orgasm. The next exercise is designed to help you deal with some fears you might have about your own expression of orgasm. *We'd like you to try this even if you feel that you don't experience these particular fears at this time.*

ROLE-PLAYING ORGASM

We call this exercise Role-Playing Orgasm. What we'd like you to do is to fantasize about a wild orgasm and act it out.

Set aside thirty minutes to one hour. Begin one of your self-pleasuring sessions in the usual way. The first time, begin role-playing orgasm after you've pleasured yourself for a while but *before* you become extremely aroused. Move around, tense your muscles, lie very rigid, do some pelvic rocking, make noises—do whatever seems really extreme to you. Moan, scratch, pummel the bed, cry—the more exaggerated the better. Stop pleasuring yourself if you want, or continue while you have your "orgasm." You will probably feel awkward doing this the first few times, but it will become easier with practice. Remember, the way you act is not really the way you would or should act. For this exercise, pretend to be the star in your own orgasmic fantasy! Try this exercise two or three times over the next week (at least once during each individual session you have). By the end of the week we expect you will be bored by this exercise but a little surer of yourself.

You may also have discovered some ways in which you were afraid to let go—movements or feelings you were afraid to let happen. After you've tried this exercise, answer these questions for yourself.

Were you aware of any thoughts or feelings that disturbed you about doing this exercise? Perhaps you associate being orgasmic with being promiscuous. When you think about being sexually responsive and uninhibited, what comes to your mind? Are you afraid that tremendous changes will take place in your life? That you will constantly think about sex or that you will want sex all the time? These fears come from early experiences that taught us that sex was bad and that sexual feelings could easily get out of control. Being sexual often meant being secretive and feeling guilty. While growing up, most of us were probably warned against having sex, and we were taught to worry about our reputations and loss of self-respect. Being a sexual person was associated with being loose or promiscuous, with being a person whom others would not respect. Not being sexual was associated with being a good girl, someone whom others would respect and value.

You are not a girl anymore, but you may still feel some conflicts about "growing up" sexually. Given the kind of upbringing most of us experienced, it's natural to feel somewhat ambivalent about making changes. You're probably worried on some level about how you'll feel about yourself, about how your partner will feel about you, and about how others will see you. Perhaps it will help if you look back on your years of growing up and dating and realize that the way you felt about sex then does not have to be the way you feel about it now. How many of us have said, "I will do this differently with my *own* life, husband, children, job, friend," and so on? We learn from the experiences of our parents and peers, and as adults we can choose to keep or discard various practices, attitudes, or beliefs as we learn to see them differently. It is possible to decide for yourself how you want to feel about sex as an adult. If you want to see sex and your own sexuality as something positive, something that makes you feel good about yourself, you can learn to feel this way. The things you have been doing as part of this program will help. Give yourself a chance to change.

YOUR PHYSICAL RESPONSES

Even though you've learned a lot about your body, you may still be feeling somewhat anxious about having your first orgasm. Will you be able to have one? When will it happen? What will it feel like?

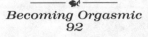

Being concerned about orgasm is natural at this stage, but worrying about it and trying too hard are the very things that may keep you from experiencing one. Worry and anxiety interfere with your body's natural responses and will distract you from focusing on sensations of pleasure and arousal. Orgasm is actually a reflex that occurs if your body is stimulated long enough and in the ways that work for you. Just as you can sometimes stop yourself from sneezing or coughing, it is possible for you to repress orgasm. At times you may find that you are so concerned about whether or not you will experience an orgasm that you take a spectator role. At these times you will be aware of watching yourself for any sign of arousal, and of course the more you watch the less likely it is that you will become aroused. The best thing to do at these times is to refocus your attention onto what you are feeling; in other words, try to get back in touch with your body and what it's telling you. The sensate focusing exercises in the previous chapter will help you to do this. Remember that you will experience orgasm when there is no pressure on you to have one. You can't will yourself to have one, just as a man can't will himself to have an erection. What you are learning now are ways to let your body experience orgasm. It's just a matter of time.

Thinking about experiencing orgasm has probably made you more aware of some of your concerns; but again, it is normal for you to be somewhat anxious. Most of us have no idea what to expect, except what we read in popular magazines and books or see in movies. Unfortunately, these are sometimes sources of inaccurate information. We feel that it's important for you to have some understanding of how your body responds to stimulation and arousal. The phases of sexual response that are described here are based on Masters and Johnson's research on human sexuality. During your sessions, you've probably noticed some of the responses we're going to discuss; however, many changes take place internally.

Look at the drawing of the female genitals before arousal. In this state, the vagina is not an open space. Rather, the walls of the vagina almost touch each other. These walls are incredibly elastic and mold themselves to accommodate the erect penis. For this reason, except for rare physical conditions, there is really no such thing as a vagina or penis that is too small or too big.

Before describing the physical stages of the sexual response cycle, we should mention the psychological "fuel" of the sexual response cycle—sexual desire. Sexual desire is a complex experience, one that sex therapists have just begun to study in the last few years. We don't yet understand completely why people differ so greatly in

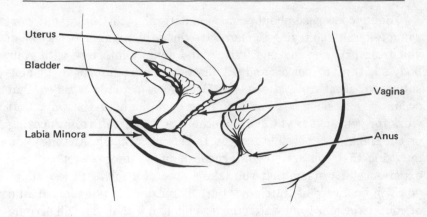

UNAROUSED PHASE

their basic level of sexual desire, with some women feeling the urge for sexual expression much more frequently than others. If you enjoyed sex before this program, you may have had sexual desire even though you did not have orgasms. However, if before beginning this program you didn't get aroused, enjoy sex, or have orgasms, you probably weren't aware of having much sexual desire. This is normal—after all, why should you feel desire for something that is not personally interesting or enjoyable? You will probably find your desire level increasing somewhat as you progress through this program. If you continue to be troubled by a low level of sexual desire, we will have some specific suggestions for dealing with it in chapter 9. Avoid pressuring yourself, at this point, to have a high level of sexual drive. Remember, for most of us, sexual drive is not a constant, high-level state. A number of current and historical experiences influence desire level, including physical health, fatigue, or stress and the emotional relationship with our sexual partner. Again, we will have more to say about these issues in chapters 9 and 12.

The first phase of sexual response (Excitement Phase) begins when you experience some erotic feelings. This triggers the walls of the vagina to secrete droplets of moisture called *vaginal lubrication*. The amount of lubrication you have depends on a number of different factors.

Certain contraceptive pills, pregnancy, and aging may increase or decrease your natural lubrication. We will talk more about these issues a bit later in this chapter. Since the vagina is a warm, moist place, bacteria and other organisms can grow within it. The natural

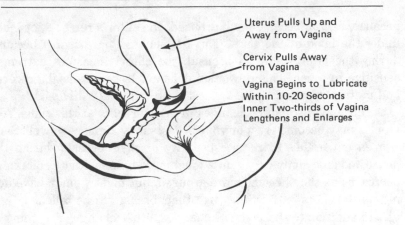

Uterus Pulls Up and
Away from Vagina

Cervix Pulls Away
from Vagina

Vagina Begins to Lubricate
Within 10-20 Seconds
Inner Two-thirds of Vagina
Lengthens and Enlarges

EXCITEMENT PHASE

acidity of the vagina usually controls this growth. However, at times infections can occur that can cause discomfort and also increase your vaginal secretions. Some of the signs of vaginal infection are itching or soreness, excessive lubrication and discharge, and unusual or disagreeable odor. Vaginal infections can sometimes be difficult to control completely. One reason for this is that oral contraceptives and antibiotics tend to make women more prone to vaginal infections. These two kinds of drugs in particular destroy the natural balance of organisms in your vagina, allowing some to take control. If you are aware of any discomfort or of a noticeable change in the amount, texture, or odor of your discharge, you should check with your doctor.

Along with these differences in lubrication, there is a wide range of *normal* variability. If penetration and intercourse are uncomfortable for you, try using a lubricating gel or cream. You need not feel embarrassed about using a vaginal lubricant during sex. This does not mean that you are abnormal, frigid, unexcited, or that you and your partner are doing something wrong. Many women put a little lubricant on their genitals or their partner's penis *each* time they have intercourse. Then, instead of worrying about how well they're lubricated, they're free really to enjoy what they're feeling.

You may experience this first phase of sexual response as a feeling of tightness or fullness in your genitals. This is because your genitals are filling with blood. This causes your labia to swell and your clitoris to become firmer or erect, just as a man's penis. You may or may not be aware of some lubrication or moisture emerging from your vagina. If you continue genital touching you'll probably notice (if you haven't already) that the clitoris seems to disappear. This is because, as you become more aroused, the clitoris retracts, or hides, under the hood of the shaft. This happens *automatically* because, during the later stages of arousal, the clitoris becomes extremely sensitive to touch. This retraction does not lessen arousal, however, and in its new position, the clitoris is still very sensitive.

You may also notice changes in your breasts at this time. Your nipples may become erect or your breasts may appear to swell. Some women experience extreme sensitivity of their breasts during this phase and enjoy only very gentle touching. This sensitivity sometimes decreases as they become more aroused, but most women have definite preferences on how they like their breasts to be touched.

In addition to these visible changes, other changes are going on inside your body. During the Excitement Phase, your uterus enlarges and rises up from its "resting" position. The vagina enlarges to accommodate the penis during intercourse.

During the second phase (the Plateau Phase), you may be aware of some "blotching" or reddish areas on your skin. This is due to changes in blood flow during arousal, and it may or may not occur. It is particularly noticeable in both men and women with fair skin. You may notice your breathing and heart rate becoming more rapid. The color of your labia minora, or inner lips, darkens, and the uterus completes its change in position while the vagina is enlarged.

During this time you may experience feelings of tension or heaviness in your genitals, legs, stomach, or arms. These sensations are

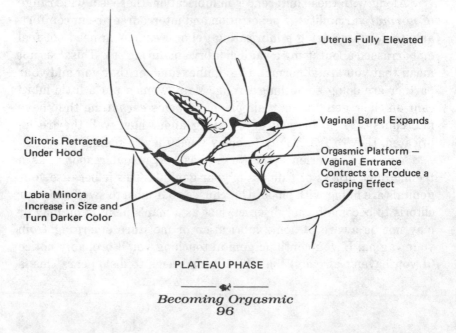

Uterus Fully Elevated

Vaginal Barrel Expands

Clitoris Retracted
Under Hood

Orgasmic Platform —
Vaginal Entrance
Contracts to Produce a
Grasping Effect

Labia Minora
Increase in Size and
Turn Darker Color

PLATEAU PHASE

Becoming Orgasmic

neither pleasant nor unpleasant. If you are not used to the feelings of arousal, you may think these feelings are somewhat scary or uncomfortable. You may feel your body is "running away with you" and that you are out of control. These are normal feelings. Over time, as you become comfortable with the feelings and emotions of arousal, you will learn to relax and trust your body, and you'll find yourself tuning in to them more and enjoying your body's responsiveness. This phase leads to the next phase, during which orgasm usually occurs, although there will be times when you may experience feelings of high arousal without orgasm. This is not a problem unless it happens frequently. Illness, drugs, and alcohol can affect how you respond. Sometimes you may not feel the desire to go on to orgasm. Having a close, loving experience with your partner may be all you desire at times. Men also as they mature experience less of a need for orgasm and ejaculation on every sexual occasion.

However, if you are only able to reach this Plateau Phase and have never experienced orgasm, you have probably felt very frustrated and physically uncomfortable from a lack of orgasmic release. Over a period of time after you've met with repeated frustration, you've learned to "turn yourself off" at the first sign of arousal. The physical signs of arousal (tension and so on) probably feel uncomfortable and make you anxious and worried about how well you'll do this time. Through these chapters, you'll get a chance to experience these feelings of arousal and, we hope, begin to enjoy these signs of your body's responsiveness to pleasure.

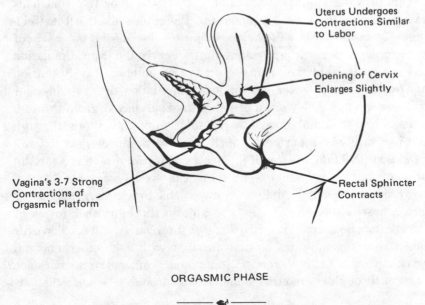

ORGASMIC PHASE

The Orgasmic Phase brings a series of rhythmic contractions to the muscles around your vagina and to the uterus itself. You may be aware of these contractions or you may not, depending on your particular pattern.

During orgasm you may respond in different ways. It's good to remember that the way you respond to stimulation and orgasm at a particular time may not be the way in which you respond the next time. What's important is to let go and enjoy the experience. Feeling good about yourself as a person means feeling free enough to do what you enjoy at the time.

You may feel like moving your body around during orgasm, or you may prefer to be absolutely still and really focus in on your feelings. You may find yourself making some noise, wanting to cry, using erotic words. You may be afraid that if you really do let go, you will grimace and appear ugly and turn your partner off. Whatever your concerns, they're no doubt interfering with the enjoyment you get from your body at *all* phases of the sexual cycle. If you have a rigid set of rules or certain expectations about sex, you're bound to lose out on the spontaneity, fun, and sense of excitement that sexual exploration can provide.

Although some women prefer intercourse stimulation, it is not always necessary for an erect penis to be in the vagina in order for women to experience orgasm. Orgasm typically results from a buildup of body tension through direct or indirect stimulation of the clitoris. During intercourse, the in-and-out motion of the penis in the vagina provides vaginal stimulation and also pulls on the labia. This causes friction between the hood and the clitoris itself. Other feelings—from the breasts (if they're being touched), from the inside of the vagina, such as the penis bumping the cervix and from stimulation to the first third of the vagina—add to this buildup of body tension and excitement. However, with enough stimulation, orgasm can occur in other ways. A few women are able to experience orgasm through intense breast stimulation only. Stimulation of the clitoris through self-pleasuring or a partner's touch can also produce orgasm. Oral-genital stimulation, the use of an electric vibrator, directing a stream of water onto your genitals—all these can produce orgasm.

Some women find it difficult or impossible to reach orgasm during intercourse, although they may be able to through other forms of stimulation. Sometimes orgasm through intercourse will develop over time, when a couple has become familiar with each other's sexual responsiveness and preferences. Some other women never experience orgasm through intercourse alone. This is probably because the particular way they fit together with their partner just doesn't provide enough clitoral stimulation to result in orgasm. In these cases, the addition of some direct clitoral touching (with finger or vibrator) during intercourse usually makes orgasm possible.

After orgasm the body gradually returns to its unaroused state. Enlargement of the breasts, clitoris, and labia diminishes. The heart rate becomes slower. The uterus descends, and the vagina returns to its unaroused size and shape. Sex flush and changes in the color of the labia fade. These changes will take a few minutes, but some swelling of the genitals can continue for thirty minutes or more.

Some women have found that stimulation during the time almost immediately after the first orgasm results in a second orgasm (or even more). This is called *multiple orgasm*. Not all women enjoy being restimulated shortly after orgasm or find that they are able to reach a second peak of arousal. When you become orgasmic, let your body be your guide.

PHYSICAL FACTORS INFLUENCING SEXUAL RESPONSE

The sexual response cycle was described above as if it were a given, almost predetermined set of reactions. In reality there are many factors that influence your sexual responsiveness. Obviously, your own psychological makeup, the way you think about sex, your feelings about your partner and your relationship, and a wide variety of other emotional issues influence your sexual response. Sexual response can also be influenced by various physical conditions, such as hormones, contraception, aging, and drugs. A full discussion of each of these issues is beyond the scope of this book, and there are suggestions for further readings in the bibliography. What we present is an overview of physical factors that influence sexual response.

Hormones

In animals, sex drive and sexual responsiveness are closely tied to hormone levels in the male (testosterone) and female (estrogen). In humans the effects of hormones are much weaker; they generally affect sexual response only when there is a medical problem, with the presence of very abnormal levels.

Many studies have been done on the effects of the menstrual cycle on women's sexual response. In general the impact of the menstrual cycle on women's sexual behavior is not very impressive—psychological issues (how well you are feeling, your feelings about your partner) usually overcome the small effect of hormonal changes during the menstrual cycle. Other studies tend to show a *small* increase in sexual desire and response around days 6–8, around ovulation (day 15), and a smaller increase again around days 22–26 of the menstrual cycle (when menstrual bleeding is counted as days 1–4). However, the late-cycle (days 22–26) increase does *not* occur for women who experience any premenstrual distress during the late part of the cycle. Again, general feelings of well-being—or a lack of well-being, in this case—take precedence over any purely cyclical hormonal effects. (For more on the menstrual cycle, see chapter 8.)

For you, a woman exploring your sexual potential, it might be interesting and worthwhile to note whether your sexual interest or responsiveness varies during your menstrual cycle. If you do notice a time of the month when you become more interested in sex or aroused more easily, don't hesitate to schedule your sessions to take advantage of this physiological assistance.

Another hormonal issue concerns the effect of oral contraception—the birth control pill—on women's sexual responsiveness. Some years ago, oral contraceptives contained much higher doses of hormones than they do now, and many women found that their sex drive declined when they were on the pill. Some women also noted breast tenderness that reduced sexual pleasure, and they had more trouble reaching orgasm. Today, with low-dose pills available, these problems are uncommon, and most women find the pill does not influence their sexual response. There are, however, some women who are *definitely* sensitive to the effects of the hormones in the pill and will have a decline in sexual desire and responsiveness. These women often notice that they are more interested in sex and have better arousal and orgasms during their pill-free week than during the rest of the month. If this is true for you, consult your gynecologist about an alternative method of birth control. You might also try a different brand of oral contraceptive, as the exact hormones differ with the brand.

Contraception

Beyond pills, none of the other methods of birth control is likely to have purely physical effects on sexual response, although some may initially inhibit your enjoyment of sex because of their mechanical or intrusive nature. A full discussion of the safety and effectiveness of

various methods of birth control can be found in the books listed in the bibliography. What we will present here are some comments on the sexual issues involved in each type of contraceptive strategy.

Intrauterine devices (IUDs). About 10 to 20 percent of women using IUDs experience unpleasant cramping of the uterus, abdominal pain, and increased menstrual bleeding. Others report uterine cramping and pain during orgasm with an IUD in place but don't have this problem when the IUD is removed. The advantage of the IUD is that it doesn't interfere with spontaneous sex and, for most women, doesn't have any negative effect on sexual arousal, pleasure, or orgasm.

Diaphragm and spermicide. Many couples use the diaphragm with a cream or jelly spermicide. Some women do experience vaginal discomfort and irritation during intercourse with the diaphragm in place. Some men also complain of bumping or rubbing their penis on the diaphragm. A few couples report that since the diaphragm takes up space and spreads the vaginal walls, neither the man nor the woman feels as much sensation during intercourse. Diaphragms must always be used in conjunction with a spermicidal cream or jelly, and some men and women report that the spermicide burns or irritates their genitals. Other couples find that the spermicide makes the vagina too lubricated, so that sensation is reduced. Of course, the diaphragm does somewhat inhibit the spontaneity of sex, as you must have it and the spermicide with you and take time out to insert it. However, with partner cooperation, its use can be incorporated without much difficulty. For many couples, who find its safety and low cost attractive, the diaphragm is an entirely satisfactory method.

A cousin of the diaphragm, the cervical cap is difficult to get in the United States. It fits securely over the cervix by means of suction. As with the diaphragm, it is used with a spermicide.

Condoms (prophylactics, or "rubbers"). Some couples report that condoms lessen the sensations of intercourse for both men and women (thus, men have described intercourse using a condom as "taking a shower in a raincoat"). The more expensive "natural," or "skin," condoms do offer better transmission of heat and sensation than do latex rubber condoms. Of course, condoms inhibit spontaneity, in the same way that the diaphragm does. One very important advantage of the condom is that it offers a woman some protection

against contracting a sexually transmitted disease, such as herpes or acquired immune deficiency syndrome (AIDS) from her partner. However, the natural skin condom does not offer this protection from disease as effectively as do rubber condoms.

Spermicides (foam, cream, jelly, or suppositories). All these spermicides offer less effective contraception than the other methods we've discussed and should only be used in conjunction with another method, such as condoms, by couples who are comfortable with an increased risk of pregnancy or by couples who find abortion an acceptable backup. The most common (and it is fairly common) sexual problem with spermicides is a burning sensation in the vagina and on the penis. Spermicides also interfere with spontaneity, like the diaphragm or condom, and many women are bothered by the spermicide leaking out of the vagina for some time after intercourse. In addition, they all taste medicinal and can therefore interfere with enjoyment of oral sex.

The sponge. The contraceptive sponge blocks the cervix, like a diaphragm, but also contains a spermicide. It offers the sexual advantage of being smaller and softer than the diaphragm, so the penis is not as likely to bump it, and it doesn't spread the vaginal walls as much. However, some women (and men) find the spermicide produces a burning sensation during intercourse. Some women also report that the sponge seems to interfere with their vaginal lubrication, perhaps by absorbing it. The safety and effectiveness of the sponge are currently under some question, and if you are considering this method, you should see your gynecologist for the latest information.

Ineffective methods. Douching is not effective as contraception, since sperm are past the cervix (and out of reach of douching) within thirty seconds of the male's climax. Similarly, *withdrawal* (coitus interruptus) is ineffective because, prior to the male's orgasm, there is usually some seepage of semen that contains active sperm. The *rhythm* method (avoiding intercourse on the woman's "fertile" days) is a marginally effective form of contraception. If the woman's cycle is unusually regular, and if the couple are extremely conscientious, rhythm can work reasonably well. If you are interested in the rhythm method for religious reasons, you should consult your gynecologist and the self-health-care books in the bibliography for the latest information on the rhythm method. As all of these marginal methods

greatly interfere with sexual spontaneity and are not truly effective, they are significantly less desirable than others.

Sterilization. Male or female sterilization is an ideal contraceptive, in terms of sexual issues, for people who do not want children. There are no side effects; sexual desire, arousal, and orgasm are unchanged, and sex can be completely spontaneous. If you are sure you don't want to become pregnant, you might think seriously about the issue of sterilization. Some techniques are reversible, but not with 100 percent certainty. We often recommend male sterilization (vasectomy) for the couples we work with, as it is less expensive, less risky, and simpler than female sterilization.

The essential issues are to decide whether you want to become pregnant or not and to make sure your partner agrees. Concerns about getting pregnant can greatly reduce your sexual desire and your enjoyment of sex. It is therefore very important to try to work out, with your partner, a method of contraception that you both find comfortable and reassuring. If you do not currently have a partner, find a contraceptive method that you like and make sure that your future partner is cooperative if your method requires his involvement. Also, don't be discouraged by the preceding material. Once people find their method, the negative side effects we mentioned are usually only experienced by a small percentage of women using each method, and most users either do not have problems or have found ways to adapt the method to their sexual lives.

Aging

The effect of aging on sexual responsiveness depends on both psychological and physical issues. If a woman believes that she is less sexual because she is growing older, she will indeed feel less sexual and probably experience diminished sexual responsiveness, for purely psychological reasons. Much of this diminished responsiveness is the result of a cultural myth, as researchers, beginning many years ago with Alfred Kinsey, have found that female sexuality actually reaches its peak in women in their late thirties and only very gradually and slightly declines thereafter. However, there are some physical changes that come with aging that do influence sexuality. These changes need not reduce your enjoyment of sex, if you are aware of them and adjust to them.

Changes in women's sexuality brought on by aging revolve around reduction in the ovaries' production of female hormones (estrogens). This reduction typically begins around age forty-five and continues through menopause itself, at age fifty-five or so, on average. At this point, lower levels of hormones remain relatively stable. We will have more to say about psychological issues involved with menopause in chapter 8; here we will discuss the physical effects.

As estrogen production declines, several things happen that may influence sexual response. The vaginal lining may become drier, thinner, and more prone to irritation during intercourse. Vaginal lubrication, which earlier in life begins within ten to thirty seconds of starting sexual activity, may take three to five minutes to begin in older women, and may not ever reach sufficient levels for enjoyable intercourse. Your skin may become less sensitive and responsive, so cuddling and hugging may not be as pleasurable as they were earlier. Clitoral sensitivity may decrease, and the clitoris may change in size with age. Orgasmic contractions may begin to include spasmodic cramping of the uterus (similar to menstrual cramps), which can be painful rather than pleasurable. As muscle tone in the urinary tract is also influenced by estrogen, some aging women may begin to lose a bit of urine at orgasm. Lest all these sound devastating, remember that many women do not experience all of these changes and that other women have them only in very minor ways that don't really interfere with sexual pleasure. Also, there is strong evidence that remaining sexually active prevents or minimizes many of these changes—sexual activity itself is a sort of tonic that promotes sexual health.

In cases in which a woman is troubled by these changes, a gynecologist can prescribe replacement estrogen, in the form of cream (which is inserted in the vagina), a pill, a skin patch, or a muscle implant. Estrogen will reverse all these aging changes very successfully in most cases. To relieve uterine cramping with orgasm, an antiprostaglandin, a type of drug also used to treat menstrual cramps, may be prescribed as well.

Some years ago, there was concern that women taking estrogen would have an elevated risk of developing cervical or breast cancer. Today, menopausal women take estrogen in low dosages and in conjunction with another hormone, progesterone (or progestin), and both drugs are withdrawn periodically so that the woman has a menstrual period. This periodic dosage has been found not to involve any elevated risk of cancer. Low-dose estrogen use, combined with progestin, has become standard medical practice for women complaining of sexual problems connected with menopause and aging. Progestins have been found to reduce the likelihood of breast and uterine cancer and,

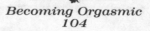

when combined with estrogens, to reduce the risk of heart disease and minimize the loss of bone mass (called osteoporosis) that usually occurs with age.

Hysterectomy

Hysterectomy (removal of the uterus) sometimes includes removal of the ovaries as well. Hysterectomies and ovariectomies are done for a variety of medical reasons and create a sort of "surgical menopause," with the same potential effects on sexuality as natural menopause. Again, estrogen-progestin replacement therapy will usually deal with these problems quite well.

If you are experiencing any decline in your sexual responsiveness and are experiencing menopause or have had a hysterectomy, you should consult your gynecologist about hormone replacement therapy. It could benefit your general health as well as some aspects of your sexual responsiveness.

Effects of Other Drugs on Female Sexuality

There are a number of medications that can negatively influence sexual response. Antianxiety or tranquilizing drugs such as Valium, antidepressant drugs, antipsychotic drugs, and sleeping medications can have the side effect of reducing sex drive, inhibiting arousal, and interfering with orgasm. Similar side effects can occur with many of the drugs used to treat heart disease or high blood pressure. Some allergy medications and some drugs used to treat ulcers can also have these effects. If you are taking any of these types of medication, you should consult with your doctor about possible sexual side effects. Again, these side effects do not happen to everyone, but if you have noticed a change in your sexuality since you began your medication, you should consult your doctor.

The most common substance that consistently interferes with sexual response and, eventually, sexual desire is alcohol. Although alcohol is *believed* to reduce sexual inhibition and enhance sexual responsiveness, it has the opposite effect. Of course, if you drink a glass of wine you may notice a more relaxed feeling and experience no noticeable difference in (or even a perceived enhancement of) arousal. This is a psychological effect. Studies have shown that if a woman consumes several drinks, with each drink her arousal level is diminished, and it takes longer for her to get highly aroused or experience orgasm. Liquor is not quicker.

ORGASM "TRIGGERS"

By now you've learned to understand your body a little better. At the times when you feel that everything goes smoothly to make for a fine session, you feel pretty good about yourself, and you're in a good mood. You find it easier to fantasize, get into, and focus on what you're doing with your body. You feel in control of how things are going and of how you're responding. You are probably aware of feelings of increasing arousal, but for some reason you don't seem to be able to have an orgasm.

At times like these it's possible to help nature's rhythm along a bit and give yourself that little extra nudge that your body seems to need. Below we've listed some suggestions that we've learned from women. Not all of these will be right for you. Again, let your body be your guide.

1. During sexual arousal, try deliberately tensing your legs, stomach, arms, or feet or exaggerating these things if you find yourself doing them. Body tension (such as pointing your toes or clenching your hands) is sometimes an automatic response, and increasing this tension often triggers orgasm.

2. Do some vaginal muscle contractions (Kegels). The squeeze-and-release movements often enhance arousal and will keep you focused on your genital sensations.

3. As you get aroused, change position so that your head is hanging back over the edge of the bed or couch. This increases blood flow to your head and changes your breathing, both of which seem to add to feelings of tension and arousal in some women.

4. Try really letting go. Begin to role-play an orgasm. Move your hips. Say some exciting words to yourself as though you were encouraging your body—"come" or "more" or whatever seems right to you at the time.

5. When you feel some arousal, try teasing yourself. Move away from the area you're concentrating on and then come back to it. Move your fingers over your breasts, nipples, and stomach as well as your clitoris. Or change the pressure of your touch or your tempo as you touch your clitoris.

6. You might try arranging a mirror so that you can watch while you're pleasuring yourself.

7. Read a favorite passage from an erotic book after you've spent some time stimulating yourself. Or try really imagining your-

self *in* your most intense fantasy. Really get into it. Let yourself go.

8.   Pick a sensuous or sexy nightgown, bra, slip, or underpants. Begin your session with this on. Feel the texture of this with your fingers. How does it feel to touch your breasts or genitals through this material? Undress yourself after a while, or continue partially dressed if you like the feeling.

9.   Try touching yourself in a different position. If you've always pleasured yourself while on your back, turn over. You might try just having your rear up and your head and chest resting on a pillow. Or lie on your side or on your back with your legs up if you've always kept them stretched out flat. Try some body movements, such as moving your pelvis in the way that you did during the pelvic exercises you've practiced.

10.   Try holding your breath for a short while or breathing heavily (panting).

How do you feel after reading these suggestions? If you want to rush and try all of them at once, remember that these suggestions are only a small part of what you do. They aren't magic. Doing these when you're not in the mood for sex, when you're distracted or tired, won't bring on an instant orgasm. Spending time on yourself, creating a sensual environment, and enjoying your body are essential for responsiveness. So, choose one or two things from our list that sound good to you. Give yourself at least three sessions to explore the possibilities you decide to try.

If you're feeling a little anxious or overwhelmed after reading our list, it's probably because you're still worried about how well you'll do. You may be thinking, If some or all of these don't work for me, then there must be something *wrong* with me. These kinds of worries are bound to interfere with your pleasure. If you do find yourself worrying about your progress, that's okay; it's natural. As you continue to practice focusing and triggers, you will slowly get more comfortable and notice some progress. Some things will not work, but with time you will be able to discover what does work for you.

Sometimes just increasing the time you spend stimulating yourself will bring about orgasm. For this reason, we're going to have you spend thirty to forty-five minutes pleasuring yourself during your sessions. The way you approach this time is very important. If you feel discouraged because it seems to be taking you so long to get aroused or to reach orgasm, try to be patient with yourself. It will not take as long later on. Earlier we mentioned that having one orgasm makes it easier and more likely that you'll have another. The more orgasms you have, the less time it will take you to feel arousal. Right now is your chance to give yourself the time you need. You have no one else's needs or desires to consider but your own. You deserve this time. Remember, you're making up for years of being out of touch with your body and its responses.

DURING YOUR SESSIONS

This week we'd like you to keep in mind the things we have discussed in this chapter. Your self-pleasuring sessions should last thirty to forty-five minutes. Try role-playing orgasm, and try some orgasm triggers when you feel yourself getting aroused. Fantasize and focus on the good feelings your body is giving you. After you have had two self-pleasuring sessions in this way, answer these questions for yourself: (1) How did you feel about these sessions? (2) Are you finding it easier to fantasize and let go, or are you running away or turning off when you experience arousal? If so, practice the fantasy exercise (chapter 5), role-playing orgasm exercise (chapter 6), and the sensate focus exercises (chapter 5) again. Think of some ways you can distract yourself when you notice you are turning off. Fantasy, erotic pictures, stories, music, or even thinking of a pleasant scene while continuing to pleasure yourself may help.

If you have orgasms, enjoy them! Continue with your individual sessions so that you can explore this new experience further. When you feel ready, move on to chapter 7.

If you have not had an orgasm, try not to focus on this in your sessions. If you feel that it is beginning to work for you, keep trying this step at least four to six times over the next two weeks. It's not unusual for it to take two to three weeks or more at this stage before orgasm may occur. If you feel that you are getting close to orgasm, and if you are highly aroused during your sessions, you may just need some more time. You are not doing anything wrong, and you haven't failed. You may just be one of the many women who need additional stimulation. If, after two to three weeks, you have *not* had an orgasm, move on to chapter 7.

7
Using a Vibrator: A Little Technology

How did today begin for you? Let us be a little presumptuous for a moment and sketch out our scenario: The alarm rang, and you reached to shut it off. Having stolen one more cozy moment, you pulled yourself from under the covers, walked to the bathroom, turned on a light, and took a quick shower. After dressing, you went to the kitchen, turned on the coffeepot, and put bread in the toaster. While the coffee was on you blow-dried your hair. Moments later you rushed to your car, switching on the radio as you headed for work or to run errands.

Perhaps some of this sounds familiar. It takes a moment to realize how much we depend on some electrical devices to enhance or maintain the quality of our lives. The larger our families are, the more important electricity becomes for saving time and preventing fatigue. Most of us take these things pretty much for granted. With the exception of wasteful uses of energy, we usually don't question the fact that such devices are generally helpful additions to our lives and that using them is okay. We don't, for instance, assume that people are lazy if they prefer electric to hand-wound alarm clocks. Nor do we usually worry about a car becoming a "crutch" for people who live only a mile from work because they should really walk.

However, many people feel differently when it comes to the area of sex. In this next phase of your personal growth program, we'd like you to feel comfortable enough to explore vibrators as another means of learning about yourself.

What is your reaction to the idea of using an electric vibrator during your individual self-stimulation sessions? Perhaps you feel you shouldn't need to—that it's not natural—or you may have fears that a vibrator will become a sexual crutch and that you will become dependent on it forever—that you will not be able to get sexual pleasure in any other way.

Often our ideas of what is natural and right in sex come from things we learned when we were younger. Perhaps you've already changed some of your ideas just by progressing through this program. For example, you probably feel somewhat different about masturbation, or self-stimulation, than you did before beginning this book. We hope that you're discovering what is right and natural for *you* sexually and that you're not putting restrictions and expectations on yourself. For instance, you may have found that relaxation exercises, reading erotic literature, or certain fantasies contribute to your ability to get into a sexual mood. And perhaps a lubricant makes touching yourself a more sensitive and pleasurable experience. Try seeing the use of a vibrator as an avenue for exploring what is right and natural for you.

Women often have concerns about experiencing orgasm with the help of a vibrator. They may feel that the orgasm will be an artificial one, something that they can't take credit for or feel good about. Actually, becoming aroused and orgasmic through the use of a vibrator is the same basic and natural physical experience as becoming aroused and orgasmic through other forms of self-stimulation. Also, remember that there is a person behind the machine! *You* are in control of the vibrator. You will find that just as you had to explore different kinds of hand strokes and touches that felt best, you will have to experiment with adjusting the pressure and focus of vibrator stimulation in a similar way. Although the vibrator provides a constant source of stimulation, *you* are the one who selects the most pleasurable means of experiencing it.

If you have a partner and are concerned about his feelings about a vibrator, you may want to have him read this chapter and exchange positive and negative feelings with him. We often suggest that the male partner try out the vibrator on his own (see the exercises below) over his whole body. Some men enjoy vibrator stimulation on their genitals; other men feel it's too intense. Either way, almost all couples can find a use for the vibrator that is pleasurable for them. We talk about several ways for couples to use the vibrator in chapter 9. Right now you may want to try to explore its nonsexual, sensual, or relaxing pleasures when you are together. Begin by using the vibrator on different muscle areas of each other's bodies (excluding the genitals)—especially the back, neck, arm, and leg muscles. Try different things and see if you can find some ways that a vibrator adds a little extra enjoyment or relaxation.

It's natural for you to have some reservations before trying something new. However, we think that it is possible for you to view the use of vibrators as you view the use of other electrical devices—as a convenience you use some of the time to make life easier, more pleasant, and more interesting.

What exactly is a vibrator? Basically, a vibrator is a relatively small machine—one that you can hold in your hand—that vibrates with a rapid, steady rhythm. Vibrators are either battery-powered or plug into electrical outlets. They come in different shapes and sizes. Some have settings for high and low speeds of vibration, attachments for massaging different body parts, and even (on the more expensive varieties) warmth for massaging sore muscles. Some you hold in your hand (see drawings B and C on page 112), and others fit over your hand and cause your fingers and hand to vibrate (drawing A).

Vibrators are wonderful for massaging your body in order to help you relax and to soothe sore muscles. And they can also provide very pleasurable sensations on your genitals. When you think about it, this isn't surprising. When you stimulate your genitals with your finger(s), you rub, stroke, and massage. This is what vibrators do at a faster rate, more steadily, and more intensely than most people can achieve with hand stimulation. Some women need this quality of genital stimulation, especially when they are learning to have orgasms.

Perhaps the biggest concern you may have about trying a vibrator is that you may enjoy it, become orgasmic, and then be hooked on using it forever. Being afraid that you may become addicted will make it hard for you to relax and be comfortable enough with using a vibrator to allow you to enjoy any pleasurable sensations that it provides.

Right now, try to relax and give yourself a chance to try it out. Once they become orgasmic with the help of a vibrator, most women are able to learn other ways of reaching orgasm. At the end of this chapter, we will discuss things that you (or, at some point, you and a partner) can do to expand your orgasmic responsiveness after you've had a few orgasms. For now, give yourself a chance to discover if this form of additional stimulation is enjoyable and will work for you.

LOCATING THE RIGHT VIBRATOR

Do some shopping around. Vibrators (sometimes they are called massagers) are sold in most department stores, through some store and mail-order catalogs, and by discount houses and pharmacies. They are very popular because of all their uses—massage, aids to relaxation, and general body stimulation—so there is no reason to feel embarrassed about purchasing one.

Try to compare a few different models. Are they comfortable to

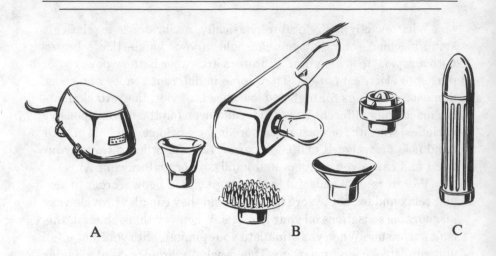

A   B   C

hold? Do they fit your hand well? How does the weight feel? Will your arm or hand tire? If you can, have each model you are considering plugged in or turned on so you can feel the vibrations. Some models will feel better to you than others. Make sure you buy a vibrator that is well built, safe, light, quiet, and not so big that it is clumsy. We do not recommend using battery-powered vibrators at this stage (drawing C), although later on you may want one as an extra. We have found two vibrators that women seem to enjoy particularly. One is an over-the-hand model, made by Oster, that is available at most department stores (drawing A). The other is a hand-held model (drawing B). Variations on these name-brand models are also available in most major store catalogs, if you prefer to shop for them by mail. If you have a partner, you might want him to shop for a vibrator with you since you will be using the vibrator together at a later point.

USING THE VIBRATOR

Set the stage as you usually do for a self-pleasuring session. Put lotion or oil on your body if you like. *Never use the vibrator around water.* Begin exploring your body with the vibrator. Explore your face, scalp, neck, shoulders, arms, hands, breasts, and so on, working down your body. After a while, move the vibrator over your genitals. You may be surprised at how intense the vibrations feel, particularly around your clitoris. Try varying pressure, movements, and placement of the vibrator. If it comes with different attachments, try them. If you have a strap-on hand vibrator, try putting one or two fingers in your vagina while you are exploring your genitals. Take your time.

Don't try for arousal. Relax and begin to learn how your body responds to this new stimulation. After you have tried this for about fifteen minutes, think about the following questions.

What differences, if any, did you notice between using the vibrator and using your fingers for stimulation?

Were there any areas that were too sensitive to touch directly with the vibrator? Some women find their nipples and clitoris too sensitive for direct stimulation. If this was true for you, try light, barely brushing types of strokes next time. If your genitals feel particularly sensitive, you might try stimulating yourself on one side of the clitoris, or through underpants, the first few times. Gradually your body will be able to tolerate more and more direct stimulation. Sometimes women use a small towel over their genitals to diffuse the intensity. If you do this, make sure that the towel does not rub your genitals in a way that absorbs your natural vaginal lubrication. This will cause redness, irritation, and burning.

Do this general body exploration at least twice. When you feel

Using a Vibrator
113

comfortable, concentrate stimulation on your genitals and remember to use fantasy, erotic literature, or the orgasm triggers to enhance your arousal. You can also use your other hand at the same time. This way you can provide additional breast or genital stimulation for yourself. Let your hips and body move rhythmically with the stimulation. Avoid holding your breath—breathe fully as the tension in your body increases.

A reasonable amount of time is probably fifteen minutes each for the first three times; then try for fifteen to thirty minutes and then thirty to forty-five minutes, if that's what your body needs. It is not unusual for thirty to forty-five minutes of intense genital stimulation to be necessary when you're learning to become orgasmic. Again, don't worry about how long it's taking you. Your body is capable of orgasm; it just needs to be encouraged. Stay at this step for at least two weeks or six individual self-pleasuring sessions that last at least thirty to forty minutes. Remember to use what you've learned in earlier chapters—fantasy, erotic literature, orgasm triggers, or whatever else works for you—in order to increase your sensual pleasure with the vibrator.

AFTER A FEW WEEKS

If you haven't had orgasm up to this point, you may feel very discouraged. If you find this happening, you may want to continue a while longer with manual and vibrator self-stimulation, particularly if you feel you may be getting close to orgasm. Or, if you have a partner, you may want to move ahead to chapter 8—some women make additional progress with their partners. Whatever you decide to do, take a moment to think about what you *have* learned and about the ways in which you have grown sexually. There is really no such thing as an unimportant change. Give yourself credit for making the gains you have made; that's a sign that with time, more changes are going to happen.

There are two very common problems that occur when vibrators are introduced. One is that the vibrator can become the center of attention. Sometimes women expect it to replace all of the other arousal techniques they have practiced. Because the vibrator stimulation is so strong and attention-getting, this is easy to allow to happen. The point is not to have a relationship with the vibrator but to use the vibrator to help create a sexual experience. The ingredients for a sexual experience include the use of fantasy, sexual thoughts and urges, sensual stimulation, and movement.

Another common problem in using a vibrator is numbness. Too much stimulation or too-intense pressure can make an area like your genitals become temporarily numb. If this happens, move the vibrator to a different area and change the type of stroke. Try teasing yourself with brief light touches from the vibrator.

Perhaps you've had an orgasm. It's not uncommon for women to be somewhat surprised by the experience. Your ideas and expectations about what orgasm would be like may or may not have been true for you. Perhaps you expected much more:

> All of a sudden the sensations just stopped and I couldn't go on. . . . it was too sensitive there. It was nice but not much to celebrate.
>
> It seemed as if I was rubbing my clitoris for about twenty minutes; then the feelings just sort of changed all of a sudden. I think it was an orgasm, but I wasn't sure.

Or perhaps you expected much less:

> I was feeling pretty turned on, and this time instead of staying at that level or stopping, I kept on using the vibrator and my hand, too. Suddenly I had this warm pulsating *strong* feeling come over me. It was terrific! I tried to do it again right away but with no luck.

It's not unusual for women to have mixed feelings about becoming orgasmic—happiness or relief, along with some feelings of disappointment. This is natural, and perhaps you've felt this way about other events in your life—such as a vacation you've planned, getting a new job, or doing anything you've looked forward to for a long time. You should feel good about yourself! You've overcome some obstacles and experienced a pleasure that is truly yours alone. Some women have excitedly called us right after their first orgasm. Other women are pleased or feel more secure about themselves but discover that orgasm really is only part of their greater sexual satisfaction. Whatever you feel, orgasm has helped you to know yourself better—and whether or not you share this knowledge with a partner, it's part of you now. You can be proud of all the changes you have experienced and assure yourself that there's more growth ahead.

IF YOU LIKED THE VIBRATOR, BUT . . .

Whether or not you've had an orgasm, we hope you feel good about what you've experienced with the vibrator. Yet, as we mentioned earlier, you may be concerned that you are or will become too dependent on it. Most women we have seen become orgasmic and enjoy the vibrator a lot, but gradually they are able to get an equal amount of satisfaction from other kinds of stimulation. Here are some suggestions to broaden your orgasmic responsiveness.

If you have experienced orgasm with a vibrator or feel that with a little more time it might happen, let yourself get used to these new sexual response patterns. Let yourself have several sessions with orgasm. Then, if you are interested in expanding your arousal to manual stimulation, gradually include more and more hand stimulation into your sessions. Expect to spend more time (vibrator arousal usually occurs more quickly) bringing yourself to high levels of arousal manually. Sometimes stronger orgasms come after longer periods of sexual arousal.

You can incorporate manual stimulation in a variety of ways. For instance, you might try letting yourself get highly aroused with your vibrator and then putting it aside and continuing with your hands. Doing this may mean that your arousal level does not continue to increase as rapidly; it may even drop some. If your arousal drops, you may be tempted to give up in discouragement. Try not to let this happen—it's natural for things to slow down when you first switch types of stimulation. And remember, you have plenty of time. Continue to give yourself manual stimulation for as long as it's pleasurable.

The next time you try switching from the vibrator to manual stimulation, you might try reaching a very high level of arousal and then changing to manual stimulation during the last few seconds before orgasm, or just as your orgasm begins, so that during orgasm you are using your hands without a vibrator. Once you have an orgasm in this way, you can try changing the point at which you concentrate on hand stimulation, gradually moving that point closer and closer to the beginning of your self-stimulation session.

Another possibility that may help you expand your ability to become aroused is to use both your hand and the vibrator simultaneously throughout your sessions. This can be very erotic, since you are providing yourself with quite a variety of sensations—different textures, tempos, and pressures. Over your sessions you can gradually begin to spend more time focusing on manual stimulation and less time focusing on vibrator stimulation. It's important to try this for short periods in the beginning. For instance, let yourself get a little aroused using both hand and vibrator, then for a few seconds just try using your hand (or both hands); go back to hand and vibrator for a minute or two, then continue without the vibrator for a few seconds longer, and so on. Slowly (over several sessions) increase the amount of time you use your hands without the vibrator. Eventually (and this may mean several weeks) you may be able to have some of your sessions with little if any use of the vibrator. During your sessions, try not to be concerned about how aroused you are. Concentrate on your physical sensations and the pleasure they are giving you.

Suppose, however, that you find, even with repeated experimentation, that you *prefer* vibrator stimulation. A number of women do find that even though they might be able to be orgasmic through manual masturbation, the intense, regular stimulation that a vibrator provides is more pleasurable. If you enjoy the vibrator and always want to use it to enhance your sexual responsiveness, that's great! You do not *have* to be able to masturbate without a vibrator, particularly if you find, as many women do, that the vibrator is a good source of sexual pleasure. Decide what you would like for yourself. The main reason we encourage women to try more than one method of stimulation is that it gives them more flexibility and freedom in sexual arousal.

8
Being Female, Being Sexual: Special Issues of the Body

So far you have become more familiar with your body. Perhaps you have begun to accept it as your own with a somewhat new perspective. Now, before we discuss ways of sharing physical pleasure, we would like to spend some time on several topics special to women. We include menstruation, pregnancy and menopause— processes that happen to our bodies, and to a great extent include changes we cannot control. We will reflect upon these events, and how they influence our feelings about being women and being sexual.

MENSTRUATION

The beginning months. Remember the first time you menstruated? Some girls were terrified because it happened without warning— perhaps because no one explained it to them. They couldn't understand what was wrong with them, why they were bleeding. Even after the fact some parents have trouble talking it over with their daughters.

> After I told my mother, she just handed me a box of Kotex and a little book. I think it was called "Personally Yours." She told me to read it and ask her questions if I wanted to. I had a lot of questions, but I was embarrassed, and I didn't think she really wanted me to ask.

Other first reactions focused on how different menstruation felt from what women expected:

> I remember how angry I was that no one ever told me how painful it was. "A little uncomfortable" was not what it felt like.
> My mother said, "Now you are a woman." She had talked to me about it, so I was prepared for this "womanhood." But I just had expected it to be different when womanhood came . . . not a chubby little twelve-year-old with a barely noticeable chest, feet that were too big, and now the crowning glory of a sanitary napkin.

———— 🐛 ————

"Now you can get pregnant," my dad told me. It sounded like a threat.

Other women report that they felt quite well prepared and had very positive reactions to their first period.

> Well, I had to wait until I was sixteen, almost the last one in my class. When it came, I was thrilled! It made me one of them.
> I was deeply proud. It sounds funny because I was a little repulsed by the blood, but at the same time felt that was the sign of something so real and important.

Perhaps you can find something in common with these reactions—some mixture of recalled pleasure and discomfort. If your reaction to getting your first period was exclusively negative, you need not feel alone or even surprised. Other cultures mark this transition with a ritual, a recognition of its importance. Our culture does not celebrate this occasion; in fact, that part of the body is often viewed as unclean and therefore treated as if it should be a secret. Colloquial terms like "on the rag," "my friend," or "the curse" try to disguise the positive power of menstruation. Indeed, as the months go on, there are times when menstruating feels cumbersome, embarrassing due to occasional odor or spotting. Perhaps you were teased. Embarrassment may have been intense.

The problem of the special importance of beginning menses is that menstruation is often the young girl's first introduction to the physical reality of her sexuality. Some girls—perhaps 15 to 30 percent—discovered genital pleasure through masturbation before their first period. Some girls have also tried pleasurable genital playing with another child. Some have had unpleasant sexual contact with a person who was sexually abusive. But, for the majority of women, the initial menses is their first confrontation with their sexual capacities and especially their genitals. So if this transformation is very negative, it can contribute to (though usually it's not the only cause of) other negative feelings about sexuality.

It is important to remember, however, that although menstruation marks an entrance into one's biological capacity for motherhood, it does not define femininity or sexuality in general. Women who have never menstruated or no longer menstruate are still women and are still sexual beings. What this means is that if you have had only extremely negative feelings and experiences about your menstrual period, you may just want to set these experiences aside, keeping an eye on them from time to time but not focusing on them exclusively. Instead, try to develop positive feelings about your genitals and body. In addition, we will discuss some steps you can take to improve your menstrual and premenstrual days, if your menstrual period is marked by discomfort and moodiness.

The Monthly Cycle: Physical Changes and Feelings

We all know what happens during the menstrual cycle. Hormone levels change, ovulation occurs in midcycle, and menstrual flow begins about every twenty-eight to thirty-six days. Nevertheless, it is only in the last twenty years that the complexity of these physical changes has been more closely examined. If you are especially interested, you may want to consult the bibliography for detailed books on this topic. Emotional changes are less clearly understood but are commonly believed to be related to an interaction of hormonal changes, cultural beliefs, and individual differences.

The two most important activities in the cycle are *ovulation* and *menstrual flow,* or menstruation. Menstrual flow marks the first day of the cycle. Estrogen increases, stimulating the growth of the egg, or *ovum.* Ovulation occurs about fourteen days later, at midcycle, when an ovum is released into a fallopian tube for its journey to the uterus.

The most important changes in the menstrual cycle are fluctuations in the levels of the female hormones estrogen and progesterone. Estrogen increases to six times its basal level from menstrual day 1 to ovulation; it then decreases and peaks again to a lesser extent about day 22 (of a twenty-eight-day cycle). Also at day 22, progesterone is dramatically higher (about six times its day-1 level). Estrogen and progesterone then decrease dramatically in the days prior to menstruation. The average menstrual-cycle length is about twenty-nine days (plus or minus two), though cycles can vary a great deal.

Many women report that they feel different during the two or three days around ovulation. It has now been documented that ovulation is a time when your various senses—especially your senses of smell, sight, and hearing—are at their high point of sensitivity. However, sensitivity to pain may be lower than usual. Some women also report that they feel better and have more energy at midcycle. Not surprisingly, this time has been noted to correspond to an increase in sexual interest for a number of women.

Hormonal changes may account for *some,* though not all, of the

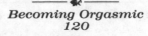

highs and lows women experience. Hormonal changes also correspond to physical changes. An increase in lubrication as well as a change in the consistency of vaginal fluid often occur at midcycle. Increased breast sensitivity and swelling, weight gain (one to five pounds), abdominal fluid retention, and even headache may occur in at least 50 percent of women during the three to five days before menstruation. Mood changes and feelings of fatigue, irritability, or restlessness may also be part of the premenstrual days—this collection of symptoms is often referred to as *premenstrual syndrome* (PMS).

Irregular Cycles

It is common for menstrual cycles to be irregular during a woman's adolescence and middle age. This seems to be a normal, gradual process of the body's reproductive organs winding up and winding down. In between those years, the regularity and length of the menstrual cycle can be related to a variety of influences, including:

Nutrition and body fat. Women who have starved themselves, as in the condition *anorexia nervosa,* stop menstruating when their body weight drops, and their cycles begin again when their body weight gets within normal range. When menstrual cycles cease, the condition is called *amenorrhea.* A minimum of body fat is needed to have one's first menstrual period, as well as to resume menstruating after a condition of starvation, either externally imposed (by war or famine, for example) or internally driven (extreme dieting strategies). Some women who are extremely physically active, such as runners or ballet dancers, may have a level of body fat that is insufficient to maintain menstrual regularity. However, normal menstruation will also be interrupted when body fat is excessive. Obese women, women 80 percent or more above their normal weight (for example, a 250-pound woman whose weight should be about 140), also have menstrual irregularities, including amenorrhea. For these women, weight loss results in the return of a more normal cycle.

Altitude. Changes in menstrual-cycle length and possibly reduced fertility have occurred to women who move to a high altitude, around 10,000 feet above sea level. It is not clear whether the menstrual cycle becomes more regular once the body has adjusted to the altitude over several years. Airplane flight attendants are also known

Being Female, Being Sexual

to have menstrual disturbances, but these may be more related to sudden shifts in time zones rather than the altitude changes.

Breast-feeding. For mothers who have recently given birth, three factors work together to determine how quickly menses will begin again: nutrition, lactation (production of breast milk), and use of a supplemental formula to combine with breast-feeding. When breast-feeding, women who are well nourished will have a quicker return of menses than will women who are less well nourished. But if women supplement their nursing with bottle feeding, menses will return more rapidly. In American women, menses may begin as soon as five to six weeks for mothers who only partially breast-feed their babies, in comparison to mothers who breast-feed exclusively, who may resume menstruation about three months after giving birth.

Sexual activity. Recent research directed by Dr. Winnifred Cutler suggests a connection between intercourse regularity and cycle regularity. In the study, women who had intercourse once a week were more likely to have a 29.5-day cycle than women who had sporadic or infrequent sex with men. One possible trigger for this is the scent, especially underarm odor, of men. While this is an idea that needs further testing, Cutler's findings support the concept that the menstrual cycle is rather finely tuned and sensitive to the woman's physical and social conditions.

Emotional upheaval and distress. Most women have a sense that if they are very upset, their periods will be affected. A common situation for some women is a fear of pregnancy delaying a period, with increased worry and tension as the late days add up. There is also evidence that women in a war situation will experience menstrual irregularity, as will women who have experienced a shock such as a family member's death. Serious depression may also interfere with cycle regularity, and it is possible that a less intense but longer-lasting stress, such as chronic fatigue from excessive work, could cause cycle-length irregularities.

Illness or disease. Occasionally, menstrual-cycle patterns can change because something specific has gone wrong with a woman's physical health. Changes in cycle length, flow, or amount; clotting; spotting between periods; or discomfort are all reasons to seek a medical checkup.

Sexuality and the Menstrual Cycle

We should not be surprised that the menstrual cycle is "sensitive" to the changes we have just discussed, since they are likely to be important if a woman conceives and bears a child: Her mental and physical health, the availability of food and resources, and the potential availability and cooperation of a partner are likely to affect the well-being of the mother and infant.

Some research evidence suggests that sexual desire is related to different phases of the menstrual cycle. However, some women do not notice any difference in their sexual desire, interest, or activity throughout the month.

Other women do experience fluctuations in their desire and activity. They are likely to be more sexual at midcycle (around ovulation), a few days before menstruation begins, and just after menstruation ends. The midcycle surge is thought to be related to the tendency for senses to be heightened, the accompanying feelings of well-being and energy, and the change in lubrication. Since ovulation is a woman's fertile time, perhaps a little push from Mother Nature at this time makes good biological sense. The premenstrual surge in desire may have to do with some increased genital congestion and lubrication increase, a decreased possibility of pregnancy, as well as an awareness of the onset menstruation, which for many couples is a less desirable time for sexual contact. Similarly, the postmenstrual peak may reflect relaxation following menstruation and desire following a period of no sex. At each of these three points, there is a likelihood that a woman will be more aware of her genitals, given a change in lubrication or in the expectation of the start or the cessation of her menstrual flow.

Some women regularly experience a change in sexual interest and ease of arousal each month at a predictable phase of their cycle. Other women occasionally notice a change, but it is never predictable. There is no single natural pattern, perhaps because other circumstances—fatigue, being in love, changes in self-esteem, emotional upsets—can override whatever tendencies may be triggered by the menstrual cycle. If your life is very stable and consistent, it may be easier for you to detect differences during your cycle.

Premenstrual Syndrome (PMS)

In the five to seven days before the beginning of the menstrual flow, it is not uncommon for women to experience irritability, depression, lethargy, and water retention (including a weight gain of one to five

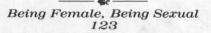

pounds). This is the primary cluster of symptoms that is called pre-menstrual syndrome (PMS). Some women also report experiencing other premenstrual symptoms, including dizziness, tension, anxiety, indecisiveness, irrationality, breast swelling and tenderness, abdominal bloating, constipation, migraine headaches, increased thirst and appetite, and cravings for sweets. Possibly anywhere from 50 to 100 percent of women experience some of these symptoms, and the intensity of the complaints varies from minor to severe.

You may have heard about the research suggesting that women are more likely to bring their children to the doctor's office and more likely to be involved in accidents and perhaps even to commit suicide during premenstrual days. In fact, these patterns affect women both before and during their flow and so may indicate that PMS combined with menstruation makes some women emotionally vulnerable.

What causes PMS? No one is really certain. It is likely that psychological and physiological factors, especially hormone-related changes, contribute. How much each of these may contribute depends on the individual woman's physiology and the culture in which she is raised. Although much is known about hormones and their effects on the body, their interactions with each other and their effects on feelings and behavior have not been carefully examined.

What can you do if you have PMS symptoms (or you think you might have them) and they bother you? First, you may want to keep a record for one or two menstrual cycles and note which, if any, of the symptoms you feel each day. Choose three physical and three psychological symptoms (and throw in a few positive choices like "energetic" or "confident" if you want to—since one study found that some women felt good before their periods). If you find that you are bothered by premenstrual physical and emotional sensitivities, there are several aspects of your life-style you can evaluate and change on your own to see if that helps.

Nutrition. If you experience fluid retention in parts of your body, have swollen and sore breasts, gain weight, feel bloated, or even have migraine headaches, changing your diet may help. Avoid sticky, sweet foods (and drinks) before your period—try to substitute fruits, nuts, plain yogurt, and bread topped with only small amounts of jam sweetened with natural fruit juice. Be careful of foods that contain large amounts of salt, such as smoked and cured meats, packaged soups, or potato chips, since high carbohydrate and high salt foods contribute to water retention. It is helpful to substitute foods that are good diuretics, that naturally remove excess water from the body.

Strawberries, pineapple, and melon are examples, as are parsley and cucumbers. Drinking water actually helps, although you might think this makes water retention worse. On the other hand, drinking caffeine-filled drinks such as coffee, tea, and various soft drinks can increase fluid retention. Finally, be careful about chocolate, as it contains both caffeine and a substance that can aggravate or initiate migraine headaches.

Incidentally, stimulating the loss of fluid may result in potassium loss. Eating fruits and vegetables will replace that loss.

And remember, if you love salty or terribly sweet foods and drink coffee by the quart, do not feel you have to give them all up. The idea is to reduce your intake of these substances, especially in the week prior to your expected period.

Alcohol. If you suffer from PMS, it may be wise to limit alcohol intake to a glass of wine or beer per day in the few premenstrual days. Alcohol is high in carbohydrates, and it appears that women are more affected by the alcohol drunk during the premenstrual phase than at other times in the cycle. Alcohol is also a depressant and may worsen existing depressive or lethargic feelings.

Exercise and relaxation. Keeping your body fit seems to be every expert's advice for every problem. While there is no evidence that exercise and fitness will stop PMS symptoms, many women seem to benefit from the overall sense of well-being and increased body capability that regular exercise seems to offer. For some women, the mood changes at the end of the cycle (especially anxiety, depression, and irritability) become less severe. You do not have to become an athlete or even an exercise enthusiast. Simply find a form of exercise that you will do regularly, will find somewhat rewarding, and that includes some aerobic conditioning. Currently most sports medicine recommendations are for three to four times per week in which twenty to thirty minutes are aerobic. Since we are not experts in this area, we suggest you check further on what types of exercise would be possible for you. Also consider what is easily available in your area and the time of day you are most apt to be able to keep appointments with yourself. Set it up so that access is easy. There are a few books for beginners in the bibliography. However if you are over thirty-five, have any physical conditions that may interfere with exercise, or take any prescription medication, you should first consult your physician. If you do not have a physician that knows you well, and you live in an area where a sports medicine clinic is available, you may consider calling them for advice, as they tend to help individuals work out ways to be active in spite of hindrances or disabilities.

While not all women are troubled by its symptoms, all women experience menopause. We will discuss exercise more in the later section on menopause. If you start an exercise routine early on in your reproductive life, your menopausal and postmenopausal years will be more pleasant, healthier, and safer.

Relaxation is almost an uncomfortable word in our society. Many of us, women and men, feel that if we aren't doing something every minute, we are not "living fully" or, worse, we are lazy. We have already discussed the importance of taking time to relax, even if this may mean taking time away from heavy commitments to others. It may be important to accept the fact that you can probably never do enough anyway—you can do only what you can do.

What does time out from pressure and external demands have to do with PMS? For one thing, research shows that in spite of the fact that some women feel lethargic and depressed in the premenstrual week, the overall activity level (in one study, measured by a pedometer) of women is actually higher then. So women may actually be increasing their burdens unknowingly and overwhelming themselves. Also important, relaxation is a skill to cultivate in and of itself, since it is a way of controlling the pace of our lives rather than letting the pace control us. Having some sense of control over life can help people feel less anxious, angry, and depressed.

Medication. If you try the above self-help techniques and they do not help, or if you are incapacitated by premenstrual symptoms, you may be helped by medication. It is wise to get a doctor's advice. Don't rely on over-the-counter, nonprescription medications as they can have side effects, long-term effects, and may interact with other medications you might be taking (not to mention alcohol).

No drugs have been found to be effective for all PMS symptoms in all women. You may have to try a few alternatives before you hit on the best solution for you. Vitamin B_6 (pyridoxine), taken three to four days prior to menstrual flow, helps some women with headache, breast tenderness, and feelings of irritability, tension, and negativity. Taking progesterone or progesterogens (synthetic, progesteronelike drugs) has helped ease some women's physical and psychological PMS symptoms. Progesterone seems to act on the brain much like a minor tranquilizer. Diuretics also relieve some other PMS symptoms.

Modifying your diet may be a better choice, given the fact that diuretics can be hard on the kidneys and may have long-term side effects.

More recently, some women have found relief by using medications that appear to reduce prostaglandins. Prostaglandins are found in most cells of the body, and one of their major functions seems to be to regulate the smooth muscles of the body. Smooth muscles are those we cannot directly control—those of the intestines, blood vessels, and uterus are examples. Prostaglandins increase during the premenstrual phase and are highest at the onset of the menstrual flow. (They seem to play a major role in menstrual cramping, which we will discuss below.) Several antiprostaglandin medications have been used for many years in the treatment of arthritic patients, therefore their long-term effects are known. Formerly only available by prescription, ibuprofen (for example, Motrin and Rufen) is now available over the counter under such brand names as Advil, Nuprin, and Medipren.

In some cases other medications may be recommended by your physician. Tranquilizers such as Librium or Valium will help keep you calm but will not directly alleviate PMS. However, the use of these tranquilizers can be habit forming. Unless your doctor has another reason besides PMS to prescribe tranquilizers for you, check out other alternatives first. You may also be prescribed antianxiety or antidepression medication (for example, Elavil, desipramine, or an MAO inhibitor). These drugs are for ongoing depression or anxiety symptoms, not for monthly PMS symptoms. If they are prescribed for you, it should be because you have a chronic mood disorder that gets worse around the premenstrual phase. Make sure you understand the reasons for, as well as the effects and side effects that may accompany, any medication your doctor prescribes.

A final word: PMS reality and illusion. Over the next few years there are likely to be changes in both the understanding and effective treatment of PMS. Meanwhile, if you experience PMS symptoms, it may take patience and trial and error on your part, but you can manage the premenstrual phase without your family, job responsibilities, and relationships suffering.

What will take more time to overcome is the cultural myth that menstruating women are the victims of raging hormones that make them unreliable, unpredictable, unreasonable, less productive, or otherwise risky. In spite of more than twenty-five years of menstrual-cycle research searching for evidence of signs of illness, violence, and

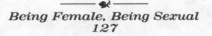

incapacity, the available evidence is rather weak and contradictory. There are probably different kinds of PMS, which vary in the type and severity of symptoms. A few women are incapacitated if they do not use one of the more recently discovered remedies. Many more women experience symptoms that usually do not noticeably interfere with their usual functioning; nevertheless, they feel better if they watch their diet, prepare for the few days before menstruation, and take into account their increased emotional sensitivity. There are also some women who are at their best during the premenstrual phase. Clearly, some percentage of women must play their winning tennis matches, run their races, sing their operatic roles and recitals, play their concert pianos, and conceive of and write their poems and novels premenstrually. It is interesting that we do not know much about how such women cope with their menstrual phase changes.

Finally, since a number of women are more sexually active during the premenstrual phase, it would be helpful to know whether women's premenstrual symptoms are related to their sexual activity in this phase. Some women and their partners may see menstruation as a time not to be sexual, others may be attuned to the increased vasocongestion in the genital area, and still others may find the premenstrual phase a time when sexual closeness makes them feel better.

Dysmenorrhea

For many years, the fact that menstrual cramps could be debilitating was not really taken seriously, even by women. Because some women experienced only minor discomfort, those who were in extreme pain were viewed suspiciously and perhaps labeled hysterical, complainers, or even doctor shoppers. Women felt they just had to suffer and not make so much fuss about their pain. With increased knowledge, however, menstrual pain has become widely acknowledged and its treatment more successful.

Menstrual pain, or *dysmenorrhea*, happens to many women, especially during the first thirty-six hours of their menstrual flow. For as many as 30 to 40 percent of women, the pain is intense enough to prevent them from carrying on their usual activities unless they take medication.

There are two types of dysmenorrhea—primary and secondary. Primary menstrual pain is due to contractions of the uterus but not to other physical abnormalities of the pelvic organs. Secondary dysmenorrhea is caused by some physical abnormality such as fibroid

tumors, pelvic inflammatory disease (PID), endometriosis, or other disorders. Fibroids are noncancerous solid growths within the muscle wall of the uterus; PID is an infection of the female organs; and endometriosis is a condition in which cells from the uterine lining become displaced to other parts of the body, such as the ovaries and fallopian tubes.

The symptoms of dysmenorrhea include cramping in the lower abdomen, backache, a sensation of aching down the inner thighs, and—less often—nausea, headache, faintness, dizziness, and waves of hot or cold sensations.

More is known about menstrual cramps than about PMS. The pain appears to be caused by strong uterine contractions. Since 1967 it has been known that women with menstrual pain had five times the amount of prostaglandins in their menstrual fluid than did women who were without pain. Different types of prostaglandins are produced in the uterus, and it appears that if one type is produced in excess, it causes the uterus to become overactive and contract excessively. Because these contractions compress the uterine blood vessels, they may cut off the blood supply. When a muscle like the uterus suffers a decrease in blood supply, there is a great deal of pain, analogous to angina, the pain experienced during a heart attack. In addition, some of the excess prostaglandins escape into the bloodstream and stimulate the digestive tract to move food along rapidly, resulting in diarrhea.

To date, the most successful treatment method for *minor* menstrual cramps is aspirin, perhaps because it has some antiprostaglandin effects. Aspirin does not relieve the pain of more severe cramps, however. Women who suffer severe cramps will usually benefit from drugs with a strong antiprostaglandin effect, such as ibuprofen. As mentioned before, these include the medications Motrin and Rufen (prescribed) or Advil, Medipren, and Nuprin (over the counter). Although these medications are relatively safe, you should read the information on side effects and warnings carefully and consult a physician regarding any complications they may cause with a current physical condition or drug regimen you are following. (Never take ibuprofen if you are allergic to aspirin or while you are taking aspirin—the two do not mix.)

There are other ways to manage pain, such as relaxation and self-hypnosis. They have not been specifically demonstrated as effective for a broad spectrum of women, but with practice you may be able to use them successfully. Further information is available in the books listed in the bibliography.

What about orgasms and menstrual cramps? Research has been done showing that some women find relief from dysmenorrhea by masturbating to orgasm. How severe these women's cramps are is not known. Since orgasm also causes the uterus to contract strongly and rhythmically, it is possible that orgasm is able to normalize the contractions away from the severe and sustained squeezing. No one has studied this, however. In addition, as some women get into their mid-thirties, they notice an opposite relationship between orgasm and cramps. When they have orgasm, especially in the last week before their period, they will have painful cramps for twenty to thirty minutes after orgasm. It is not clear why this happens, and if you notice this, you need to inform your physician, as there may be an underlying physical problem.

Very little is known about medication and sexual response during menstruation. Some of the women we have seen have tried a variety of remedies for cramps. Several have noticed that when they take antiprostaglandins, it takes somewhat longer to have an orgasm and orgasms feel less intense.

Women may be told that cramps become less painful or even disappear after childbirth. This is true only for some women; others continue to have severe pain during menstruation.

A final word on dysmenorrhea. Pain is a very special phenomenon that is only partially understood. Because it is usually a sign that something is wrong, it is important to understand it, take care of it, and remove the cause. In this case, we need to treat only the pain. You should have a medical checkup whenever you have pain that you cannot easily explain or manage, just to make sure that nothing else is wrong. If your physician does not seem to hear you, to take you seriously, or to regard your pain as real, you may want to get a second opinion or change physicians.

SELF-HEALTH CARE
AND CHOOSING A PHYSICIAN

Your health will be enhanced if you take three basic steps. First: Try to keep informed about what "healthy" and "unhealthy" mean in terms of your body. Reading books and articles about women's bodies and reproductive systems, written in everyday language, is a start. So is getting familiar with what is normal for your own body.

This leads us to the second point: Be aware of your body and its changes over the course of your life. One easy self-exam is a breast exam. To do this, lie down and use two fingers to feel the tissue in the breast opposite your hand (left breast with right hand, right with left). Feel under the skin for any solid lumps. If you have cystic breast tissue, you will learn how your breasts feel over time and can therefore notice any change. Cysts are small lumps that feel like movable firm-to-hard marbles in the breast, and they can enlarge closer to menses and be tender or painful. To cover the entire breast, start with a small circular movement at the nipple and move in a spiral to the outside of the breast. Then stand and look in the mirror for any bulges or puckers in the breast or nipple area. Repeat while raising your hands over your head and pressing them together, and then while pressing your hands down on your hips. Do this once a month, after your period is over if you still menstruate monthly. Breast cancer is the second leading killer of women, but it is usually curable if detected early. The earliest detection can be done with mammography (X rays of the breast), and currently nonradiation techniques are being explored. Many women are even fearful about self-examination because of the possibilities of detecting breast cancer and the likelihood of breast removal (mastectomy). If breast cancer is detected early enough, mastectomy may not be necessary, and tumors can be removed with only small scars remaining in most cases.

A final self-care step that many of us take for granted is finding a physician. For general gynecological care you may want a general practitioner, an internist, a gynecologist, or an obstetrician-gynecologist. You need someone knowledgeable and competent and with whom you can develop a good working relationship. You should feel that you and your physician are on the same team, looking for the reasons for any problem or distress. Your doctor should be willing to answer your questions (prepare them in advance, or you may forget them in the rush of the moment). Don't expect your physician to spend time explaining things to you unless you ask (some patients do not want to know). And when it comes time for a major decision, such as those centering on childbirth or hysterectomy, try to understand the rationale behind the decision and see if you agree. If surgery is being recommended that is not urgent, do get a second opinion. Many insurance companies now also suggest second opinions.

WHEN MENSTRUATION STOPS NATURALLY: PREGNANCY AND MENOPAUSE

Pregnancy

It is difficult to talk "just a little" about pregnancy. In this book we certainly cannot do justice to all of the physical, psychological, and interpersonal changes that accompany pregnancy and childbirth. What we would like to do is discuss those aspects of pregnancy that are related to sexual response and functioning. If pregnancy interests you, we suggest you continue your reading among the more special-ized selections offered in the bibliography.

Sexuality during pregnancy should take two things into account: what is safe and what is comfortable. Any decisions should be tailored to the pregnancy and couple involved.

Let's consider comfort first. If women don't desire sexual con-tact, they won't feel comfortable being sexual. The first question is, What happens to sexual desire, interest, and frequency during preg-nancy? Most research findings agree that frequency of sex and sexual desire decrease during the latter part of the third trimester—the last month or two before delivery. There is less agreement on sexual response during the rest of pregnancy. Several patterns have been reported. For example, some women (compared to their prepregnancy levels) have less interest, activity, and responsiveness in the first trimester (the first three months) and greater interest in the second trimester and the first half of the third. Other women show a slow but steady decline of sexual interest throughout the entire pregnancy. Still other women notice increased orgasmic responsiveness, perhaps even multiple orgasms, beginning in the second trimester.

What may be influencing such changes in sexual desire and re-sponsiveness? Several possibilities exist.

Hormones. Massive increases in sex hormones occur during pregnancy. Estrogen increases and then levels off in the second tri-mester, with a second escalation later in the third trimester. At deliv-ery, estrogen is ten times above its normal level. Progesterone in-creases, with acceleration in late pregnancy. By the time of delivery, progesterone has increased to twenty-five times its prepregnancy norm. Both estrogen and progesterone are suspected of lowering sexual desire, though they increase the blood supply to the pelvic area and thus may make women feel increased need for release of sexual tension. Meanwhile, the mother's androgen (male hormone) levels rise progressively throughout pregnancy, perhaps counteracting the sex-ual depressant effects of progesterone and estrogen.

Body image, self-image. According to several studies, a majority of women become dissatisfied with their appearance during preg-nancy. Given what we have already discussed about our society's addiction to lithe, slim bodies, some uneasiness about a ballooning pregnancy is predictable. A woman who feels less attractive may feel less sexual.

On the other hand, some women feel they look wonderful during

pregnancy and are captivated (especially in their first pregnancies) by the changes in their bodies. One woman we saw in treatment for orgasm problems had always battled her weight, trying to get thinner and more "perfect," though she was a slender, very attractive person, deeply loved by her husband. When she became pregnant, much to everyone's surprise, she said she felt good about her body: "It's getting bigger, but it feels full. I even like how my stomach feels as the skin stretches."

Partners. Some men find pregnancy a time of worry, of questioning their capacity to be a father (of a first child) or to support later children. An unplanned baby may also make a man withdraw for a while. In addition, some men really like how their wives' bodies look during pregnancy; other men don't. Wives of men who are turned off by pregnancy may find it very difficult not to feel rejected, uneasy about their own sexual attractiveness, and in need of some reassurance. It is true that a number of men have affairs during their wives' pregnancies, though the state of their relationships in general and each person's sexual values appear to be more important than the pregnancy itself in producing extramarital sex during this period.

If you are pregnant and your partner is turned off or not very aroused by the look of the pregnancy, try not to see it as your problem but rather as a difficulty he has with appreciating your pregnant body. He will not be able to change if you or anyone else tries to get him to feel differently. He may, however, have some erroneous ideas about whether the baby will be hurt, or that sex and parenthood don't mix. Try to find some ways to be physically intimate that are comfortable for both of you. Sometimes, taking Lamaze classes and discussing the baby more, including talking to it (the fetus can hear after six months!), will help shift the emphasis from your shape to the mystery of the process.

Mood and health. Some women feel physically or psychologically distressed at various stages of their pregnancy. This discomfort is a major reason many women lose interest in sex. Again, it is important to let your partner know how you are feeling when you refuse or don't initiate sex, since he can also feel rejected and left out of the pregnancy process. For a number of couples, pregnancy can be a time of conflicted feelings and sometimes intense emotions. New worries, new relationship demands, self-expectations, and self-doubts about parenting adequacy are among the many sources of mixed emotions that can occur during pregnancy or after delivery. It is sometimes more difficult for partners to express their doubts and negative feelings, since people often believe that they should feel only delighted.

What about the safety of sex during pregnancy? Advice to pregnant couples over the last 100 years has ranged from "all sex is unsafe" to "do whatever you feel like doing." In fact, most of the research on the topic comes to an inconclusive answer. Decisions need to be made based on each specific pregnancy, each woman and man.

Between 10 and 15 percent of all pregnancies end in miscarriage, but rarely because of physical trauma or injury. The fetus seems to be protected from most jars and bumps by the fluid cushion within the uterus. Coitus and other sexual activities are extremely unlikely to cause miscarriage, except under certain medical conditions:

- If the cervix begins to open prematurely, or there are other signs of premature labor and delivery
- If the woman has had previous miscarriages due to uterine defects
- If either partner has a sexually transmitted disease or is carrying certain other bacteria that can be transmitted through genital contact
- Forceful blowing of air into the vagina during oral sex is very dangerous for women; it can cause air embolisms (bubbles in the blood vessel system) and result in maternal death

Another consideration is whether the woman is bearing her first child. One study has shown a slightly higher incidence of fetal distress among first-time mothers who had been more sexually active in the last month of pregnancy, compared to less sexually active first-time mothers.

So, if you are pregnant and do not have any of the above conditions, sexual activity is very likely to be safe for you and your baby. Most couples have sex during the first eight months, though some changes in position and activity are necessary.

We have seen some couples for sexual counseling during pregnancy. Sexuality during this time can take on a different meaning— for example, it may seem less like pure pleasure than before, it may seem more serious, more an act of commitment to the marriage and a future.

Usually couples come up with fairly natural solutions to any sexual complications caused by the woman's body enlarging. Unless the couple lies side by side, face-to-face positions become more awkward and sometimes uncomfortable as the pregnancy advances. Other positions enjoyed by very pregnant women and their partners include a "spoons" position (see chapter 11), in which the man lies behind the woman holding and caressing her while having intercourse from the rear. Alternatively, rear entry with the woman on her knees and supported with pillows under her chest and belly can be pleasurable.

During pregnancy, the woman may feel sensations somewhat differently. Therefore, a very important guideline to sexual activity during this period is to explore what types of contact provide the most satisfaction rather than to assume that sexual preferences and stimulation will remain the same. There may be times when just caressing is all that you want, or vaginal-penile contact without thrusting.

Many women become very self-conscious about their physical appearance during pregnancy. While it is important for you to appreciate your body, you may not be able to convince yourself that you look wildly sexy. If that's the case, try to focus less on how you look and more on other senses: how you feel, how touching feels to you, and how your partner responds to your touch. If you are uncomfortable physically, do not force yourself to be sexual just "for him," but let him know what you are experiencing.

Some women feel they need to be sexual for their partner's sake, especially during pregnancy. However, it is still important, during pregnancy as at other times, to have some reason of your own to engage in sex, some motivation that is for you—whether it be closeness, comfort, a sense of safety, sexual arousal, orgasm, or a variety of other reasons.

After Delivery

Babies change people's lives dramatically, and no one can know exactly how he or she will react until the baby is born. Being at the service of, and totally available to, an infant can be a difficult adjustment for both parents. Women often experience this more directly, since they have birthed the infant and are often breast-feeding.

In addition to the personal and social shock of adjusting to the birth, the mother's physical condition changes rapidly. Within three days after delivery, estrogen and progesterone levels drop dramatically from their very high pregnancy levels to very low levels. This decline is similar to the premenstrual pattern, though of a far greater magnitude (in fact, the hormones decline to a level close to that of

postmenopausal women). In this time, there can be strong mood changes.

In fact, most (estimates range from 60 to 85 percent) women experience a brief period of "postpartum blues," or minor depression, including mood swings and crying for about two weeks after delivery. It appears that this reaction is related to both the physical and interpersonal changes brought about by a baby. About 25 percent of women experience depressive symptoms for several months, though some depressive symptoms (such as sleep disturbance, fatigue, or lack of enjoyment of usually pleasurable activities) are difficult to separate from the reality of living with a newborn. Finally, a smaller percentage—less than 10 percent—of women experience severe depression and psychotic symptoms after birth. For women in the latter two groups, a psychiatric consultation should be considered if the symptoms are severe, disturbing, or making functioning very difficult.

We mention these issues for two reasons. First, it has been shown in some research that a partner who is very involved in the pregnancy, delivery, and aftercare seems to help the woman adjust—she will show fewer or less severe mood symptoms afterwards. This is not always the case, however, especially among women who suffer severe PMS or have a predisposition to experience depression.

The second reason for mentioning this adjustment period is that a woman may not feel much like having sex for a while after the physical recovery from birth (usually three to six weeks). This is all expected and natural; it's best not to force sexual feelings. Sex may also feel different at first. Initially there may be some physical discomfort when resuming sex after delivery. For example, the type of care given to the *episiotomy*, the incision made to enlarge the vaginal opening just before the baby's head emerges, influences whether the woman has pain for several months after delivery. Currently, it is recommended that episiotomies not be performed routinely, and if they are, they should be midline episiotomies with fine suture materials. You may want to discuss this procedure with your physician, so he or she knows your concerns. Vaginal discharge and residual bleeding may also delay resumption of coitus. Before resuming sexual intercourse, you may want to try other methods of sexual exchange. When you feel emotionally ready, and assuming there are no medical indications against coitus, you may want to examine your episiotomy scar with a hand mirror and, with clean fingers or a tampon, explore the opening and inside of the vagina for soreness. Your partner could

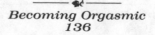

join you if you feel comfortable and as long as you can control the quality of the touching during the first few attempts. You and your partner may want to try intercourse gradually over several occasions, beginning with partial insertion of the penis, then trying full entry without movement, and gradually increasing to freer movements.

Vaginal soreness is not the only issue. Some women feel that their vagina is larger after delivery. To help maintain muscle tone and health of the genital and urinary area, it is recommended that you start doing Kegel exercises (see chapter 3) within a few days of delivery. During intercourse, try different positions to improve sensation and stimulation.

Breast-feeding has several effects on a woman's sexuality. A hormone called prolactin is responsible for milk production. Prolactin helps delay the renewal of the menstrual cycle by influencing the production of hormones that regulate menstruation. Prolactin directly inhibits estrogen production, and estrogen keeps the vagina lubricated. Therefore, nursing women may need a vaginal lubricant such as K-Y jelly until nursing stops.

Nursing itself can be accompanied by sexual responses. Common reactions include nipple erection, a feeling of breast warmth, clitoral sensations, and uterine contractions. A woman's nipples are very sensitive during the first month or so after delivery. A feeling of sexual arousal may occur along with these sensations, though this does not always happen.

Sexual arousal or breast stimulation (including nursing) may trigger milk ejections—producing drops or even brief squirts of milk. This makes good sense from nature's point of view—the infant depends on mother's milk initially, and the fact that nursing can evoke pleasurable sensations, and pleasurable sensations can evoke milk production, helps to keep the pair involved in this activity.

However, some couples find the production of milk during sexual activity embarrassing or a nuisance. Some are relieved to know it is a healthy and natural response. Other women may want to nurse just prior to sexual contact, may wear a bra with absorbent pads, or may keep a soft towel on the bed.

The sexual response patterns of vaginal vasocongestion, lubrication, and distension as well as orgasmic intensity seem to take eight to twelve weeks after delivery to return to prepregnancy patterns. Some women report that childbearing increases their sexual arousal and orgasm capacity, though most women report their sexual responsiveness is unchanged.

Menopause

We have heard a variety of comments about menopause from our friends and other women we have known. One menopausal woman, commenting on a friend's daughter who had just begun to have periods, said, "It's hard to start and it's hard to stop." A woman almost finished with menopause commented, "Well, I like the freedom. But I miss those predictable highs and lows I used to feel as the month progressed. It's so even, so flat now."

And from a forty-eight-year-old woman:

> I dreaded menopause because I had such emotional tailspins during my periods.
>
> I was right. Sweating day and night, unpredictable, leg aches, headaches. Anxiety, too. I did not have that before. I feel like a hypochondriac. . . . I think I sound and am seen by others as a complaining, aging, neurotic woman. I remember my mother, who had similar complaints and couldn't stand to be around us [children] for several years. . . . The physical feelings are real and focusing on them does two things: It makes them worse and it makes me aware of my body and how much older it is.

Although every woman goes through menopause, every woman's menopause is not identical. You may notice shorter cycles, irregular cycles, or an increase or decrease in your flow. Cycles may become very infrequent. This is the beginning of "the change of life."

Actually, menopause is a process made up of many physical and some emotional changes. Based on research of the past two decades, we know much more about the complexity of menopause and a little more about how to manage its difficulties. Several excellent resources, listed in the bibliography, go into these issues in greater detail. Here we will discuss briefly some facts about menopause itself and how sexuality is affected by menopause.

What happens during menopause? As a woman ages, her reproductive system goes through changes. Part of the process includes the shrinking of her ovaries and the decline of estrogen, progesterone, and other hormones. These changes are *gradual,* beginning about six to seven years (usually in a woman's early forties) before her last menstrual flow. As a young girl's body undergoes changes years before she experiences her first menstrual period, a similar gradual winding down seems to occur before the last menstrual period. This is a natural process; if it occurred overnight, the sudden

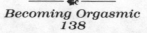

Becoming Orgasmic

physical changes and withdrawal from hormones would be much more uncomfortable.

What are the symptoms? Change may occur to the time between periods, the length of periods, or the amount of flow each month. In addition, about 80 to 85 percent of women experience one or more other symptoms: hot flashes (a sudden rush of heat experienced over the body, accompanied by sweating), night sweats (waking up at night drenched in sweat), headaches, dizziness, and insomnia. Mood changes such as depression and anxiety can also be present. Actually, only hot flashes and night sweats are directly related to the menopause. The other symptoms may occur throughout a woman's life and just become more prominent during menopause.

Even after menstrual periods stop, hormone levels continue to decrease, and a woman may experience symptoms for several additional years.

What happens to the body? Your ovaries will decrease in size and produce less estrogen while continuing to produce androgen. Androgens are hormones that are associated with higher energy levels and increased sex drive. Men have them in much higher concentration than women.

The decrease in estrogen appears to be related to a variety of other changes. Skin aging is accelerated, particularly the loss of muscle tone and thickening of the skin tissue. Aging also reduces cells, called *melanocytes*, which manufacture the pigment causing skin to tan. Thus, women become increasingly susceptible to sunburn if they are unprotected.

The skin lining and muscle tone of the urinary tract and the vagina also diminish. A woman may have some loss of bladder control, which Kegel exercises will help correct. Vaginal changes may also include less lubrication and more sensitive tissue, subject to small abrasions or tears during intercourse unless some lubricant or hormonal replacement is used (more on this in a moment).

It is interesting that several different reports have shown that menopausal women who are sexually active have less deterioration of vaginal tissue. Keeping sexually active seems to help maintain an older woman's vaginal health. No one knows if nonintercourse sexual activities have a similar effect.

There are a variety of other menopausal changes a woman may experience. Hair may become a bit coarser and thinner; breasts may begin to lose their fullness (this is especially noticeable in women with large breasts). These changes are also primarily due to a decrease in estrogens.

How common is bone loss? Recent studies show that at least 50 percent of women, in every country studied, show some signs of bone loss by age sixty. This bone loss goes on throughout the menopausal years, and its greatest decline is between the mid-forties and mid-seventies. Bone loss has dramatic consequences—by the time a woman reaches eighty, she may have lost more than one-third of her bone mass. Under these conditions, a woman's chances of bone fractures are great, whether in response to a fall; a sharp, abrupt movement; or even the sudden pressure of someone grabbing her to prevent a fall.

This decrease of bone density is *osteoporosis.* It means an increase in bone porosity—a decrease in the density of the bones. Bones are not what they seem to most of us—unchanging, solid, and fixed. They have blood vessels and nerve tissues and are constantly part of a process of deterioration and rebuilding. A major ingredient of bone tissue is calcium. Every day some calcium leaves the bone tissue, and new calcium is picked up from the blood and added to the bone.

We now know that estrogen plays a very essential role in the exchange process between the blood and the bone. When estrogen levels decline, as they do at menopause, the bones become endangered and begin to disintegrate. This loss does not happen to all women at the same rate, but some degree of change has taken place in most women who reach their seventieth birthday. (Bone loss occurs in men, too, but they tend to have fewer breaks, perhaps because their original bone mass is greater than women's.)

The most common result of osteoporosis is hip fracture, occurring to almost one-third of women over sixty-five. Spinal bones are also frequently affected, especially at the points where the spine naturally curves, since these are the spine's weaker points. Women with spinal fractures generally lose several inches in height and may form a protrusion in the upper back, creating a humpback appearance (called a "dowager's hump"). It appears that fair-skinned, thin women of Northern European descent are more likely to suffer some of the effects of osteoporosis than are Asian and black women.

It used to be that a woman had to wait until she suffered a broken bone or a loss in height before bone loss could be diagnosed. That is no longer the case. A variety of painless techniques are now available for early diagnosis, and all women can benefit from some preventive measures.

Being a menopausal woman (not to mention an aging woman) does not sound like fun. No wonder they have emotional symptoms, too. Is this really such a terrible part of a woman's life? Some women do experience depressive feelings, such as loss of self-worth and feelings of uselessness, tearfulness, and lack of interest in daily living. Some may also experience sleep problems, appetite loss, low energy, an inability to function, and an overwhelming sense of hopelessness. In part, depression or anxiety can be related to the hormonal changes that take place during menopause.

There are also psychological changes associated with this time in a woman's life. It means many different things to different women: a loss of fertility, a loss of youth, a sense of decreasing desirability, becoming a woman "like my mother," or sometimes threat of abandonment by a partner.

One friend in her early forties remembered: "I've never depended on my looks to get along in the world, at least I didn't think so. I'm only moderately attractive. Yet I've had a tough time getting used to being treated [by men] in a way that middle-aged women are treated."

Many women also have to deal with mixed feelings about their children leaving home. Others can't stand having physical ailments— they are not used to and do not tolerate discomfort very easily (especially when it's unpredictable).

We discussed earlier how negative our culture is about aging. Older means loss, doing less, winding down, and decreasing resources, none of which our society is very tolerant of, let alone positive about. Menopause is a dramatic "change" signal for women that "older" is really going to happen.

In contrast to our negative view, in other cultures, including many American Indian tribes, people are not considered real adults (wise enough, grown-up enough) until they are about fifty-five or sixty. In our culture, youth and productivity are primary and connected values, and fifty-five is the beginning of the descent into old age. Finding a positive identity and maintaining self-esteem as one ages may be difficult.

The combination of the cultural meaning, the social transition, and the physical symptoms of menopause weigh down on a woman. For many women menopause looks and feels like a disaster.

But this need not be the case. Treatments are available to help alleviate symptoms, and if we reexamine the world around us we find plenty of evidence that, as the famous anthropologist Margaret Mead noticed, "The most creative force in the world is the menopausal woman with zest."

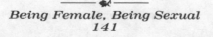

Being Female, Being Sexual

What changes in sexual functioning can be expected? Not many, as it turns out. Less lubrication perhaps, which may decrease some of the sensations of genital stimulation. Wetness increases our ability to perceive stroking in the vaginal area. So you may get aroused a bit more slowly. There are no changes in orgasms until you are much older, say in your seventies, when they may become less intense.

Sexual activity does decrease over time, but very gradually except in case of illness, disease, or injury. The frequency of sexual activity depends on the continued desire for sex, the availability and interest of a sexual partner, and adequate health. The ability to discuss changes in desire or activity is very important.

Several different studies have shown that women who have regular sexual contact in the years after forty are less likely to suffer from sexual problems, including vaginal dryness and discomfort during sex. Should you be in this age range and not have a partner, continue to provide self-stimulation. When you meet a partner, go slowly until you and your body feel relaxed and responsive.

Keeping Healthy Before, During, and After Menopause

Menopause and its consequences sound something like a natural disaster, nature's version of a physiological and psychological aging cyclone. In fact, many of its consequences can be managed quite successfully. Though aging itself will occur, it is possible to minimize the physical risk and discomfort associated with menopausal changes. Let's summarize what is currently known about useful treatments and their pros and cons.

Hormone replacement therapy (HRT). An obvious way to mitigate the effects of hormone withdrawal is to reintroduce hormones. Replacing some estrogens will relieve hot flashes, improve skin moisture and elasticity, help vaginal lubrication, dramatically decrease and perhaps halt bone deterioration, decrease skin itching and sensitivity to certain fabrics, and improve general mood and well-being. Women taking estrogens also have less incidence of heart disease, reduced cholesterol levels, and have no blood pressure elevation.

In earlier decades, use of estrogen in HRT (as well as in birth control pills) showed an increase in some types of cancer. At current recommended low doses, greater cancer risk is not linked to estrogen use except under certain conditions. Low doses of estrogen alternated with low doses of progestins are thought to decrease the chances of

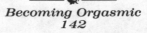

endometrial (uterine-lining) and breast cancer, compared to women taking only estrogens.

Certain diseases and conditions are sure signs that you should not take HRT: vascular thromboses (sudden blood vessel clots), visual system blood vessel disease, high blood pressure, breast cancer, or undiagnosed vaginal bleeding. Other conditions warrant proceeding with caution in undergoing HRT: diabetes, a past history of certain cancers that are hormone dependent, endometriosis, uterine fibroids, gallbladder disease, varicose veins, heavy smoking, or being more than 30 percent over your normal weight.

The decision to go on hormones and remain there should be based on your own history and the most recent information available to your doctor. Frequent medical checkups, at least once a year, may be an important part of the treatment.

Other drugs and medical procedures. In general, minor and major tranquilizers, sometimes prescribed for nervousness, irritability, and sleep problems, are not recommended to treat menopausal symptoms. They are more appropriate for time-limited, acute conditions.

Hysterectomy, the surgical removal of the uterus, may be considered good prevention by some people since the uterus and cervix can be cancer sites. However, it is not recommended unless there are other signs of uterine trouble, such as fibroid tumors or troublesome bleeding. In addition, the ovaries provide some hormone production even after menopause. Current recommendations are to keep your ovaries unless there is some clear indication to do otherwise. It is always good practice to seek a second opinion before proceeding with surgery.

Diet, nutrition, and exercise. The advice for a healthy diet continues to be revised annually. What remains true are two approaches: balance and moderation. A few additional special guidelines are currently being recommended. High-fiber, low-fat diets are considered good in general and especially good to help prevent breast cancer (though part of breast cancer proneness seems to be inherited). A calcium intake of about 800 milligrams per day (the equivalent of about two glasses of milk) until the mid-forties and gradually increasing to about 1,200 milligrams per day is considered important to counteract the progress of osteoporosis. Vitamin D through pills (up to 400 international units) or through fifteen minutes of sun per day helps to extract the calcium from the intestines and so is often recommended in addition to calcium. Too much calcium is not good for the arteries, and too much vitamin D may have a decalcifying effect. New discoveries are made each year, so it is important to keep yourself informed about new dietary theories.

Caffeine is thought to increase benign breast cysts. Since caffeine, especially more than two cups of coffee per day or equivalent amounts, also seems to be correlated with premenstrual breast tenderness and more severe menstrual cramps, reducing your intake of this chemical early in life might be wise.

Maintaining a level of physical activity that keeps muscles toned and the body in movement may help decrease bone loss. Exercise alone will not prevent osteoporosis, however. It will promote general well-being, strength, cardiovascular functioning, increased bone mass, and overall balance and condition. Feeling better physically is usually associated with good sexual health as well.

9
Sharing Self-Discoveries with Your Partner

U ntil now, your partner has only been able to participate indirectly in your feelings and discoveries. He may be unfamiliar with the things you have been practicing for these past sessions. The exercises in this chapter will give you a chance to share your discoveries with your partner. His involvement is very important, and it will help if he reads these chapters along with you.

Before we talk about this step, we would like to note where you might be in your sexual growth right now. You may not have experienced your first orgasm yet—that is really not essential. What is most important is that you have learned how to give yourself a fairly high level of sexually arousing pleasure. Continue to use your individual masturbation sessions to teach yourself about what feels good, and keep your sexual arousal high. Some women experience their first orgasm with their partner, and this might happen to you.

This step is a challenging one, for you will gradually be teaching your partner about what kinds of stimulation give you pleasure. At first you may just want to discuss what works for you, the kinds of stimulation you need—such as vibrators, manual stimulation, certain strokes and pressures—and then you will try a self pleasuring session with your partner next to you. Your partner will also share with you his patterns of masturbation. This is a unique opportunity for you both to learn how each of you gives your own body pleasure so that you can learn more about pleasuring each other.

How do you feel about masturbating in front of your partner? Many people initially find this a rather peculiar idea. At the very least, it seems that having someone else in the room would be distracting. It may also be somewhat embarrassing, since most of us have grown up with a taboo against doing anything sexual in front of another person. You may be worried about what your partner will think—whether or not he will like this new aspect of you—especially if many of your past sexual experiences together have been unsatisfying. Watching your partner may seem improper or even competitive if he is easily aroused or moves from arousal to orgasm quickly.

———— ❧ ————

For now, whatever your feelings, feel confident that it is completely natural to have mixed emotions about sharing your changes with a partner. The most important aspect of your future sexual experiences together is that you try to give each other encouragement and support—both physically and emotionally—and that you have a sense of being on the same team. Support involves providing understanding and encouragement without pressure or criticism. We will offer some specific suggestions in a moment that will make it easier for you both to create a supportive atmosphere in which to try this exercise.

Before you decide whether or not you want to try this exercise, we would like you and your partner to talk over any expectations or apprehensions that you may have. We would like to make the following suggestions: Imagine that you are going to begin pleasuring yourself in front of each other. What concerns do you think you would have? What concerns do you think your partner would have? Whether or not you "guess right" about your partner is less important than just exchanging your concerns about each other's feelings. Talk about each feeling in terms of what each of you can do to maximize the pleasure and minimize the mutual worries. Share your fears and hopes for this experience.

This mutual exploration of feelings will give you a clearer idea of how each of you feels about doing this exercise, whatever those feelings might be. It should also give you an idea of what you are each hoping to gain from this experience.

You might also consider how you *both* see masturbation as part of your total sexual relationship. Do you see it only as something to be done in "emergencies"—when one partner is away or sick? Spend a few minutes discussing this, because we will come back to it later.

If you decide that masturbation really has very little or no place in your sexual relationship, you may initially hesitate to share this activity. You do not have to believe that masturbation is enjoyable or valuable to your sexual relationship in order to do this exercise. The primary purpose here is simple: to show your partner what you've learned about yourself. Right now, only you know how to give yourself the kind of stimulation you need to become sexually aroused. You are your partner's best teacher of what gives you pleasure. Although it may be difficult at first, we have seen couples grow sexually and emotionally from this experience.

In speaking with couples in therapy, we noticed that their concerns and reservations have had several recurrent themes. We'd like to suggest that you talk about these if you haven't already, especially

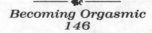

if you found it somewhat difficult to express your feelings and exchange them with each other.

From the woman's point of view. What does it mean to you to touch yourself or give yourself pleasure with your partner watching you? Are you pleased, frightened, titillated, uncertain, or just curious? Expect your feelings to be a mixture of interest and hesitation: interest because this is something that you have never shared before, and hesitation because you don't really know how difficult or easy it will be with him present, and perhaps also because you do not know how he will respond to you in this new situation. If you feel your partner will be somehow critical, discuss this with him. What *exactly* are you afraid that he might think or say?

As we mentioned earlier, trying this step may conflict with some of the sexual values that you learned while growing up. In most homes masturbation is not regarded as an acceptable form of sexual expression. It is usually done in private, if not on the sly. Therefore, masturbating with someone else present may feel a bit like being "caught in the act." Several things can be done to reduce these feelings. One is sharing and supporting each other's attempts in the positive ways you have discussed above. Another is just to try—repeated attempts will help you reevaluate some of the old values you have gathered throughout your development.

Another sexual value that may contribute to some uneasiness is the notion that couples are not supposed to masturbate. Masturbation is thought to be detrimental or unnecessary if a partner is available, and masturbation is seen as a second- or third-rate sexual activity, in comparison to intercourse and other types of mutual stimulation. Often, masturbation is thought to be detrimental because of the belief that sexual desire or energy will be used up and result in a loss of desire for couple sex. This is not true. Research on female sexuality has found that women who masturbate are more likely to be orgasmic and to engage in sexual expression in all forms. In fact, more than 30 percent of men and women *do* masturbate after marriage. Remember, masturbation is not the goal, it is simply another sexual avenue to explore and grow with, particularly since it will permit you to share positive changes with your partner.

From the man's point of view. Which aspects of this step are you looking forward to, and which do you think will be more difficult? Even the most enthusiastic male partners often have some reservations before doing this exercise. Usually these reservations revolve around the following concerns: *(a)* the man feels left out, unimportant, and uninvolved in the woman's self-pleasuring; and *(b)* as a result, he has a nagging suspicion that he is somehow replaceable—that his partner will prefer her own stimulation to his.

With almost all the couples that we have seen in therapy, the woman does learn to enjoy self-pleasuring but wants primarily to have sex with her partner. What she learns about her body during her own sessions will make it easier for her to teach you the most pleasurable ways to stimulate her. And, as we have mentioned, masturbation for many women seems to enhance sexual desire rather than detract from sex with a partner.

There are ways in which you can increase your involvement with your partner. A very important aspect of the next few sexual sessions you do together is for you to let her show and tell you what gives her pleasure. That may sound easy, but our experience has shown us that this is a difficult thing to put into practice. Our culture expects men to know what to do sexually with their partners at all times, and not knowing somehow reflects on their competence as men and as lovers. Of course, this is unreasonable—the same sexual technique will not be equally pleasurable to all women, and we have tried to stress that the same woman also varies in her preferences at different times. Nevertheless, you may occasionally have to remind yourself that a good lover is one who tries to pleasure his partner in a way that is specifically good for her. This involves communication and forms the foundation from which you can eventually expand your sexuality as a couple.

Men are influenced by the same cultural values about masturbation as women. Years of believing that one should not be caught in the act, or that it is not right to combine masturbation and a close relationship with someone else, are not going to disappear automatically. Also, the cultural expectation that men are supposed to be supersexual is an added burden on men. This expectation suggests that any sexual experience, including shared masturbation, should be easy for men. Actually, many men do not find it easy to masturbate in front of their partners. If this is true for you, try to express your reservations about this to your partner. In any case, the woman's encouragement and support—in whatever ways are best for you—are very important. Let her know what she can do to make this experience a positive one for you both.

If one or both of you feel strongly that you do not want to do this sharing exercise, or if you attempt it but feel extremely uncomfortable or upset afterward, that's okay; it means that this particular learning experience is not suited to your needs. Finish reading this chapter, since other information is included, and then go on to chapter 10. In other words, this exercise is encouraged but optional—one that you both should feel comfortable about trying. It is normal to feel somewhat awkward, uncomfortable, or even silly, but not horrified and miserable. In this latter case, read through the next section, paying special attention to "Bridges Between Nonsexual and Sexual Interactions."

SPECIFIC SUGGESTIONS FOR SELF-PLEASURING WITH YOUR PARTNER

It is normal to feel awkward or somewhat uncomfortable touching yourself in front of your mate. You shouldn't feel that you are "performing" but rather that you are teaching. Talking about ways to decrease your discomfort is a first step. There are also several things you can do to enhance your session. The first time that you try these suggestions, it may feel a bit strange for both of you. This, after all, is still a period of mutual discovery—not a demonstration of expertise.

In working with more than 150 women and their partners on the inability to have orgasms, we have found that the teaching and learning that are the purposes of this exercise are most effective if the man first demonstrates his arousal for the woman. There are several reasons why we recommend that the man be first.

One reason is that the man is likely to have masturbated for many years, typically since adolescence. The woman may only have masturbated since beginning to use this book. Thus, the man is usually more relaxed about masturbation, and initially is more able to share his arousal technique and orgasm with his partner.

Second, watching her partner masturbate to arousal and orgasm can be a tremendously valuable experience for a woman who is trying to develop her own sexual responsiveness. Aside from learning about him, having watched him masturbate tends greatly to reduce her embarrassment and apprehension when she is showing him her own arousal and orgasm.

A number of women we have worked with were unable to masturbate to arousal or orgasm with their partner present until he first masturbated with her watching. This seems to be a liberating experience for women who have been inhibited about their own sexual

arousal, and it makes it possible for them to be more sexual with their partner. It also provides men with a perspective on how their partners may initially feel uneasy about "showing" their sexual arousal. For these reasons, we recommend that the man be first in demonstrating his own arousal techniques and orgasms in this exercise.

Your partner is not expected to arouse you sexually; he (or she) is expected to make it as easy as possible for you to arouse yourself. The following are specific suggestions that have helped other couples who followed this program. We hope that you will find some that feel right for you or that you will make up your own.

1.   Both of you help set the mood for this session. You may want soft light or candlelight in the room to make the atmosphere seem warmer and more private. You need enough light so that you can see each other, but not so much that you will feel uncomfortable.

Some couples like to just sit and talk a while or to have a glass of wine together before they begin. This is not a good time to solve daily problems or crises, however. Try to talk about pleasant topics or discuss any feelings of anticipation you may have about what you are about to try.

2.   Both of you should be nude or almost nude. A shower together is one way to get nude comfortably. Warm water and soapsuds help put people in a relaxed and sensual mood. Or, if you don't want to shower, you might want to undress each other slowly and caress each other as you do.

If you are not used to being nude in front of your partner, you might wear a loose-fitting shirt or nightgown. It should be something that you feel good about wearing and something that will still allow your partner easily to see your particular techniques of masturbating. You may find that you gradually become more comfortable during your session together, and eventually you should try to be completely undressed. But if this is a bit scary, go slowly. Once again, practice and partner support will help you feel more at ease.

3.   Begin with some mutual exchange of pleasure—hugging, kissing, light stroking of each other's face or body, and whatever else you like. Concentrate on feeling good and on the physical sensations that your body is providing. As we have suggested previously, the man should go first and demonstrate how he masturbates, becomes aroused, and has an orgasm. When the woman is ready, she can begin to show her partner the ways in which she touches herself that give her pleasure. This may be during the same session or during the next session.

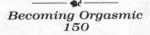

People differ in their needs for partner support while masturbating—for example, you may want your partner touching you, holding you, or just lying next to you as you masturbate. Do whatever makes you feel most comfortable, and ask what your partner prefers. This helps both partners to feel involved.

4. You may want to try this exercise again, so don't worry if you can't see everything your partner is doing. What you should pay attention to initially is your partner's movements, the various areas of his or her body that he or she caresses, and the kinds of touches that are used.

5. End the session with some mutual affection, and then talk to each other about how you felt during this exercise. Also ask questions. For instance, "What kind of stroke were you using on your clitoris?" "Did your fingers also go inside your vagina? How far?" "How hard were you pressing on your breasts? Clitoris?" And, "How much time did you spend touching your scrotum?" "How strong was your grip on your penis?" If you decide to repeat this exercise, use what you learned from the first session in order to improve the experience. Each time you do self-pleasuring with each other, notice what your partner repeats during each session, and also notice what she or he does differently. It is important for you to realize that you both have different needs and responses and that you will not respond exactly the same way during each sexual experience.

POTENTIAL DIFFICULTIES

Some women find it difficult to experience feelings of pleasure during this exercise. They are either distracted by their partner's presence or worried about his reaction to their sexual responses. If this happens to you, there are several ways you might deal with it. You might have him move into a position that is more supportive and less distracting, perhaps with him sitting behind you and holding you (see chapter 10). Alternatively, you may find his touch distracting at this time; you may like him just to be near you. Another technique to help you concentrate is to close your eyes and create a fantasy— you might even imagine that you are alone rather than with your partner.

You might want to try masturbating by yourself, with your partner in another room nearby. If you become aroused, you can then call him to come in and join you. Some women we have worked with have found this procedure helpful in overcoming initial difficulties in becoming aroused with their partner present.

Remember that trying for orgasm will only make things more difficult for you. It is not necessary for you to have an orgasm during these sessions. Instead, try to feel comfortable showing your partner what you like, and then gradually let yourself become more expressive in his presence. It may take a while, so give yourself time. *Whatever* you are able to do is a sign of change to build on. Enjoy yourself for what you can do, and don't fall into the trap of judging (or letting your partner judge) your progress by where you think you ought to be.

Some women, on the other hand, have no difficulty feeling pleasure or even becoming aroused during their first sharing experience. If you did become aroused or experienced orgasm, were you surprised? Pleased? You should be! Did you like the way your partner responded to your self-pleasuring? If so, let him know. Particularly let him know the ways in which he helped you feel at ease enough to be sexually expressive with him beside you. If he didn't respond in a way that made you feel good, think about what you can tell him to do or say that would make a difference to you.

The man who has had his first experience seeing his partner become aroused or have an orgasm may not know quite how to respond or what to feel. It's not uncommon for men to feel somewhat awkward or left out, even if you talked this over earlier and didn't expect him to react this way. Another possible reaction for the male partner is some apprehension about seeing his partner being sexually responsive, especially if this is a first. What does it mean for her to be sexual and enjoy it?

Some men are concerned that a sexually responsive woman will want sex all the time. The thought of a "supersexual" partner can scare a man, since most men have some concerns about their own performance; or he may worry that she will seek sex with a lot of different partners in addition to himself. Worries about out-of-control sexual urges can be a concern for women also—they sometimes think that after a few orgasms they will want sex all the time and never be satisfied. In point of fact, based on the couples we have seen in sex therapy, the frequency of sex and the choice of sexual partners is not really related to whether the woman is orgasmic or not. What does change is the amount of pleasure both partners derive from each sexual encounter. Their increased satisfaction seems only partly related to the fact that the woman is able to have orgasms and more

related to greater comfort and to the ability to communicate sexual needs mutually.

POTENTIAL GAINS

There are several new doors that we hope will be opened by taking this step. Sharing pleasure is a very intimate experience, and sharing personal sexual pleasure means that trust and understanding are an important part of a couple's feelings for each other. Perhaps with increased openness about sharing the pleasure you've found, your mutual feelings of trust have deepened. A number of couples we have seen have benefited from recognizing that arousal and orgasm belong to the person experiencing those feelings—the partner can facilitate them or not, join with them or not, but the partner cannot cause or force them to happen. We hope that this has been a useful transitory step as well as an experience that broadens the range of sexual activities that you can do with one another. You may find this a very pleasurable experience that you will want to include among the sexual things you do together. And finally, we hope your ability to try this builds a sense of *personal* satisfaction for you both.

BRIDGES BETWEEN NONSEXUAL
AND SEXUAL INTERACTIONS
Initiation and Refusal

A common area in which many couples want to improve is their pattern of initiating and refusing sexual activities. Although you may not find this to be a problem at the moment, you have probably had experiences in which feeling more comfortable and confident about initiating and refusing would benefit you both.

Think for a moment about how your partner usually initiates sex. With a kiss? A touch? A look? A grab? A joke? A few words? Initiating and refusing sexual advances are very important aspects of sexual communication, ones that cause difficulty for almost everyone. Generally, the problem seems to be: How do you manage to get two people in the mood at the same time and at a time when sex is possible?

It's natural for two people to have differences as to when and how

often sex is desired. For women, desire for sex can increase and decrease at times during the menstrual cycle (see chapter 8). However, these changes in sexual desire do not seem to be very consistent, and some women do not notice any fluctuations in desire that are related to their cycle. The same statements are true for birth control pills, with some women reporting greater desire and others reporting less desire after being on the pill for a while.

Other influences on sexual desire include illness, pregnancy, depression, and aging. You've probably noticed that when you are ill, uncomfortable, or upset, your interest in sex decreases. This may or may not occur during pregnancy and menopause, since some women feel very good at these times and others feel physically or emotionally distressed. Also, although there is no physiological reason to avoid sex during a woman's menstrual flow, some women have pain or discomfort at this time; other women do not experience discomfort and enjoy the closeness of sex at this time.

With variations in sexual desire, there are times when one partner initiates and the other refuses in any relationship. But there may be other influences affecting whether one person initiates and the other says yes or no. What we would like you to do is to "brainstorm" on what the problems are for you two on the issue of initiating and refusing sex—mention many different ideas without criticizing them. Just let your ideas flow. Think about who usually initiates. Would you like the other person to do more? Who usually refuses, and how does this make you both feel? Talk about what makes it difficult to get sex started: for instance, the presence of children, feeling tired at the end of the day, or having household chores to do first.

Certainly a very basic consideration is timing. One woman who was in therapy complained that her husband always began "fooling around" with her while she was doing dishes or scrubbing the bathtub—not exactly a time when she felt very sexy.

More frequently, couples tend to put sex off until the very end of their day, when they are tired. If this describes your situation, you may want to think about any adjustments you could make in your schedules to spend more time together earlier. The question is one of priorities: If sex is important to both of you, then it shouldn't be last on your list of activities. This will probably mean that you have to help each other free up some time. The man, for instance, might share some of the housework and help take care of the children's needs if that has been primarily the woman's responsibility and usually keeps her busy in the evenings. The woman may, on the other hand, help guarantee some uninterrupted time for her partner so that he can finish his responsibilities.

Sometimes one partner initiates in a way that does not appeal to the other. Blowing in his ear or nibbling on her neck may do nothing to encourage, and may even discourage, his or her interest. One couple we saw rarely had sex in part because of the man's way of initiating sex. With all loving intentions, he would, as she labeled it, "cutesy" her (tell her how adorable her ears were, call her "little peach"), which, sweet as it may sound, drove her out of any sexual mood. She was sensitive about her small size and felt she was being treated as a child rather than a woman.

We have found a very useful exercise you can do together that will help you both learn good ways to initiate sex ("good" in terms of what your partner likes). We would like you to reverse role-play: To do this, pretend you are your partner and that your partner is you, and act out what you consider to be a poor initiation of sex. Set the typical scene (such as in the living room or the bedroom) as well as the action (a grab for the breast, a quick kiss). Then tell your partner what you would prefer and why. Be specific. Physically and verbally demonstrate to the other person how sex could be initiated so that you would feel good about the initiation. Now have your partner practice different good initiations a few times with your help. Take turns, so that you both get a chance to demonstrate what kinds of initiations are good and bad for you, and why.

But even the best initiation will not always be accepted. Have you ever had the feeling that you couldn't tell your partner no, or have you ever felt resentful about accepting? It is possible to say no in a way that's not hurtful. Indicating that you care about your partner, or that you'd like to be with him or her but don't feel like sex, or discussing why you aren't in the mood now but would like to after you finish your work or tomorrow morning are some possibilities. A blunt no or "I'm tired" is likely to make the other person feel hurt and rejected, and it can cause a fight.

So, as you did before, pretend you are your partner and role-play a bad refusal—some way that makes you feel angry or resentful when you initiate and are refused. Again set the scene, and act out the words or gestures your partner uses. Then point out what would make it a good refusal, and act that out. Let your partner try it, too. Practice so that you understand what your partner means by a good refusal. Have your partner practice accepting the refusal as well. Saying something that shows that you acknowledge and accept that your partner cannot have or doesn't want sex right now helps relieve feelings of tension and guilt.

There are two other areas that contribute to good initiation or refusal communication. We have found that often couples benefit from discussing how frequently (approximately) each of them would like to have sex. Here, both partners should be clear on whether sex always includes intercourse. There may be times when nonsexual affection, sensual pleasuring with a vibrator, or manual or oral stimulation to orgasm would be preferred by your partner.

Often one partner wants sex more frequently than the other. If this is the case, one partner is going to be initiating a lot, while the other partner is refusing a lot. It sometimes helps to reach a reasonable compromise on about how often to have sex so that initiations are less frequent and thus are more likely to be accepted.

Another area that couples often find to be a problem is the pattern of one person doing most of the initiating. There are various reasons why this causes difficulty: *(a)* It can leave one partner feeling less desired if he or she is always taking the first step; *(b)* it tends to make sexual activities more dependent on just one person's mood and needs; *(c)* it sets up roles whereby one person's responsibility is to

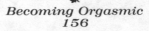

decide when to have sex, while the other person always holds the stamp of acceptance or refusal; and *(d)* sometimes, because the pattern is so predictable and the roles are set, it can contribute to making your sex life boring. However, many couples do have a preferred pattern in which one person does almost all of the initiating. If this is your pattern, and you *both* like it, there is no reason to change as long as the less-frequent initiator can feel free to initiate when sex is desired.

If, however, you would like to initiate more or have your partner initiate more, you can work on making this possible. First, try talking about why you would like yourself or your partner to initiate more. Some couples just like the idea of equalizing their sexual initiations—it makes sex seem more mutual and can make one partner feel less at the whim of the other. Whatever your reasons, talk them over together.

Second, the person who is to increase his or her initiating probably has some concerns about doing so. One concern is how your partner will respond—what if your partner turns down your initiation? Talk about your reservations and what you can do to maximize, at least at first, your chances of not being refused (the better time, place, mood). Keep in mind what we discussed earlier about refusals not being a rejection of you as a person.

And third, for women who are learning to initiate more, there are some special difficulties. In our culture, women are taught that the male should initiate more often, and even though they would personally like to change their own pattern, they are in conflict about it. Discuss this with your partner. Give him a chance to tell you why he would like it and to reassure you about any fears you have, such as feeling too aggressive or "unfeminine." Men usually welcome the chance to have their partner initiate sex. A major motivation for many women to be more assertive sexually is simply the freedom to be able to express themselves—to be able to say what they would like to do. You will be doing more of this in your sexual activities as a couple as you continue through the next few chapters.

Relationship Patterns: The General and the Sexual

For some couples, how much, how often, and how pleasurable their sex life is remain fairly separate from how they get along in general. "We leave all the troubles outside the bedroom door," one woman told us, and they almost always did.

For other couples, as the overall feeling about the relationship goes, so goes their sex life. One could say that for them sex is a kind of barometer, signaling how troubled, pressured, or stormy the relationship is at any particular time.

So there are no absolute rules about when sex should reflect the general feeling of the relationship and when it should be independent. But you and your partner probably have your own rules (rules you may not have discussed or even been very aware of) as to when sex is impossible and when it's very likely. We would like you to reflect on and discuss this by considering the following factors as starting points. We select these because their importance has been emphasized by couples in the past in proceeding with this program.

How committed are you both to this relationship? You do not have to be committed to having satisfying sex or making progress in this program. But if each of you is differently committed (one very, the other not at all) or you are on the verge of divorce, working together will be extremely difficult. If one of you is hedging or feeling very unsure about staying in the relationship, this may be influencing your sense of trust, which in turn may influence how easy you find it to be sexual with each other.

What is your ideal of closeness? Measure it right now by sitting as close to one another as feels right (not too close, not too distant) first for you and then for your partner. Note differences in your choices. How do each of you get more closeness when you need it? More distance? Some people get into arguments a lot, which, among other things, helps to regulate the distance between them, keeping some people very close by fighting a lot (fighting is very intense involvement) and keeping other people distant by fighting a lot. Usually, sex signals less distance and more closeness, but after a sexual encounter, one person may suddenly need more distance while the other wants to maintain that level of closeness.

If too many or too few arguments are problems in your relationship, try to discuss how fighting can affect the relationship and your distance from each other.

In general, you do not have to feel wonderful toward one another in order to have sex or to try any of the activities we suggest in this book. However, consistent hostility and bitterness on one or both parts will make sexual growth difficult.

How near is the past? If you have been together for a while, you have some common history with smooth and rough periods. Do you

find you keep a running tab on the mistakes and hurts your partner has committed, remembering all the old ones with each new and seemingly related problem? If your answer is yes, you may want to consider the burden this collecting method (natural and understandable though it may be) puts on you, your partner's efforts to change, and the relationship. If something upsetting happens, especially during your sexual contact, and you feel yourself saying or thinking, "You always . . . ," "Every time I say X you do Y . . . ," or "Can't you ever . . . ," you are using the past to damn the present. Be careful: Initiating change is a delicate matter. It needs encouragement rather than threats that change will not happen, will never be enough, or never convince you it is enough. Look for small, positive changes in your partner, and ignore some of the old patterns of response. Shift your eyes toward what's different and away from what's the same—it will give change a chance.

"Wait, slow down, I know I said I wanted change, but . . ." It is very common to say, "I want to have a good sex life," and then as change begins, one or both of you gets worried and wants to stop or does things to slow the process without realizing it. Change is uncertain, and this worry makes sense. Try to discuss your uneasiness; you may have more worries in common than you think.

PROBLEMS IN SEXUAL DRIVE LEVEL

In the past several years, we have worked with a great many couples whose problem is not a lack of orgasm but rather a lack of sexual drive or desire. Therapists refer to this problem as "inhibited sexual desire" or "aversion to sex." In fact, inhibition is very different from aversion, a bit like the difference between "not pleasurable" and "unpleasant." Our work with couples who are uninterested in sex has given us some insights that may be beneficial if you also have a problem in this area.

It's important to realize that a low level of desire is to be expected if you are not enjoying sex and don't get aroused enough to have an orgasm. After all, if you don't enjoy sex, why would you want to do it? It's likely that learning to become aroused and have orgasm will pretty much solve the problem. The exercises suggested previously under "Initiation and Refusal" deal with most other issues in this area.

However, there are some women who can become aroused and

have orgasm and yet still have an inhibition of their sexual drive. These women report that sex is good for them when they have it, but they only rarely feel the urge to make love. If the woman's partner has a higher level of sexual interest, this can develop into a real problem.

Often, couples who are troubled about different levels of sexual desire ask, "What is a normal level of sex drive?" Rather than looking for an arbitrary set of numbers by which to judge whether the man is "oversexed" or the woman is "inhibited," it's important for you and your partner to work out what is "normal" *for the two of you*. There is a wide range of what happily married, sexually well-adjusted couples report as their usual frequency of sex. Age, years married, socio-economic class, degree of religiosity, living circumstances, and a host of other factors all influence couples' sexual frequency. Depending on these factors, a normal frequency of sex can be less than once a month or more than once a day.

Minor discrepancies in desire level are usually resolved when the couple has the discussions about their relationship and about initiation and refusal we suggested earlier in this chapter. However, there are women who, in progressing through this program, find that their desire level remains quite low even though they have successfully arrived at this point in our sexual growth program. If this describes your situation, there are some additional issues for you to think about in regard to your sexual desire.

In working with many orgasmic (and nonorgasmic) women with low sexual desire, we have found some commonly recurring issues that seem to inhibit a woman's sexual drive. While reading about these influences, think about yourself and whether each cause might apply to you.

Negative messages about female sexuality. As well as inhibiting arousal and orgasm, these messages can also inhibit desire level. Sometimes women learn to have orgasm, but the negative cultural and religious messages continue to inhibit desire. A clue here is whether you still feel any vague embarrassment, guilt, or shame about initiating sex with your partner or about masturbation.

The work ethic. Sex is an expression of love and affection, and it is also a form of play or fun. Are you a very hard-working, organized, achievement-oriented person? Do you feel you must be more successful and make more money, or have the cleverest children and the cleanest, most fashionable house? Some women with this ap-

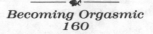

proach to life find it difficult to acknowledge their more playful, frivolous side and therefore never get in touch with their own sex drive. If nothing else, putting sex at the end of your schedule of required duties for the day pretty much ensures that it will feel like the least important duty. Over time you may enjoy it less and be less motivated to participate in sexual activity.

Unpleasant reactions during sex. Some women's sexual drive is inhibited because unpleasant emotions are activated when they engage in sex. Some of these women were sexually traumatized by being molested as a child or raped as an adult. Engaging in sex signals or cues memories of this trauma and makes sex itself unpleasant. (We will discuss these issues in more depth in chapter 12.) Other women, who have not been previously molested, have their desire level inhibited because making love with their partner includes some specific activities they find unpleasant. For example, the man may insist on oral sex, which the woman really doesn't enjoy at this point in her sexual development. If this applies to you, a discussion with your partner is needed. Point out to him that for your desire to grow, you need to know that making love doesn't have to mean doing something you don't enjoy.

Fear of loss of control over sex drive. Some women who become orgasmic are afraid that if they let themselves feel sexual desire, they will be unable to control themselves. They fear they will become immoral, insatiable, and wanton if they let any of their sexual drive out, so they automatically turn off. As we've stressed all along, letting yourself feel desire, arousal, and orgasm won't make you into a different person, it will be a part of you. You will decide how to act. Our gothic romance image of desire is that it will take us over. In fact, desire exists or doesn't, and people decide to give into it or not. You won't be a different person unless you want to become a different person.

Fear of pregnancy; contraceptive issues. This is very obvious, yet it's a surprisingly common cause of a woman's inhibited desire. If you are not actively trying to have a baby, you and your partner should be using a safe, effective method of birth control. This method should be one that doesn't interfere with the quality of your sexual relationship, is a minimal health risk, and accommodates your future plans for a family. Male sterilization and oral contraception are the safest, least bothersome methods for many couples. Female steriliza-

tion (tubal ligation) is also an option, though it carries more surgical risk. Combinations of diaphragm, condoms, and spermicidal creams are also effective but can detract from sexual enjoyment. Each method has pros and cons that need to be evaluated. In any case, discuss this issue fully with your partner, and be sure you are at ease about the issues of pregnancy and contraception.

Depression. It is well established that even a mild case of depression will dramatically interfere with sexual drive. If you are feeling depressed much of the time, it is unrealistic to expect your desire level to be normal. Symptoms of depression include feelings of sadness, low self-esteem, low energy level, problems with sleeping, eating, and digestion. If you are depressed, you should consider getting some help with this problem. There are some suggestions for locating a therapist in chapter 14.

Hormonal and medical issues. Abnormalities in levels of the various sex hormones are rarely a cause of low sexual desire, but do occur occasionally. High levels of estrogen or progesterone can inhibit sexual desire. Thyroid problems can also be a cause of low desire. If you have any other symptoms of hormonal problems (for example, menstrual irregularity, breast tenderness, problems in fluid retention, hot flashes), you should see your gynecologist or an endocrinologist (a hormone specialist) for an examination. There are a variety of medicines that can also inhibit sexual desire. Some women report that oral birth control pills have this effect on them. These days, the pills have a much lower dosage of hormones than was the case ten or even five years ago, so this is not a common problem anymore. However, if you have noticed a change in your desire level over the course of being on the pill, see your gynecologist.

Many psychologically active drugs suppress sexual desire. The mild tranquilizers like Valium and Librium can have these effects, as can most of the antidepressant drugs and the more powerful major tranquilizers. If you are taking any of these drugs and have noticed a change in your desire level, see your prescribing physician.

Finally, alcohol and other recreational drugs like marijuana all have the effect of greatly suppressing sex drive in people who use them frequently or people who occasionally use large amounts.

Body image and aging concerns. If you are over eighteen, you may be a victim of our cultural stereotype that only very young, very thin, and very beautiful women qualify as truly sexy. We've discussed this cultural trap and the ease of falling into it in chapter 2. If you feel

very negative about your age, your appearance, and your sexual attractiveness, your sexual desire is likely to become inhibited.

Partner-attraction issues. Are there some things about your partner that might be inhibiting your sexual desire? For many women, their desire level can be inhibited if their partner has poor hygiene. Bad breath, dirt, body odor, a scratchy beard stubble, and other issues of poor personal hygiene can be a cause of a woman's low drive. Similarly, if he is very overweight or underweight, or doesn't take good care of his body in other ways, this can influence low desire.

There is a slight variation on this theme, in that some women's desire level is inhibited not by their partner's physical attractiveness but by his lack of sexual skill (thus the rather angry bumper sticker that reads, "There are no frigid women, only clumsy men"). If you previously didn't enjoy sex, get aroused, or share orgasms with your partner, you probably didn't know how much of the problem was in you and how much was related to the way he makes love. Now, for the first time, you know enough about yourself to be able to teach him what pleases you.

Of course, issues of personal attractiveness and sexual technique are very sensitive for most men, and you must be thoughtful in how you raise these issues with your partner. Always phrase things in a positive way that avoids accusing or blaming the partner for past mistakes. Instead, tell him in a positive way what he can do differently that will make sex better for both of you. The reason to do this is not to protect him but to foster change—few people are motivated to change by their partner's blame and criticism.

Some examples:

Negative: "Your bad breath is revolting." *Positive:* "I like kissing you, but it's important to me that we both brush our teeth first."

Negative: "You are too rough when you touch me." *Positive:* "Easy; try to just lightly brush your fingers across my clitoris, like this. That feels good."

Life-style issues and marital conflicts. We have discussed these issues earlier in this chapter. Let us just repeat that it's unreasonable to expect to have much of a sex drive if your life-style leaves you chronically tired and stressed. Similarly, if you are unhappy in your marriage, your sex drive is at risk. We most often see inhibited sexual desire in women who feel powerless in their marriages. By powerless, we mean that the woman feels her partner is dominant and overbear-

ing, without mutual give-and-take in conflict resolution and decision making.

Feelings of vulnerability and issues of trust. We have seen some women whose sexual drive is inhibited by their fears about being emotionally vulnerable to their partners. For these women, making love gets them in touch with their love for their partner and with their feelings of needing him emotionally. While these should be pleasant emotions, they can be frightening ones if you don't quite trust your partner to be there for you when you need him, to stay in the relationship, or be considerate of your emotional vulnerability. These frightening feelings are avoided by a suppressed sex drive. Though you may try to feel desire, it does not happen. Women who have these concerns sometimes come from a family in which they saw their mother treated badly by their father, or they have had a disastrous experience in a previous relationship. If trust is an issue for you, the following suggestions about using cognitive therapy techniques to cope with these fears may be especially applicable.

Couple differences in need for personal space. Some women need more personal space than others. By personal space we mean time alone, away from your partner, separate friends and interests, and so forth. This need for space is no problem (and indeed is an asset in a marriage) provided your partner has a similar need for space. However, if your partner wants more closeness and less space, and pursues you, this may have the effect of inhibiting your sex drive. You may even get into a vicious pursuer-distancer cycle, in which the efforts of the pursuer drive the distancer even further away, and the relationship ends up with more emotional distance and tension than either person wants. If you feel this is an issue for you, you need to discuss with your partner what your need for space *means.* Once he understands that it doesn't mean you don't love him as much as he does you (a common, yet catastrophic assumption many people make), it may be possible to work this issue out. The material in the "Relationship Patterns" section in this chapter may help.

DEALING WITH THE CAUSES OF INHIBITED DESIRE

As is apparent from the list of possible causes, low sexual desire can be a very complex issue. If you found that some of the causes we have discussed apply to you, you will need to work on those issues. Com-

plex issues like major marital difficulties may require you to work with a therapist to solve the problems that are inhibiting your sexual desire. While we have made some specific suggestions above for dealing with particular causes, you can also use the problem-solving cognitive therapy approach we discussed in chapter 4 for dealing with negative feelings. We believe that the sex drive is a basic biological need and is part of our nature. When a person is not feeling this drive, it means some emotions are blocking it. Many women with inhibited desire are initially unaware of any negative feelings—they report they just feel neutral about sex and aren't interested. We believe that this neutral feeling is a protective umbrella-emotion—that is, it covers up the underlying negative emotion.

Using the framework for cognitive therapy presented earlier, you can try to understand and work through the issues that are inhibiting your desire. Specifically, first try to identify any negative emotions that might be hidden under the umbrella of just feeling uninterested in sex. You can do this by reexamining your sexual history and the role sex plays in your life and your relationship. Try closing your eyes and visualizing a fantasy in which you have a high sex drive and are actively seeking sex. Does this fantasy make you frightened or uncomfortable? Ask yourself what would be bad or risky or frightening about having a higher sex drive. These exercises may get you in touch with the negative emotions that are blocking your sex drive. Try to label the emotions specifically as fear, anxiety, shame, anger, resentment, and so on.

Next, try to identify where the emotions came from, as discussed on page 159. As the next step, reexamine the basis for the negative feelings, and try to develop a set of coping statements to address the issues that are inhibiting your sexual drive.

Once you have worked with the cognitive therapy procedures, you can try an additional set of procedures that we have found helpful in getting women in touch with their sex drive. We call these procedures *cuing*.

Cuing refers to the fact that many of our basic biological drives require an environmental cue or signal to make us aware of them. For example, if you are busy and distracted, you may not realize that you are physiologically hungry until you smell food or look at your watch and realize it's way past mealtime. Sex drive works even more strongly in this way—it takes some real-life cue to make you aware of your sexual needs. Such cues include seeing romantic and erotic films, reading erotic books, and consciously deciding to spin out a sexual fantasy for yourself. You may want to try cuing your own sexual drive. Several times a week, try some of these cues:

- Read an erotic book or magazine (see suggestions in chapter 7).
- Look at some erotic films or pictures.
- Write out a sexual fantasy, making it as erotic as you can.
- Do something physical that gets you in touch with your body. This could be sunbathing, dancing, exercise, or similar activities.
- Raise the level of physical affection between you and your partner. This should be sensual pleasure rather than sexual and should not be part of initiating sex. What we mean here are brief kisses and hugs, holding hands or sitting close while watching television, showering together, walking, dancing, sunbathing, playing a sport together, and so forth.

If you have gained the ability to become aroused and have orgasm and you try the cognitive and cuing exercises we suggest, you will gradually experience an increase in your sex drive. Don't expect an overnight miracle, as this issue takes some time to work through. If, after a few months of work, you are still troubled by a low level of desire, we suggest you consider working with a therapist on this problem. There are some suggestions for locating a therapist in chapter 14.

10
Pleasuring Each Other

I n some ways you and your partner are aware of the areas of each other's body and the types of touch that please one another. Yet this pleasuring phase will go better if you don't presume to know anything about the other's preferences. Act as if it is all to be discovered.

Pleasuring each other is a process of exploration and growth similar to that of getting in touch with your own body. The first step is becoming comfortable enough to explore new possibilities for pleasure that your body and your partner's touch can give you. In order to feel really free to do this, you both need first to consider your expectations for your sessions together.

EXPECTATIONS

Do you have any expectations about how your sessions together will be in comparison with your individual sessions? It's natural for you to think about this. If you were able to become highly aroused or orgasmic through individual self-stimulation, you may be expecting the same thing to happen automatically in your couple sessions. Or perhaps you are not expecting your couple sessions to live up to your individual sessions. Perhaps you were not able to reach orgasm through self-stimulation. You may be thinking that arousal and orgasm will be easier with your partner present. Whatever your expectations are, they are likely to affect what happens between the two of you. You may find yourself overly concerned with tracking your own or your partner's level of arousal and lose touch with any feelings of pleasure within yourself. You may begin putting pressure on yourself or your partner to perform or respond in certain ways, and old feelings of frustration and self-doubt may reappear.

What are some positive expectations for your sessions together? You can expect the process of learning new ways to pleasure each other to take time and understanding. Exploration, discovery, guidance, learning, trust, and communication are all necessary for sexual growth. With time and understanding, you are likely to enrich and deepen the intimacy between the two of you. You will probably see improvements in other areas of your relationship with growth in your sexual relationship.

You can now take more responsibility for when sessions occur and for what happens during a session. You each need to participate actively in the process of changing as a couple. Feeling free to initiate and refuse a sexual encounter makes for a more mutual physical and emotional relationship.

During a session, you will find yourself giving as well as receiving pleasure. Keep in mind that how you respond sexually can change from sexual encounter to sexual encounter as well as at any given time within a particular session. What feels good at one time may be neutral or even unpleasant at another time. For example, some women find breast stimulation painful or neutral (not particularly pleasant or unpleasant) early in a session but extremely enjoyable after they become somewhat aroused. Also, some men find having their nipples touched or kissed pleasurable once aroused, whereas this may feel "ticklish" at other times. Some women want to avoid breast caressing completely before or during the early part of their menstrual period because their breasts are tender. These normal variations in personal preferences make communication extremely important.

VERBAL AND NONVERBAL COMMUNICATION

People can communicate in many different ways. Infants can make themselves understood with a few grunts or cries. We all encounter situations daily in which the look in a person's eyes or a person's facial expression communicates feelings such as pleasure, disapproval, delight, or anger. In the next few sessions, you will be focusing on using verbal and nonverbal communication to help guide your partner in pleasuring you. For example, if the woman's breasts are being kissed or touched, she might say, "That feels good," or perhaps, "Stroking the nipple hurts; try stroking around the nipple." However, rather than speak, the woman might try placing her hand over her partner's hand and guiding it so that he is touching her in the way that feels most pleasant. Both verbal and nonverbal forms of communication are important. As you practice stimulating each other, you should try using both means of communicating.

Learning to communicate so that you both learn from each other and can respond to each other's desires ensures, as we mentioned, that each sexual experience is unique and spontaneous. If you can learn to tell each other what you want during sex, you are less likely to fall into a routine. Getting into a rut sexually usually takes away from feelings of excited anticipation that add so much to the experience.

Perhaps you have talked of likes and dislikes before, or you may have kept silent during sex because you were afraid that you might hurt your partner's feelings. There is a lot of pressure on men and women (particularly on men) to be experts at sex; many believe that if they are "good lovers," they will know (without being told) the right thing to do to please their partner. This kind of situation only increases worries and tensions that interfere with really enjoying oneself sexually. You may feel you have to be a mind reader and be constantly looking for signs and clues as to what your partner wants or is feeling (the spectator role again). You may feel responsible for your partner's sexuality and see his or her sexual responsiveness and whether or not he or she has an orgasm, as reflections on you.

Actually, you cannot *give* your partner an orgasm. Giving and receiving pleasure means the physical and emotional involvement of you both. As a couple, you must share the responsibility for making your sexual encounters as rewarding as possible. You can provide feelings of pleasure and arousal in an environment of comfort, warmth, and caring that may allow your partner to feel like going on to experience orgasm. Sharing involves communicating and trusting, trusting each other to communicate verbally or nonverbally what it is you feel and what it is you would like to do. Trust allows you both to feel free to focus on your own pleasure.

It would be natural to feel somewhat uneasy when you first communicate directly about things that have to do with sex. Most of us were not given much chance to practice sexual communication while growing up. Recognizing this will make it easier for you to offer each other support. Saying such things as, "I know you feel embarrassed, I do too," or, "That was hard for me to say," gives your partner encouragement and support because it aids understanding and caring. Communicating positively, such as, "If you would touch me this way that would feel really good," rather than negatively, "I don't like that," is important. A positive statement shows that you want your partner to try and indirectly says you think he or she *can* learn how to please you. Also, the particular example here gives your partner something specific to try—your message has important information that only you can provide. Communicating your needs is a vital ingredient for the continued renewal and expansion of your sexuality. It keeps sex interesting and alive.

Again, it may be hard for you both not to compare these early couple sessions with your individual sessions. If you were highly aroused or orgasmic during your self-pleasuring sessions, you may be watching yourself for signs of arousal. It's natural for you to feel disappointed if you don't get aroused or as aroused as you do in your individual sessions. This doesn't mean that something is wrong. Give yourself and your partner time to learn to get in tune sexually, just as you gave yourself time.

Some women who have not reached orgasm up to this step do experience orgasm through manual or vibrator stimulation with their partner present. If you weren't orgasmic through the self-stimulation sessions, you may begin to put pressure on yourself and your partner and feelings of frustration and self-doubt may result. You may feel your partner is judging you and watching for any signs of arousal. One thing that will help is for you to continue your individual self-stimulation sessions at other times during the week, so that you continue to grow sexually as an individual as well as part of a couple. Taking the pressure off yourself and your partner—letting yourselves relax and enjoy your sessions together—makes it more likely that you will experience orgasm either through your own or your partner's stimulation during the next few weeks. Talking with your partner prior to your sessions about some of the concerns you each have is also an important way to deal with those reservations.

YOUR SESSIONS: HOW TO BEGIN

Lying close, kissing, massaging, and running your hands along each other's bodies will help set the mood. When you both feel comfortable, one of you can begin exploring the other's body with your hands and mouth. Try some tentative touching and kissing of the breasts or chest, ears, back of the neck, inner thighs—any part of the body that gives pleasure. The partner being pleasured should be giving gentle positive communication about what he or she likes. What is said and the tone of your voice should indicate whether you like what is being done, and if not, what the person doing the pleasuring should try.

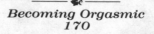
Becoming Orgasmic
170

Your whole body is involved in sexual response, so take your time and communicate about what does or doesn't feel good.

The process of exploring and communicating can be done one at a time or together, as long as each of you has a chance to pay attention to what you're feeling and help guide your partner in stimulating you. Sometimes you may want to get involved in just pleasuring your partner or in being pleasured. At other times, you will want to pleasure at the same time. Let your partner know.

Gradually include the genitals in your explorations. At first it is probably better for you to take turns giving and receiving pleasure. When you are touching or stimulating your partner's genitals, either manually or with a vibrator, try to recreate the movements, pressures, and pace your partner likes when stimulating him- or herself. The first few times you do this you will probably find you need lots of guidance, but it's the best way to learn. Have the partner who is being pleasured verbally or nonverbally communicate to you what feels best. A nonverbal communication, again, might be placing your hand over your partner's hand and moving or pressing down in order to indicate the kind of stroke you like.

We recommend that you do not try intercourse yet. It is easier to explore new patterns of touching and communicating without moving on to intercourse.

Positions

There are a number of possibilities to try. You may want to (1) lie on your sides facing each other as you do this, or (2) lie head to feet so that you can see each other's genitals. Another choice (3) is to take turns, with the pleasurer sitting down next to his or her partner's genitals. Consider (4) having your partner lie down or sit with his or her back supported against a wall or pillow. The partner who is doing the pleasuring sits between the other's legs so that he or she can easily see and touch his or her partner's genitals, while the person receiving stimulation can totally focus on his or her own pleasure. For pleasuring the female, (5) the male can sit with his back propped up or leaning against the wall. The woman then sits between his legs facing away from him. Her back is against his chest. In this position the male can encircle the woman with his arms and touch her breasts and genitals, as well as kiss her neck and hair. The woman can lean back against her partner for support and is free to concentrate on her own pleasure. It is important to become familiar with the different parts of each other's bodies. Take your time—the idea is not to arouse each other. As a matter of fact, it would probably interfere with a shared experience for you to try for arousal at this point.

Try to have at least three to six sessions where you focus on teaching and learning the most effective ways of communicating and giving pleasure. Seeing where you are touching is a good idea the first few times you do this. If after two sessions you feel comfortable with stimulating each other, have a session where you both use what you've learned. During this session, do whatever things you like to pleasure each other except intercourse. You should probably allow thirty minutes to one hour for each couple session. If orgasm happens, that's fine, but do not expect it or try for it at first. The important thing is to make each session as pleasurable and rewarding as possible. Orgasm does not have to be the goal of your sessions. Rather, you will experience some good feelings, be able to help your partner experience good feelings, and feel closer as a couple. Orgasm will come in time if you continue to be attuned to your feelings of sexual pleasure and to share those feelings in an atmosphere of warmth.

Things to Think About and Talk Over with Each Other

1. What do you feel you still need to work on?
2. Where do you see progress being made?
3. If you have not reached orgasm yet, how do you or your partner feel about this?

After having several couple sessions you may find you are thinking about or feeling concerned about certain things. We'd like to help you begin to explore some of these thoughts and feelings.

How do you feel about sex without intercourse? Perhaps you feel some satisfaction with whatever gains you've made up to this point. You may be eager to go on to intercourse and see pleasuring through other means as a poor substitute. Such feelings may be causing you to rush through your sessions, and they probably make it hard for you to relax and enjoy what your body is experiencing. You may feel better if you keep in mind that the things you are learning will make intercourse a more enjoyable experience. These foreplay or pleasuring techniques can be a prelude to intercourse or ends in themselves. We will talk more about this in the following chapter on intercourse.

If you engaged in petting and genital touching before marriage and felt guilty about it, it would be natural for you to have some of those same reservations now, even though you're older, married, or

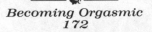

in a stable relationship. You may still associate genital touching with shame, guilt, or anxiety, even though circumstances have changed.

Talking about these feelings with a supportive partner may help. It is possible to change your attitudes and ideas about what you do sexually, especially if you see some advantage in this. One advantage is that broadening the range or variety of sexual activities you and your partner enjoy can only add to the spontaneity and genuineness of your sessions. Another advantage is being able to enjoy each other fully without rigid expectations for what you can or cannot do. This means that at times—perhaps the majority of times—you may wish to include intercourse in your sessions. However, there may be times when one or both of you would like to experience the pleasurable feelings of manual, oral, or vibrator stimulation to orgasm. At times you may want to pleasure yourself in front of your partner or have your partner pleasure him or herself either as part of foreplay or to lead to orgasm.

For the woman. What would happen if you "let go" in front of your partner? Concerns about how your partner will respond when you experience orgasm may be causing you to stop yourself when you reach a certain level of arousal. You may find that at these times your mind wanders, other thoughts distract you, or you lose the good feelings that you were experiencing. Dealing with some of your worries will enable you to move past this point.

If you have not yet experienced orgasm, the first thing you should do is get in touch with some of your fears. Go back to chapter 6 and reread the section on orgasm role-play and triggers. Try to repeat some of these suggestions in your next two or three individual sessions.

Can you put some of your fears into words? Try sharing them with your partner, even if it seems a bit awkward. Reassurance and support are important for both of you at this point. For example, if arousal is accompanied by the feeling that you may urinate, share this fear with your partner. Your partner needs to know that it is not unusual for women to urinate a little during their first few orgasms, but control automatically develops fairly quickly. Discuss ways that you could handle this as a couple (keeping a towel near the bed) in case this happens.

The next step is to role-play orgasm during a few of your couple sessions. The first time you try this, each of you act as if you're having an exaggerated orgasm early in your session before you feel aroused. Do this one at a time so that the partner who is not role-playing can say or do some supportive things. Saying things like, "Go ahead," "Let go," "Come," or just being close and maintaining some contact, such as holding hands, can reassure and encourage your partner.

Repeat this until you both feel you've really acted out some of your worst fears. You will probably find that you feel embarrassed and silly doing this; that's all right. After a few times you both will probably be less concerned about letting go and enjoying what your body is feeling. The next time you find yourself "stuck" at a plateau of sexual arousal, try role-playing orgasm along with some of the other orgasm triggers discussed in chapter 6.

Something else that can interfere with your couple sessions is any uncomfortable or negative feelings you may have about your partner's genitals. Often women have these feelings because they are just unfamiliar with male anatomy.

Just as often, however, women's feelings regarding male genitals may be related to negative attitudes about sex in general, or about men in particular, that were learned while growing up. For

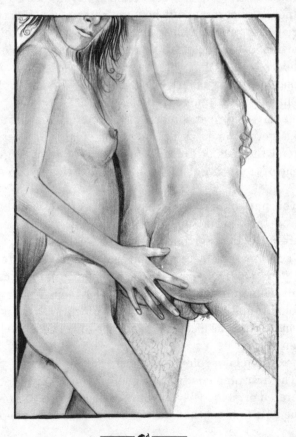

example, one woman in sex therapy remembered first learning about conception at age fifteen and being petrified by the idea of intercourse. The idea that a man's penis enters the woman's body was upsetting because she thought it would be painful. Also, because she was unfamiliar with male anatomy (she had never seen a male nude), she imagined a penis of enormous proportions. Before learning to pleasure her partner, this woman had to deal with her feelings about male genitals. We will discuss some ways to do this in a moment.

Of course, there are other ways in which women may learn to be sexually cautious of men. One woman we interviewed had a father who refused to let her date until her late teens. When she did begin to date, he constantly warned her to be on guard because "Men are only interested in one thing." When this woman grew older she found that she couldn't relax and trust any man sexually. For her, men had become associated with distrust and possible harm. Our feelings about sex, then, are not something we are born with—we learn them from our experiences with our family and our friends; from things we read, see, or hear; and from the men we get to know. Feelings may be based on information given to us gradually (like parental attitudes) or on a particular experience (like rape). Since feelings about sexuality are learned, it is possible to unlearn them. So, if you feel uncomfortable about the thought, sight, or touch of a man's genitals, you can, with time and an atmosphere of warmth and caring, learn to feel differently. Here are some suggestions to try. Some should be done with your partner. Others are best done on your own during your individual sessions.

1. Think about the sources from which you might have learned these feelings. Who did they come from? Do you ever remember feeling differently? What accounted for the change?

2. When you feel ready, talk about your feelings with your partner. Give him a chance to understand where your feelings are coming from. This will make it easier for him to give you encouragement, support, and the time to make changes. Changing is a slow, uneven process. In return, it will be important for you to reassure your partner that your negative feelings do not stem from feelings about him as a person.

3. You may find looking at pictures of male genitals less uncomfortable than looking at the real thing. We suggest that you buy a magazine that features nude males. These magazines are widely available in drugstores and on magazine stands—you do not need to go to a pornography shop for them. You may be somewhat embar-

rassed to buy one of these magazines, but if you look at their circulation figures inside the front cover, you'll find that you are not alone. These magazines will have lots of pictures of men, some of which show their genitals. Start slowly by paging through an issue until you find a picture that you like. Let your eyes linger over the upper body and face before looking at the genitals. Look at the genitals for as long as you're comfortable and then stop. Come back to the pictures a little longer each time, until you feel you can look at pictures of male genitals without feeling uncomfortable.

4. If the last suggestion doesn't appeal to you, you may prefer to try an exercise that specifically includes your partner's genitals. Select a time when you are feeling pretty good about your partner (not when you've just had a disagreement or when you are tired). You may like some kissing and caressing as you begin or you may not. Either way, communicate this to your partner.

The first time, just try looking at his genitals without touching them. If you are uncomfortable, you may want to take just a brief look and then continue touching and enjoying other parts of his body. Try this several times and gradually spend longer periods of time looking at his genitals. Talk to your partner about how easy or difficult it is for you—what you or he could do to make it easier.

When you can look at your partner's genitals comfortably, begin touching. The purpose is not for you to arouse your partner or even to give him pleasure. It is for you to learn about him through touching. Remember when you first began touching yourself? Try thinking of this as the same type of learning experience.

You may want your partner to lie still during this time and perhaps close his eyes so you won't feel that he is watching you. Make any suggestions that you feel will make you more relaxed and comfortable. Closing your own eyes for short periods while touching may help you tune into the feelings your hands and fingers are receiving. As you touch, try relating what you feel to other *good* touch sensations. For example: The skin on this part of the penis is soft and smooth, almost silky. Also, try to compare the various textures of his genitals to other parts of his body—does the scrotal skin feel at all like the skin on his chest or abdomen? Does the penile skin around the glans feel like his lips? And finally, how do his genital textures compare to your own genitals? Notice similarities and tell your partner what you are noticing.

5. The Name Game: Sexual words often carry positive or negative connotations and can relate to how you feel about your own and your partner's genitals. One couple, for example, used "pussy" in a

positive affectionate way, while "cunt" was more likely to be used when one partner was angry. Another couple may say "cunt" in a positive way when referring to female genitals. Playing this game with your partner can be fun as well as help you feel more at ease using sexual words.

How to play: Each of you say out loud or make lists of all the slang terms you know for the words below. You will want to share or list as many synonyms as you can think of:

Vagina
Intercourse
Breasts
Penis
Masturbation (for men, for women)
Testicles
Clitoris
Menstruation
Ejaculation
Oral-genital sex (for men, for women)

After you've traded terms (and, we hope, exchanged a few laughs), try talking about which words on your lists you feel positive and negative about. Can you help your partner understand what it is about the word and the image it produces that you like or that bothers you? As a couple, see if you can come up with your own vocabulary, which you both feel good about, for communicating sexually. You might even want to make up special words of your own.

The purpose of this is to find sexual words that have *positive*

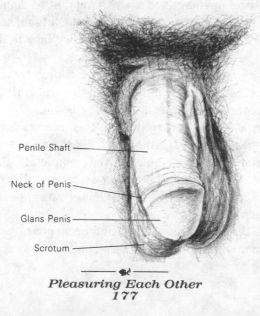

Penile Shaft

Neck of Penis

Glans Penis

Scrotum

meanings and images for you. You may feel more comfortable thinking about or referring to your partner's penis, for example, as his "dick" rather than his "penis." Some couples even adopt affectionate nicknames for each other's genitals. If this is an idea you both like, try it!

6. Learning about male sexual anatomy and functioning will make your partner's body seem less frightening and foreign to you. For this reason we have included a drawing of male genitals that labels the various anatomical parts. We have also provided you with drawings on the sequence of changes that occur during the male's sexual response cycle. In order to become better acquainted with what happens during male sexual arousal and orgasm, we would like to spend some time briefly describing some of the internal and external changes that take place.

As the male becomes aroused (the *Excitement Phase*), sexual tension increases blood flow to the pelvic area and penis and the process of penile erection begins. As the penis becomes erect it increases in length and diameter, and the testes elevate. A smaller penis tends to increase more than a larger penis relative to its unstimulated size. Breathing becomes more rapid as heart rate increases. Some men experience nipple erection.

With greater arousal (the *Plateau Phase*), a flush may appear on the skin over certain areas of the body, blood pressure increases, and the penis usually becomes a darker red with increased vasocongestion. Heart rate may double its normal pace. The testes elevate fully and increase in size while the skin of the scrotal sack (which supports the testes) thickens somewhat. The glans of the penis enlarges, as does the urethral opening, and a small amount of seminal fluid may escape. This preejaculatory secretion often contains sperm. Just before orgasm, there is a feeling of ejaculatory inevitability that indicates the process of ejaculation has begun.

During orgasm (the *Orgasmic Phase*) contractions of a series of muscles propel seminal fluid out through the urethral opening. These contractions cannot be stopped once they begin.

After orgasm has occurred (the *Resolution Phase*), the penis quickly becomes less erect, although full loss of erection often takes a while. Men vary in how quickly and completely they lose their erection after ejaculation. The testes descend and become smaller. The sex flush, heart rate, and other changes disappear or return to their unstimulated state.

Over all, the phases of arousal and orgasm are very similar for men and women. Exceptions to these similarities are that the male

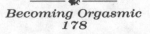

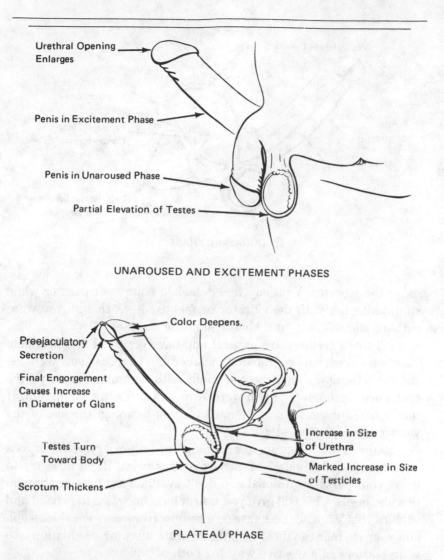

Urethral Opening Enlarges

Penis in Excitement Phase

Penis in Unaroused Phase

Partial Elevation of Testes

UNAROUSED AND EXCITEMENT PHASES

Color Deepens.

Preejaculatory Secretion

Final Engorgement Causes Increase in Diameter of Glans

Testes Turn Toward Body

Scrotum Thickens

Increase in Size of Urethra

Marked Increase in Size of Testicles

PLATEAU PHASE

ejaculates and almost always has a period of time following orgasm during which another erection or orgasm is not possible. It is hoped that the information we've discussed about male sexual response will help you to feel more comfortable exploring your partner's body.

For the man. If you are learning to use an electric vibrator to pleasure your partner, you may have concerns about this. Some of these concerns were probably shared by your partner when she began using the vibrator herself. Reading chapter 7 and talking with her may help reassure you. You may worry that your partner will prefer this form of stimulation to anything you could provide, or you may be dismayed if your partner experiences orgasm for the first time while

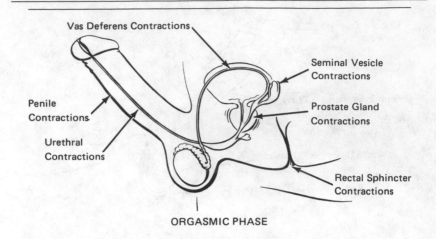

Vas Deferens Contractions

Seminal Vesicle
Contractions

Penile
Contractions

Prostate Gland
Contractions

Urethral
Contractions

Rectal Sphincter
Contractions

ORGASMIC PHASE

using the vibrator. You may feel detached from your partner while stimulating her with the vibrator or feel used—as though you were nothing more than a "machine behind the machine."

All these feelings are natural and have occurred in other men. Your sexual education probably included the idea that *you* were responsible for how things went sexually with a woman. She may have controlled the limits, but you were responsible for turning her on. If this is true for you, it may be hard for you to accept the use of the vibrator as a positive step.

Rather than seeing its use as a sign of failure, try seeing it as a convenience and a source of variety at this point. Right now, try to enjoy your partner's arousal and don't evaluate the type of stimulation she needs. This will give you a firm base on which to expand and explore your growing sexuality as a couple. Here are some things you and your partner can do to help incorporate vibrator stimulation into your sessions in a positive way for both of you.

1. Get comfortable with the vibrator. Try using the vibrator on yourself or have your partner use it on your head, back, arms, legs, feet, and so on, as well as on your genitals. This will give you some idea of how strong the vibrations are and whether or not they provide you with pleasurable sensations. Most males enjoy some vibrator stimulation of their genitals, but it is important to learn where, how, and how much before you start teaching your partner.

2. Try to use the type of vibrator that you both enjoy. Chapter 7 illustrates and explains some types of vibrators that are available. Try the one that the woman prefers, if this is the type of stimulation

she has found pleasurable. There is also no reason why (if you can afford it) you can't have two vibrators—one for the woman to use on herself and one for you to use on her. Since they take a while to learn to use with ease, try each one more than once. Also, you should give each other some feedback on which type feels best on you.

3.   Let the vibrator be an option, an enrichment of your sexual repertoire. This means that you won't necessarily use the vibrator each time you make love (although you may choose to do just that). By now you've learned a variety of ways to pleasure your partner. The vibrator can be thought of as an extension of yourself; by itself it is just an object, but used with care it is an instrument for pleasure. Keep the vibrator nearby (in a dresser or nightstand drawer or plugged in and under the bed), so that getting at it isn't too distracting. Practice ways in which you both can initiate using it, for instance, "How about the vibrator now?" or "I'd like you to touch me with the vibrator." At times, though, you may want to stimulate your partner only with your hands or mouth and not use the vibrator. At other times you can alternate using the vibrator, your hands, and mouth in your lovemaking.

4.   Stimulate your partner in other ways while using the vibrator. Kissing a woman's breasts while giving her genital stimulation can be extremely pleasurable. While using the vibrator on the male's penis, a woman can caress his testicles with her mouth or other hand. Be inventive. Reading chapter 13 ("Enhancement") may give you more ideas.

Sometimes during vibrator stimulation, watching your partner and gently encouraging her to get into her feelings may be all you want and need to do to feel that you are greatly involved in her pleasuring. That you have provided an atmosphere of trust and caring that allows your partner to experience pleasure means a great deal. The vibrator cannot provide this atmosphere—it's you who makes it possible.

It is not uncommon for women to have difficulty becoming aroused through nonvibrator types of stimulation after they have learned to become aroused or orgasmic with a vibrator. This is not surprising, since vibrators provide intense stimulation. If, as a couple, you have had success achieving arousal or orgasm with vibrator stimulation of the woman, you may want to become more skillful at other kinds of stimulation (see chapter 13).

The following suggestions can be tried after the woman finds it relatively easy to experience arousal with a vibrator in front of her partner. This is to make sure that you have overcome most of your inhibitions about showing arousal in front of each other.

1.   Try alternating the vibrator with other forms of stimulation. Allow the woman to become highly aroused or close to orgasm, and then begin vigorous manual or oral stimulation. This technique will take a lot of patience and practice to go smoothly. Since discontinuing one form of stimulation and beginning another may stop orgasm in the woman, you both have to expect some restimulation to be necessary and possibly some feelings of frustration to occur. Let her be the guide about how many times she wants to try this technique in a given session. If the experience is too upsetting or too frustrating, discontinue it. Try it again another time.

2.   For some women, more stimulation after an orgasm feels great, while others are extremely sensitive after an orgasm (particularly if a vibrator was used), and any additional stimulation is painful. If the woman is able to have an orgasm with the use of the vibrator, she can try stimulating herself manually or having you stimulate her manually soon after orgasm (thirty seconds to two minutes). If the feelings are pleasant, it may be easier to produce arousal manually or orally at this time, since her genitals will still be in an aroused state. Again, let the woman determine what should be done and for how long.

For you both. At this stage, people often experience concerns about stimulating or pleasuring their partner or letting themselves be pleasured. You may feel that you or your partner requires an undue amount of stimulation in order to feel pleasure, arousal, or orgasm. Women in particular tend to feel that they are "abnormal" because of the amount or kind of stimulation that they need. They may feel that they are being selfish and fear that their partner is feeling bored, detached, or resentful. Fears and worries of this kind can put tremendous strain on your sexual sessions and it can prevent you from feeling pleasure or even experiencing orgasm. Knowing what is "normal" helps to relieve many of these fears. From our experience in helping women learn to have orgasms, we have noticed that when a woman first becomes orgasmic, it is not unusual for her to want and need a substantial amount of time and stimulation—an hour is not unusual. When we say stimulation, we are including hugging, kissing, massage, and breast and other body area pleasuring. Genital stimulation itself may vary from a few minutes to forty-five minutes. (We are not including intercourse here; we will talk about intercourse in chapter 11).

Alternating pleasuring, being pleasured, and mutual pleasuring will help ensure that both of you are *involved*. If all the attention is geared toward the woman having an orgasm, feelings of resentment and impatience on the male's part, and frustration and guilt on the female's part, are bound to occur. And, as we mentioned before, the pressure on both partners to perform makes pleasure impossible. Rather, try to focus on your own pleasure and remember that you can't force an orgasm. Communication is crucial at this stage. You will both want to make sure you are getting the kind of pleasurable stimulation that feels good to you. Also, at this time, try to give lots of positive feedback to your partner. Feelings of boredom and detachment usually occur when one partner is feeling left out and unsure of what the other is feeling. Reassuring your partner may mean nothing more than a grunt or moan to indicate satisfaction. Saying a few words—such as "nice," "more," or "that feels so good"—also contributes to feelings of intimacy and involvement.

Earlier, we talked about arousal and orgasm as natural responses that many women have *learned* to ignore or suppress. Throughout the exercises in this book, you (as individuals and as a couple) have been learning how to help your bodies experience these sensations. We like to view this knowledge as learned skills you will improve, expand, and embellish with time and experience. As you become more comfortable and skillful with different forms of sexual pleasuring, it will become easier and easier to experience arousal.

Usually the more orgasms a woman has had, the easier it is to have more. Why? No one is exactly sure. One physiological reason may be that stimulation that leads to arousal and orgasm increases the flow of blood to the genitals. Increased blood flow may result in the formation of additional small capillaries (vessels that carry blood). This additional blood supply may make it easier for blood to rush to the genitals and hence for pleasurable feelings to occur sooner. This process takes time, obviously, so don't be discouraged.

The important thing is to give yourselves time and lots of opportunities to learn. Specifically, how much genital and clitoral stimulation a woman wants and needs depends on the woman. Some men are surprised to find that the most pleasurable stimulation for their partner is a very repetitious, continuous movement at some spot on the genitals—for example, a circular massaging motion on the side of the clitoris. If the movement is stopped, the building arousal often subsides. So don't be surprised if your partner is very choosy about what kind of stimulation he or she desires. You have learned a lot about yourselves—and for both of you this knowledge is just beginning to expand. Give yourselves the chance to teach each other about your needs, and you will find it becomes easier for you to participate and to share in your partner's pleasure.

FANTASY

Fantasy can also increase the pleasure you and your partner get out of your sexual experiences together. (See chapter 5 for fantasy as an aid to enhancing the woman's individual sessions.) We hope that you have become more comfortable about the idea of fantasy as a way to expand and increase your sexual responsiveness. However, you may feel differently about using fantasy while having sex with a partner, than about using it during masturbation.

Two particularly frequent areas of concern seem to be: (1) What does it mean about myself or my partner if I use fantasy during our lovemaking? (2) How will using fantasy affect our sexual relationship? Some women feel that there is something wrong with them or with their sexual relationship if they imagine sex with someone other than their partner—"Shouldn't he be enough to turn me on?" Others are concerned that they may only be able to become aroused through fantasy, that sex with their partner will be less satisfying than their imaginary sexual activities, and that eventually sex with their partner will not be satisfying at all. Actually, recent studies on female sexuality have shown that more than 50 percent of married women fantasize at least some of the time during sexual activities with their partner. Women who fantasize also tend to have sexual daydreams at times when they are not actually doing anything sexual; and they are often imaginative and creative people. Most women who fantasize frequently enjoy their fantasies and have what they describe as a satisfying sexual relationship with their partner.

Fantasy seems to give people the opportunity to enjoy thinking about having sex in a variety of circumstances. Imagining ourselves in all sorts of sexual situations can be exciting and fun—just as imagining going on a world cruise might be fun. Also, many fantasies include activities that we would never really engage in. Such fantasies add interest and allow us to satisfy our curiosity, while protecting us (and other people) from doing something we really don't want to do.

Of course, the content of fantasies varies a lot from person to

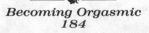

person, as you can see from reading Nancy Friday's *My Secret Garden* or *Forbidden Flowers*. Some women remember past lovemaking. Some women include their sexual partner in their fantasies but change the place (to a beach, a car, a party, a shower, the desert, a cabin in the woods), change the number of other people present (ménage à trois, orgies, mate swapping), or change the kinds of activities (spanking, aggression, force, submission). Other women imagine these situations without ever including their partner in their fantasies.

If you are concerned about the themes of your fantasies, or that they do not include your partner, one way in which you can deal with these feelings is to think about the positive effects your fantasies have on you and your sexual relationship with your partner. For instance: *(a)* They may enhance your feelings of arousal and make you feel more sexual—the increased arousal is something that you do share with your partner and something that he enjoys, too. *(b)* Fantasy can be another way of getting into a sexual mood and focusing on sex rather than worrying about what happened during your day or how much you have to do tomorrow. *(c)* Your fantasies are another way you can take responsibility for letting yourself become aroused rather than expecting your partner to do everything to turn you on physically and mentally.

Fantasies are part of your personal sexual expression. If they include some activity like whipping or orgies, you may never really want to act them out, but you may just like and find exciting the forbidden quality of certain sexual scenes. Remember that as we were growing up and discovering what sexuality meant, the whole idea of sex was taught to be something somewhat forbidden. So it's not surprising that some of us want to retain that element of intrigue. However, you may be able to include some parts of your fantasies in your lovemaking. You might look at Alex Comfort's *Joy of Sex* to get ideas for how to do this in a fun and loving way.

Another way you can deal with your negative feelings about fantasy is to try discussing some of these feelings with your partner. You may want to try telling one of your fantasies to your partner and have him do the same. Some couples also like to try constructing a joint fantasy—a kind of erotic story—just to see what they can put together. These are both ways of sharing and getting more comfortable with the idea of having fantasies in the presence of your partner. Alternatively, you may decide *not* to share your fantasies. Often the secretiveness of the fantasy is what makes it special—if this is true for you, it's fine to keep it for yourself. What is important is to communicate to your partner your mutual acceptance of the fantasy side of his or her sexuality, to reassure him or her that fantasy enhances your sexuality and is therefore likely to continue having a positive influence on your growing sexuality as a couple.

In sharing fantasy, one common issue is concern over your partner fantasizing about someone else. While most people aren't too upset by their partner having sexual fantasies about a movie star or magazine centerfold, many people are worried, jealous, or upset to hear that their partner has sexual fantasies about someone he or she actually knows personally. If you have such fantasies, you may not want to share them with your partner. If you do share them with your partner, make it clear that these are just fantasies, that you are not going to act on them. You should both remember that it is normal to be sexually attracted to other people. Such attraction does not mean that you are not attracted to your partner, nor does it mean that you are promiscuous or likely to act out the fantasy. We discussed these issues earlier, in chapter 5, and you might want to review that section now.

Remember, too, that if you don't fantasize during sex and don't particularly want to, that's fine, too. Just focusing on your physical enjoyment and your partner's enjoyment can be equally pleasurable, as long as it's satisfying for you.

WHAT'S NATURAL FOR YOU

It is very important for you both to give yourselves time and to accept each other's sexual needs and desires. Comparing yourselves to others is self-defeating. The idea of sexual growth implies a variety of means and ways to grow. If arousal and orgasm are only possible through the strong rapid motion of a vibrator, then that is what's right and natural for you right now. Given time, your needs and desires may change; but let it be a natural change rather than a change due to insecurities and pressures about what *should* happen.

11
Intercourse: Another Form of Mutual Pleasure

O ften when we hear the word *sex* we automatically assume that sexual intercourse, or coitus, is being discussed. One reason for this is that intercourse is an extremely important part of our sexuality.

Certainly, in terms of biology, this is true: Conception almost always involves intercourse. The significance of conception and the rights and responsibilities of parenthood set intercourse apart from other sexual activities. Partly for this reason, regulations concerning intercourse are included in moral, religious, and legal standards governing sex. These standards emphasize the importance of intercourse and generally restrict, at least in our culture, its occurrence to marriage. Restriction of desirable activities tends to increase our interest in them.

Given the contributions of biology and culture, many of us have learned to feel that intercourse is better than other forms of sexual expression, and that once we are married or involved in a loving relationship, all good sexual encounters should end with intercourse.

These kinds of feelings can influence your sexual growth in many ways. For example, you may not feel free to explore a full range of sexual activities if you or your partner believe that you must have intercourse every time you have sex. Foreplay under these conditions may become boring and perfunctory—a brief preliminary that automatically precedes intercourse rather than a pleasure of its own.

Similarly, you may feel guilty about those times when you cannot or don't want to have intercourse. Intercourse may not be desired, for instance, during the woman's menstrual period, when the man has difficulty getting and maintaining an erection, or when one partner is tired. Since other activities are seen as second best, resentments and feelings of frustration often develop.

Another problem that can result from overemphasizing intercourse is the tendency to judge your sexual relationship and your sexual competence on the basis of what happens during intercourse. We have seen couples who feel there is something desperately wrong

---

with them if intercourse is not as enjoyable for them as manual stimulation. Some of the women we see are orgasmic through self-stimulation, and through manual and sometimes oral stimulation by their partner, but not during intercourse. Rather than seeing arousal and orgasm during intercourse as another skill that people learn, the man or woman may believe that lack of coital orgasm is a symptom of an emotional or physical problem. This leads to all kinds of concerns about such things as penis size, size of the vagina, size of the clitoris and hood, as well as doubts about the relationship itself, and about oneself as a person (does this mean that one can't give love?).

Talking with your partner and trying to sort out your feelings is a first step. Once you're in touch with your feelings, beliefs, or expectations concerning intercourse, you'll be in a better position to make those changes that will contribute to positive sexual growth as a couple.

Here are some questions to consider when sharing your feelings:

1. Is either of you dissatisfied if a sexual encounter doesn't include intercourse? Why? Where and how did you learn to feel the way you do?
2. What else beside genital sensations is pleasurable for you both during intercourse? For instance, do you feel emotionally closer?
3. Is it very important for you both that the male partner ejaculate during intercourse? What if ejaculation occurs during some other activity such as oral or manual pleasuring, or not at all? How does this change the experience for you?
4. If the woman experiences orgasm before or after, rather than during, intercourse, how does this make each of you feel?

Perhaps in discussing the above questions together you found that you and your partner were more flexible than you had thought. You may both be willing to reevaluate your feelings about intercourse and orgasm during intercourse. You might try having a few sessions that exclude intercourse entirely and see what you can discover about other erotic pleasures. Or you might have intercourse in the middle of a session and then go on to orgasm through another form of stimulation. One advantage of these alternatives is that they reduce feelings of pressure to have orgasm during intercourse and allow you to make the experience slow and sensual. Alternating sensual movement with no movement, and really focusing on the warm sensations of physical closeness, can enrich your sexual communication. Give yourself the chance to experience intercourse as a form of lovemaking that has special qualities of its own. Intercourse need not be a race to orgasm nor a requirement for you to feel good about yourself, your partner, and your sexuality.

Perhaps one of you prefers intercourse more than the other. Often, the male finds intercourse somewhat more stimulating than the female (we will talk about this more fully in a moment). There are other reasons too—one being the long-standing feeling that sex *is* intercourse. What we ask you to think about, if this is your feeling, is that sex is usually more than just genital stimulation: Through sex you may express your pleasure in another person, your caring for him or her, your concern, and your desire to share intimacy and affection, as well as your sense of responsibility and commitment to maintaining the relationship. Since sex involves both of you, you must be sensitive to giving in a way that your partner can appreciate. This means being attuned to what the other person would like. Each of you will probably want to experience some activities that are more stimulating for your partner (intercourse may be one of these) than for yourself; at other times you may decide on something that is more stimulating to you. Other activities will be equally pleasurable for both of you.

When you have learned something about your own body and your partner's body, and when you have learned ways to communicate those discoveries to each other, you are ready to integrate intercourse into your sessions as another natural and loving activity for giving each other pleasure. To do this, you may need to learn new ways to make intercourse as pleasing as possible for each of you so that you can both share the experience. It may sound simple, but sexual communication is as complex as the changing needs of the people involved. You will find it takes patience and consideration and the expectation that it does *not* happen automatically.

Start by looking at where you are now. You may have experienced orgasm, either through your own stimulation, your partner's stimulation, or both. If you haven't yet had an orgasm, this does not mean that something is "wrong" with you. It may mean that you need to spend more time practicing earlier steps. If you are getting aroused at least some of the time, then you are on your way.

If you find that you're getting more aroused in your mutual pleasuring than in your self-pleasuring sessions, then you may want to spend more time in your mutual sessions. If your individual sessions seem to be going better than those with your partner, you might want to slow down on your partner sessions to concentrate on yourself. Different women make progress in different ways: Some women find that becoming aroused is easier when they are alone because they feel less distracted and more able to focus on themselves without feeling self-conscious; other women find that their partner's presence enhances their own ability to become aroused.

We recommend that you hold off on having intercourse until you are feeling at least some arousal during either your individual or couple sessions with your partner. It is not necessary for you to have had an orgasm. However, if *you* feel you would not like to try intercourse without first feeling more aroused or experiencing orgasm, that's fine too. Discuss these feelings with your partner.

Before we describe what we would like you to try, we want to share with you some feelings and concerns that other couples have had at this point. Read through them, and if any are particularly relevant to either or both of you, it will help your sessions if you talk about your reactions.

Unhappy memories. At times, one or both partners feel nervous about trying new things during intercourse because of unsatisfying or frustrating experiences they have had in the past. In these cases, intercourse was usually accompanied by pressure to perform. You may have felt inadequate in the past for not reaching orgasm; your partner may have felt similarly if he ejaculated too fast or too slowly. Resentment and feelings of failure and disappointment usually grow naturally out of such situations. If you have unhappy memories, it will be very important to reassure each other that you are going to try not to let these situations repeat themselves. Sharing your feelings and taking any pressure for orgasm off each other will help.

He or she will never really change. Some changes in the area of sex will be easy for you to make. Sometimes, however, partners realize that there are some areas in which they are unwilling or find it difficult to change. If the particular issue is rather minor, sometimes the other partner can just accept the difference and not let it interfere with more important concerns. However, if you reach a stalemate on a major issue, it may prevent you from even trying to work together sexually. If talking about it does not seem to help, let us make a few general suggestions that can apply to changes you want to make in any area of your life.

1. Try to maintain a sense, as mentioned in the last chapter, that your common goal is to change your sexual relationship, *not* to change one another. People usually feel more like changing if they are not being told what to do and what's wrong with them but are being asked to contribute to changing a situation.

2.   First work on those areas in which you and your partner both agree that there is a need for change. This, again, makes it more likely that you will succeed, since you are both interested in making the changes.

3.   Be specific about the changes that need to be made. For example, say: "I would like it if you initiated sex a couple of times this week," rather than, "I would like you to be more enthused about sex."

4.   Rather than attack the problem as a whole, you could try compromising on one small aspect of it. People find it very tempting to try to overcome a difficulty as completely and quickly as possible, and sometimes there is too much to solve all at once. It's best to start with a small change that your partner feels he or she will be able to make rather than to expect drastic changes overnight. Starting small also makes it more likely that you will succeed rather than disappoint each other. An example of this would be: "I'd really like you to kiss me more during foreplay," rather than, "I'd like it if you'd be more romantic."

5.   Share what each of you finds rewarding or pleasurable, and show your interest and enthusiasm about any progress that is made toward the changes you desire. This is extremely important. You have no doubt experienced discouragement and felt like giving up when efforts you were making went unrecognized. Recognizing and appreciating another person's efforts to change encourages further change.

Throughout our lives, appreciation is shown to us in different ways. As kids, we might get a pat on the head, a hug, "You're terrific," or a special little present. As adults, too, both material (a gift, money) and nonmaterial (a touch, words, a smile) acknowledgment can be very encouraging. Sometimes just hearing someone say, "That really means a lot to me," can make us feel tremendously appreciated. It's important to acknowledge *any* effort toward change, because it will help encourage the person making the change. Of course, you need to know what meaningful forms of appreciation are for each of you. People often differ on how they would like their partners to acknowledge and reward their efforts. For example, a man may find it very rewarding to have his partner say that she loves him. However, a more meaningful way for him to communicate appreciation for *her* might be through actions rather than words. For example, his putting the children to sleep or spontaneously suggesting a night out may be far more rewarding to her than a verbal statement of love. You both should talk over the important ways your partner can show his or her appreciation toward you.

6.   Both of you have a responsibility to try to make changes in your own behavior. Sometimes this is difficult, and a couple may get caught up in the issue of who's going to change first. Rather than either partner taking a risk and feeling vulnerable, they may find themselves engaged in a power struggle while the situation remains the same. To avoid this problem, it helps for *both* partners to agree to work on some changes *each* needs to make. You will probably find that your partner is more willing to try hard to change in ways you consider important if at the same time you are trying hard to make the changes he or she wants.

If you encounter an obstacle in an area where you disagree about the need for change, consider the reasons why one of you doesn't want to change. Patterns sometimes feel safe even if they are silly or harmful. Are you afraid of what might happen if you change? Or of what your partner's response might be? In what specific ways do you think your partner may be making it difficult for you to change? How could he or she make it easier? Try discussing the situation from this perspective, and see if you can make some headway. If you are not able to get anywhere at all, you may want to consider brief intensive sex or marriage therapy to deal with this area of your relationship. We will talk about ways to seek outside help in chapter 12.

Physical concerns and problems. A frequent worry of men, at some stage in their development, is that their penis is too small. Less frequently, but often enough, women mention that they think their vagina may be too large or too small. Genital size does vary among individuals, but it should not influence a person's ability to experience arousal or to arouse his or her partner.

If you go back and look at the drawings in chapter 2 showing the female sexual response cycle, you will see that the vagina is a sort of closed organ, or what is called a *potential space.* When the penis enters the vagina, the vagina accommodates the size and shape of the penis. Women can also learn to contract their vaginal muscles to provide maximum contact between the penis and vagina (Kegel exercises). Only about the first third of the vagina is sensitive to touch, the back part being almost totally insensitive. Most of the stimulation for the woman during intercourse comes from stimulation of the clitoris, either directly through touching or indirectly through pulling on the vaginal lips during thrusting. It is not necessary to have deep penetration during intercourse for the woman to experience pleasure or orgasm. Other pleasurable feelings may come from full body contact, from feelings of pressure or of fullness in the vagina, from contact

Becoming Orgasmic
192

between the head of the penis and the cervix (although some women find this uncomfortable), and, of course, from the sight, smell, and sounds of their partner. Also, variations in position produce sensations by providing deep or shallow penetration of the vagina (see page 171).

It is not necessary, then, that the male's penis be a particular size or shape or the woman's vagina be a particular size or shape, in order to experience pleasure and arousal. Pleasure and stimulation depend on what you do and feel for each other, not on the size of your sexual equipment. It is possible, of course, that size might be a psychological turn-on for someone, but that alone is not sufficient for a good sexual experience.

Another fairly common concern of women is the occasional experience of some sort of pain or discomfort during intercourse. This can be caused by a variety of factors. Certain positions for intercourse are sometimes uncomfortable because of the angle or depth of penile thrusts. A urinary or vaginal infection can cause irritation or burning sensations during or after intercourse. If you think you might have one, you should see your physician or gynecologist.

If you are tense during sex, your vaginal muscles may be tight and make penetration uncomfortable. More practice in general relaxation usually helps. Having a relaxation session before your couple sessions is something you might try. Continuing with your Kegel exercises will also give you more control over your vaginal muscles. It will make it easier for you to relax these muscles, just as you learned to relax the rest of your body. If at the time of penetration you feel tense, try a few Kegels and then guide the penis into your vagina when you feel your muscles are more relaxed. You should guide the penis into your vagina slowly. Some women find that a slight bearing down of their vaginal muscles during insertion helps because it prevents them from tightening up, since it is impossible to do both at the same time.

Also, find some positions for insertion that make this step easier. You may want to insert the penis while you're in one position (female on top, for example) and then maneuver yourselves into another position before beginning intercourse movements. This takes practice, so expect to feel clumsy and awkward for a while. Finally, a lack of lubrication can cause significant irritation—try using K-Y jelly or Astroglide on both the penis and the vaginal opening. If slow, relaxing foreplay and penetration and discussion with your partner do not help your discomfort, you should see a physician who can treat you or refer you for sex therapy.

ENJOYING INTERCOURSE

It is not unusual for a man to get more enjoyment from intercourse than a woman. This varies with the couple, how well their bodies "fit" together, and the position that is used for intercourse. The penis is usually receiving direct stimulation, while stimulation to the clitoris may be indirect. For some women, indirect stimulation of the clitoris during intercourse is sufficient for becoming aroused and experiencing orgasms. However, in order to experience sexual arousal and orgasm, many women need some additional manual or vibrator stimulation to their clitoral area during intercourse.

Even though many women need this extra stimulation during intercourse, there is a strong tendency for them, and often for their partners, to feel that this is abnormal or wrong. If you have these feelings, think about them for a moment, consider where you might have developed them, and see if you can put them in a slightly different perspective. Here are a few facts that should help you begin to reevaluate your ideas.

First, most women are taught that the vagina is their primary sexual organ and that it is the greatest source of sexual pleasure. Women in our society often do not know what a clitoris is, where it is, or why they have one until long after they have learned about their vaginas. So, even though the clitoris is far more sensitive than the vagina, its presence tends to be ignored as a woman develops sexually. The message we can easily get from this is that the clitoris is, or should be, unimportant to good sex, and that if we like the feelings we get there, something is strange about us.

Keep in mind that in desiring clitoral stimulation during lovemaking, you are asking for the same kind of stimulation that provides your male partner with sexual pleasure—during intercourse he receives direct stimulation to the sensitive glans area of his penis. It makes sense that you should be able to experience direct stimulation of your clitoral glans also.

At those times when you don't desire additional stimulation during intercourse, it's a good idea to allow yourself to get highly aroused before penetration takes place. Also, it is very important here for the woman to let her partner know (verbally or nonverbally) when she would like him to enter her and how hard or rapidly he should thrust to maintain her arousal. (Ways to prolong intercourse will be discussed in chapter 13.) One way that many couples use to trigger orgasm during intercourse is this: After the woman becomes very aroused—almost to the point of orgasm—the male begins either very

rapid or very strong and deep thrusting. The woman can use her hands to guide the pace and depth of her partner's movements.

If you still feel restricted by always needing manual or vibrator stimulation during intercourse, you might try the following.

Let yourself become very aroused with other forms of stimulation (manual, oral, or masturbation), and after penetration, let your partner know what kinds of thrusting feel best. Use a position that allows you to use your arms to guide his thrusting, as well as one that allows you to move your hips to adjust the tempo and the pressure to your needs. You may initially lose *some* of your arousal during the few moments you change to intercourse stimulation. Don't be concerned about this, because once you have reached and remain at a fairly high level of arousal for a short time, your body takes quite a while (anywhere from five minutes to an hour or more) to return to where it was before arousal. So it may *feel* as if you've "lost it," but actually your body is still aroused.

Another variation of working toward intercourse stimulation alone is for you to reach a high level of arousal during intercourse with the additional clitoral stimulation you need. When you are highly aroused and very close to orgasm (with time, you will be able to know this), discontinue the additional stimulation and, again, guide your partner's thrusts to provide you with the best stimulation. If this works for you, over the various times you have intercourse, let the time at which you stop the additional stimulation gradually become earlier and earlier during your arousal. You may eventually be able to learn to get more pleasure from intercourse without simultaneous manual or vibrator stimulation, although you will probably always enjoy and need some direct clitoral stimulation prior to intercourse.

Whatever you decide to do, these changes take time, lots of patience, and a good deal of cooperation from your partner. It's important that he understand the necessity of your guidance. If you try this, make sure he reads this section and you both talk over your concerns before a session—and your reactions afterward.

Remember that you do not *have* to have additional clitoral stimulation during intercourse—some women do find that indirect stimulation is more pleasurable. Also, at times you may be more sensitive or less sensitive around your clitoris and vaginal opening (for example, at certain times in your menstrual cycle). You may find that you like a slightly different pressure or stroke for maximal stimulation at these times. Don't expect your partner to know automatically what feels good. By guiding him and using verbal and nonverbal communication, you can let him know when you are experiencing pleasure.

Another expectation that many couples have is that they should experience their orgasms at the same time. Simultaneous orgasm occurs more often with some couples than others, but it rarely happens regularly. It would be unrealistic at this time for you to expect simultaneous orgasms—in fact, it might even be detrimental to your sexual expression. Why? Because, again, this would put pressure on you and your partner to "go after" orgasm instead of just enjoying pleasurable feelings. The pressure would be on both of you to hold back or speed up. By doing this you would be distracting yourself from the natural buildup of erotic pleasure you could be experiencing. You would also be putting more emphasis on orgasm than on your own or your partner's enjoyment and might miss many of the rich erotic sensations that lead to orgasm. For the woman in particular, emphasizing the timing of orgasm may actually prevent her from reaching satisfaction.

We are not trying to play down the delights of simultaneous orgasm. We are just suggesting that it not be sought as the ultimate sexual experience. With this in mind, you can enjoy this when it occurs, but do not be disappointed or inhibit other aspects of your lovemaking if it doesn't. Also, having your partner experience his or her orgasm separately from your own has its own rewards—it allows you to appreciate each orgasm completely. Feeling sexual excitement build, hearing his or her sounds, and being physically and emotionally close at the moment of your partner's orgasm can be a very special and intimate experience of its own.

ORGASM DURING INTERCOURSE

We have briefly mentioned the desire for orgasm during intercourse earlier in this book. At this point, you may be ready to think about this issue in more detail.

Many women and their partners enter a program for sexual growth with the woman being able to reach orgasm during intercourse as the specific goal. Both people may consider it a "problem" that orgasm happens at other times but not during coitus. Physically, the orgasmic response appears to be very similar regardless of the type of stimulation (hand, mouth, penis, or vibrator) that a partner provides. A great many psychological studies have shown conclusively that there are no differences in femininity, sexual adjustment,

maturity, or psychological health between women who have orgasms during intercourse and those who have their orgasms in other ways. Similarly, the man's masculinity, skill as a lover, and penis size do not have anything to do with whether or not his partner has orgasm during intercourse. Simply stated, we don't really understand why about 50 percent of women regularly have orgasm during intercourse and about 50 percent do not. There may simply be natural differences in how sensitive some women's vaginas are to touch and pressure. There may also be differences in how well the couple's pelvises fit together, so that some couples produce more indirect stimulation of the clitoris during intercourse by the man's pelvic bones and lower abdomen than do others. Rhythmic movements can also be better or more poorly coordinated, and sometimes one person's "natural" preference for speed and duration of movement is very different from another's. Learning new ways is possible, but they can take a while to feel natural.

Perhaps the most important erotic ingredient, feeding into all of the physical factors, is a person's thoughts and feelings about the value, importance, and sexuality of intercourse. If a person believes this to be the most sexually arousing act, it will help ignite whatever physical stimulation occurs. On the other hand, if intercourse is felt to be an invasion, all for the man's pleasure, or an obligation, it will not be an activity in which stimulation is enhanced by the subjective sense of arousal.

The important question for you and your partner to ask yourselves is, Why do you want to have orgasm during intercourse? If you feel that not doing so means there is something wrong with one or the other of you, you need to talk this out and be convinced that this is not the case. On the other hand, if you are feeling okay about your progress in reaching orgasm in other ways and would just like to try to have an orgasm during intercourse as another experience, there are some specific techniques you can try. Before describing these techniques, however, let us caution you that they are somewhat mechanical training procedures that take a good deal of planned practice and can reduce your enjoyment of spontaneous lovemaking. Many couples who try these techniques for having orgasm during intercourse find them to be more trouble than they are worth. As one of our clients put it, "Before, I was having great orgasms from him touching me, and I was really enjoying intercourse. Now, by trying to make both happen at the same time, I'm not enjoying either one as much as before." We encouraged this couple to reexamine how important it was to have orgasm specifically during intercourse. They were able to recapture their more erotic, spontaneous lovemaking once they stopped trying for orgasm during intercourse.

If you do want to experiment a bit and see if you can have orgasm during intercourse, there are three techniques you can try.

1. As we have discussed above, simply try continuing direct stimulation of your clitoris during intercourse. Later in this chapter, we discuss some positions for intercourse in which you and your partner can easily reach your clitoris during intercourse. Don't be embarrassed or inhibited by ideas that it is somehow wrong for you to touch yourself, or your partner to touch you, or to use a vibrator during intercourse. Remember, we know that the clitoris is the focus of orgasm for most women, and touching it directly (rather than only indirectly stimulating it by pressure of the man's pubic bones) is only logical if you want orgasm during intercourse.

However, some women find that simply continuing direct clitoral stimulation during intercourse doesn't work for them. Your clitoris may lose some pleasurable sensitivity or even become so sensitive that direct touching becomes unpleasant during intercourse.

2. Some women find that once intercourse begins, direct touching of the clitoris is no longer highly arousing. For these women, we often suggest a gradual "fading" procedure—a series of small steps, gradually blending the way you can have orgasm now into the goal of orgasm during intercourse. We can explain this most clearly with a case example:

> One woman we worked with (let's call her Ann) could have orgasm by masturbating. She masturbated by rubbing her clitoris directly. She also could have orgasm from her husband, Tom, touching her clitoris directly. She was now enjoying intercourse as well, but she couldn't have orgasm during intercourse and seemed to lose her arousal if she or Tom directly caressed her clitoris during intercourse.
>
> As a first step, we had Ann resume masturbating alone, but with a small change. Instead of just caressing her clitoris, she also put one of her fingers in her vagina *before* she began to masturbate. By putting her finger in her vagina before beginning to masturbate, instead of waiting until she was highly aroused, she didn't lose sensitivity in her clitoris, which occurred with clitoral stimulation during intercourse. In a few sessions, she was able to masturbate to orgasm with her own finger in her vagina. This was an important learning experience, as orgasmic contractions often feel somewhat different when there is something in the vagina for the muscles to contract against.

Next, Ann began to move her finger in and out of her vagina while she masturbated. Again, in a few sessions, she learned to have orgasm in this way. For the next small change, Ann masturbated to orgasm this way, but with Tom present in the room.

For the next step, Tom gently inserted his finger in Ann's vagina, again *before* they began any touching of her clitoris. After a few sessions like this, Ann was able to masturbate to orgasm with Tom's finger in her vagina. Over the next few sessions, Tom began to move his finger in and out of Ann's vagina, and he began to caress her clitoris as well. Again, after a few sessions, Ann became able to have orgasm this way.

As the next step, Tom inserted his penis into Ann's vagina and simply lay still while he and Ann both caressed her clitoris. When she could have orgasm in this way, Ann began to move her body, so that Tom's penis was moving in and out of her vagina. Finally, Tom was allowed to move as well, and they became able to have orgasm during intercourse.

As you can see from this example, this gradual fading procedure takes a good bit of time, patience, and willingness to follow a plan during each lovemaking session, instead of being spontaneous and playful. You should think carefully about just how important orgasm during intercourse is for you before beginning this sort of approach, as it can be a lot of work! If you decide to try this program, try to find eight to ten intermediate steps between the way you can now have orgasm and the goal of orgasm through intercourse. Practice each step several times, and don't be discouraged if it takes several tries to learn to have orgasm at each new step. Try to treat it a bit like a cross between a game and an experiment, rather than something you must do to feel good about yourself.

3. A third approach works best for women who can only have orgasm in a way that does not lend itself to gradual fading to intercourse. We call this procedure the *rapid switching* technique, and again, a case example will make the procedure clear:

Bill and Sue had progressed to the point where Sue could have orgasms easily, but only while Bill caressed her clitoris orally. Obviously, you can't orally caress and have intercourse at the same time, and it's not clear just what would be "fading" steps between oral caressing and intercourse. For these reasons, we had Bill and Sue try the rapid switching technique. This technique attempts to generalize arousal and orgasm from oral caressing to other sexual activities.

As a first step, Bill and Sue tried oral caressing until Sue just began to have her orgasm. At that moment they stopped the oral caressing, and instead Bill caressed her genitals with his hand while her orgasm continued. Although Sue had not had an orgasm when Bill used his hand, once an orgasm begins, it won't suddenly stop because of a change in stimulation. At first Sue had less intense and rather brief orgasms, but after some more sessions like this, she was able to have a full, intense orgasm.

As the next step, Bill and Sue began to make the switch from oral to hand stimulation *before* her orgasm began. Specifically, they would use oral stimulation until Sue was very highly aroused and then switch to hand caressing of her clitoris for only ten or fifteen seconds. If her arousal level started to decrease, they quickly switched back to oral sex for thirty seconds or so. Bill and Sue would switch back and forth between oral and hand caressing many times during each lovemaking session, and gradually, manual caressing came to be as arousing as oral stimulation. She eventually came to be able to trigger her orgasms during hand caressing as well as during oral stimulation.

Next, intercourse became a part of the rapid switching. During lovemaking, Bill and Sue would switch between hand caressing, oral caressing, and intercourse every thirty seconds or so. In this way the high pleasure and arousal from oral and hand caressing was carried over into intercourse. As soon as Sue's orgasm was triggered by either oral or hand stimulation, they immediately inserted Bill's penis in her vagina, so that most of the orgasm occurred during intercourse. After many sessions of this repeated and rapid switching, Sue began to have orgasms with continued direct hand caressing of her clitoris during intercourse, and they were able to discontinue the program of rapid switching.

Like the fading procedure, this procedure is also very programmed and mechanical, and it frankly works only when the couple has a sense of humor about it. The procedure is a bit like a speeded-up comedy movie, with both of you switching positions and actions every few seconds. Many couples find that this procedure is a distraction from enjoying their lovemaking, and they reevaluate their wish for orgasm during intercourse.

If you do decide to try it, be aware that it will require several—or even a great many—sessions of rapid switching in the way we've described to reach your goal.

After you and your partner have read about the three techniques for having orgasm during intercourse, try to decide if you want to use any of these techniques and, if so, which one seems to fit your current situation best. If you don't find one technique to be working, try one or both of the others. If you work at all three of the techniques and

don't progress, we would not suggest you make a crusade out of your search for orgasms during intercourse. Instead, relax and enjoy your lovemaking. Enjoy your orgasms and intercourse separately, as separate and equally valuable parts of your sex life.

YOUR SESSIONS

As you begin, we would like you just to get comfortable with each other and do whatever is pleasurable for you both (for now, be guided by the woman's preferences). This may include some talking, mutual massage, cuddling, kissing, stroking, or whatever else you like. If you have found the vibrator enjoyable, it, too, can be included in some general body stimulation. This period of time is very important both to set a comfortable atmosphere and to be sensual, to be affectionate, and along the way, to become aroused. You should not rush foreplay: Let it go on for as much time as you like—an hour is not too long. It depends on you both. For now, let the woman decide when to begin intercourse. Feeling "ready" might depend on how aroused you are or how lubricated you are—but you do not have to be either highly aroused or very wet around your genital area. Just wait until you *want* to begin intercourse.

It is important at first for you to guide the entry of the penis into your vagina. If you are not lubricated enough for the penis to enter comfortably, you may use some K-Y jelly and smooth it over your partner's penis and the inside of your vagina (you can make this fun and stimulating with a little practice). When the penis is inside your vagina, don't feel you have to rush into rapid thrusting. Take your time.

At first you can try just lying together without moving at all while the penis is contained vaginally. During this time, you can talk or stroke other parts of each other's bodies. Try a few vaginal squeezes around the penis and see if your partner can feel them. For a while you might try caressing each other's genitals with your hands: The clitoris, breasts, and testicles will probably all be within reach. As you do begin to move, try slow, gentle body movement at first. The woman should guide the extent of pelvic thrusting and tell her partner so that you both learn how *deep* the penis can go without hurting, how *rapid* the rhythm of movements should be, and how *long* thrusting should continue. There is no way for one partner to be able to *know* these things without the other partner's verbal or nonverbal guidance. You will find that your preferences differ at different times and in different positions—so you must involve your partner and indicate to him what feels good and what doesn't.

At the same time that you are having intercourse, it is important for your partner or yourself to be stimulating your genital area. He may do this either manually or with a vibrator, depending on what works best for you (try both eventually). Remember to let your feelings flow and to guide his hand or give him feedback, just as you have done earlier.

If you have not tried intercourse with manual stimulation before, you will find this awkward at first. Learning to arrange bodies and arms and hands takes a while. There are several positions that will make this easier and that other people have found are fun. Each position has special satisfactions—discover the ones that best meet your mutual needs and desires.

One position is when the woman is astride and on top of the man as he is lying on his back. This gives the man access to the woman's breasts and genitals while she is able to stimulate his chest, thighs, and testicles as well. This position gives you both a good opportunity to talk to and look at each other while caressing. Hugging and kissing are more difficult, since the woman is in a seated position. One of the most important benefits of the woman being in this position is that it allows her freedom to move around during intercourse—something that is more difficult when her partner is on top of her. She can easily guide the penis into her vagina, control how quickly and deeply the penis enters, and direct the tempo of thrusting. If your male partner becomes very quickly aroused and you both want to delay his ejaculation, you can just slip the penis out of your vagina, and continue nongenital caressing until he is ready to begin intercourse again. Another possibility is just to pause and remain still with the penis inside the vagina. It is important here for the man to be able to judge when stimulation needs to be stopped or slowed down. Once the urge to ejaculate is felt, it is too late to stop the ejaculatory reflex. Experience is the best teacher for this—expect that while you are practicing there will be times when ejaculation will occur too quickly. Chapter 13 gives more detail on ways to increase ejaculatory control.

Another situation is also common: If he loses his erection, you can take the penis from your vagina and resume pleasuring genital and nongenital areas until you desire to insert the penis again. If his penis remains erect during intercourse but still slips out of your vagina, don't worry about it. Just guide it back inside, or, while the penis is

slippery, try rubbing your labia and clitoris along the length of his penis for some extra stimulation.

Another position is one we call the *spoons* position—in which both people lie on their sides with the woman's back against the man's chest. Although this position does not allow you to look at each other, it does provide the man with easy access to the woman's genitals and breasts and allows him to kiss or orally caress her neck and shoulders. It can also be a very cuddly position that provides feelings of closeness for you both. This is a good position for using the vibrator, too. When his hand is touching your genitals, you can put your hand over his, as you have done before, to adjust the tempo and pressure of his touch.

In what is unromantically known as the lateral position, the couple face each other while on their sides. Your legs intertwine like scissors, and you will have to adjust yourselves in order to find a comfortable way for the vagina to hold the penis. Once you figure that out, this position allows you to do a lot of different kinds of pleasuring. Since neither of you is supporting the other person's weight, you have freedom to touch and stroke each other over the face, upper body, and genitals and can do it together, although the woman should for now direct it more, so that she doesn't feel rushed or uncomfortable. This is a fun part of this position, since you will have a chance to wiggle around and laugh at yourselves when the penis (as it is likely to do at first) slips out. Once you begin moving and thrusting, you may want to hold onto each other's buttocks—this helps to keep the penis in

Intercourse
203

place and provides some pressure to the genital area that both partners usually like. However, the woman is likely to need more clitoral touching, too, so the man should also try different ways of touching her genitals during intercourse in this position.

A rear-entry position, with the male entering the female from behind while she is on her knees, is a good position for genital stimulation of the woman, as the man can reach around her hips and touch her clitoris easily. This position is surrounded by a number of sexual myths. One is that this is more of an "animalistic" than human position, because many animals have coitus in this way. A better way to look at this position is that it provides another opportunity to share different kinds of pleasurable feelings. Some cultures regard rear entry as one of the more preferred positions. Another myth about this position is that it is a homosexual pattern. This actually refers to the practice of anal intercourse, in which the penis is contained in the anus. Although anal intercourse can be stimulating and enjoyable, and is used by many heterosexual couples, it is *not* the same as rear entry into the vagina.

The rear-entry position allows for extra penile depth (so go slowly at first) plus buttock stimulation and easy access to the female's breasts and clitoris. Also, many men find the rear view of their partner to be an added pleasure (notice that the spoons position is a variation of rear entry). Rear entry can be done in several ways. The two most common ways are: (1) The woman supports herself on her knees and hands while the male kneels and enters from behind. His hands are free to clasp her thighs and hips or to caress her breasts and clitoris. (2) The woman can rest her upper body on the edge of a bed or couch and kneel on the floor (use a pillow to make her knees comfortable). The male enters from a kneeling or squatting position. Although rear entry does not allow the woman as much total body movement as some of the other positions, it does allow her to move her hips freely and to receive a good deal of manual stimulation to her clitoris. If you are hesitant about trying this or any of the other positions, remember to share your reservations with your partner. Try making suggestions that might reduce your negative feelings, so that at least you feel comfortable exploring new forms of stimulation with each other.

Finally, there is the old favorite, the man-on-top position. It has attracted a variety of nicknames over the years, including "missionary," "matrimonial," and "Adam and Eve." This position seems to be one that a majority of couples include in their lovemaking a great deal of the time. It has some unique advantages. It provides a great deal

of full-body contact and plenty of opportunity to hug, kiss, and nuzzle throughout your lovemaking. It allows the couple to look at each other during sex if they want to. Some women like the feeling of a man's weight (but usually not all of it) pressing against them. The stimulation from his pelvic thrusting, however, may or may not be enough to arouse the woman highly. As a couple, you should explore different ways to continue caressing the clitoris during the time that the penis is in the vagina. Clitoral stroking is a bit more difficult for the male to maneuver in this position, but it can be done if he supports himself on one elbow or arm and will become less awkward with practice. At some point during clitoral stimulation, the woman may want just pelvic thrusting movements. Or she may want to continue with direct clitoral stimulation.

Communication is especially important in this position. The man actually has more physical control of thrusting and movement, so in order to make the experience as mutual as possible, the woman must express her needs and he must be tuned into her signals. This can make the difference between a frustrating and satisfying lovemaking experience. Keep in mind that one day is not the same as the next: Sexual needs and desires vary, so don't expect a particularly enjoyable pattern to be enjoyable forever.

There are many variations that may help make this position more arousing for you. Placing pillows under the woman's buttocks may allow her to receive added clitoral stimulation from thrusting. The woman can vary the position of her legs, opening or closing them tightly, so the penis gets additional stimulation. If she wants to move a lot, he can support himself with his arms so she can rise up to meet him. You can help control each other's thrusting by gripping each other's buttocks. In addition to pelvic movements, almost everyone likes kissing and caressing over the rest of his or her body. Some people like to say sexual words or just make noise. Since this is a position you have probably tried, before you try it again, talk to each other about what you like and dislike about it. What changes would you like to make? How do you feel about trying extra clitoral stimulation in this position?

BEFORE YOU BEGIN

We suggest that before you actually use these positions in a session, you have some fun just trying each of them for practice and seeing which ones seem most interesting and comfortable for you. This will also help reduce the awkwardness of finding out where arms and legs have to go. Don't forget to discuss reservations you might have about certain positions—you won't enjoy trying if you feel you have just to grin and bear it.

Don't feel confined to these positions. Your body shapes and preferences may be suited to other variations. You might want to look at Alex Comfort's book, *The Joy of Sex*, to give you some more ideas. Feel free to invent your own. The important thing to remember is to accompany penile stimulation with manual stimulation, depending of course on your particular needs.

Give yourselves four or five sessions to explore positions for pleasurable stimulation. During each session, we would like you to take your time. After insertion, try just lying together without moving for a few moments while the penis is in the vagina; then try slow, gentle body movement for a while before you build up to more rapid, powerful stimulation. Depending on your position, slow shallow thrusting, deep strong thrusting, or sensuous circular pelvic movements may give the most pleasure. Try to focus on what you are feeling rather than worrying about how you are doing. Give positive verbal and nonverbal communication about what you like, keep tuned into each other's signals, and ask each other what feels good. Remember, this is exploration. Try each position on several different occasions—as you become more comfortable, you will discover new things about each other.

A lot of couples assume that once intercourse begins, it must continue until one or both partners have an orgasm. This doesn't have to be the case: You can have intercourse in the middle of your session and then try manual, vibrator, or oral-genital stimulation; or you can just hug and tumble around and then go back to intercourse. Intercourse, as we mentioned earlier, does not have to be the last activity you do together. For a change, you might want to end with manual or oral-genital stimulation, or with each of you stimulating yourselves. Treating intercourse as another form of stimulation will help add variety and pleasure to your sessions. Viewing intercourse in this way will also help take pressure off both of you to get aroused and have orgasms through intercourse.

If you have been orgasmic in masturbation, see if you can let yourself have an orgasm with your partner. This may or may not happen easily. It's best not to get discouraged if progress is slow. Instead, try to concentrate on the small gains, the little improvements that you make each time you are together. All the things you have learned about yourself and your partner are important. Try the or-

gasm triggers if you find yourself getting very aroused but can't let go. At times you may lose yourself in a fantasy for a while. Your attention will drift from outward focus on your partner and your movements to inward focus on your feelings and sensations. Don't let yourself feel responsible for your partner's pleasure; doing so could put pressure on him and distract you from your own enjoyment. Remember that he is probably getting pleasure from your experience, and that at times he, too, will lose himself in his own feelings.

AFTERWARD

The afterplay following intercourse is also an important part of lovemaking. What happens at this time may vary, depending on whether you have had an orgasm or not and on your mood.

At times you may want to enjoy the sensations of intercourse but withdraw after a while and come to orgasm manually or with the stimulation of a vibrator. If the woman is multiply orgasmic, the man may want to give her some additional manual or oral stimulation after intercourse to make a second orgasm possible.

Often, you may want just to cuddle and talk or lie quietly and stroke each other before going to sleep. Try to become sensitive to your partner's mood during this time. Lots of hurt feelings have been caused by one partner turning over and going to sleep immediately after intercourse. Find out what your partner would like, so that you can share this time as part of lovemaking.

12
Sex in the Modern World: Real-Life Relationship Issues

Ours is not the first generation to have to confront complexities and dangers in sexual relationships. One hundred years ago, our great-grandmothers were far more likely to die in childbirth, and therefore pregnancy and intercourse carried a very significant health risk. In Victorian England the upper classes considered sex to be a burden for women, and husbands were polite if they frequented prostitutes and spared their wives their sexual desires. Syphilis, a sexually transmitted degenerative disease that ultimately kills people, was without even semieffective treatment before 1909. Gonorrhea, serious if left untreated, was not manageable with drugs until 1935. Many men carried one of these diseases: It was estimated that 25 to 50 percent of men in the armed forces in 1914 had either syphilis or gonorrhea. This made sex with a serviceman a very risky activity for a girlfriend or wife.

Now, as we near the end of this century, we face different pressures. Pregnancy is safer but also more complicated, with the new possibilities of genetic testing, fertilization techniques, and surrogate mothering. AIDS is with us and certain to stay for a while, with threats of becoming an even more widespread epidemic. The rate of rape is higher in the United States than in any other industrialized country. The sexual abuse of children, while definitely not exclusively a modern phenomenon, may happen to as many as one out of five girls and one out of ten boys.

With these conditions, we all attempt to develop a sexual life that is meaningful and satisfying. For some people the path to a satisfying sexual relationship is quite straightforward. However, most people stumble from time to time and need to accommodate or make a change. We would like to discuss three common problems that we feel are related to modern pressures: moving on from past sexual trauma, finding sexual partners, and living in long-term sexual relationships.

MOVING ON FROM SEXUAL TRAUMA

Were you engaged in sexual activity with an adult before you were twelve? According to current research, between 15 and 20 percent of women in the United States would answer yes. For males the figures appear to be much lower, but that may be because boys are less likely to tell anyone. In addition, research showed that between 5 and 25 percent of adult women are raped during their lifetimes (these figures are difficult to establish because many rapes are not reported). Both of the above activities are considered to be sexually assaultive behavior, molestation, or sexual abuse, to underscore the fact that one person's rights to refuse physical contact were violated. In the case of children under twelve, it is not important whether they did or did not resist the sexual contact, since a child is not considered capable of giving an adult fully informed consent. Children may not understand, and if they do, they still cannot freely say yes or no because of the power differential between adults and children.

If you were not involved in any type of sexual assault, you may want to go on to the next section of this chapter. If sexual assault is part of your history, we hope the following will be a useful start toward understanding your reactions to what happened and beginning to put its effects aside. You may also want to read it if you have a friend to whom this has happened. More detailed self-help information is available in the bibliography.

Remembering what happened. One of the more difficult aspects of sexual molestation is remembering what happened. Some women can't stand to think about it. Some have forgotten it as a way to protect themselves from their feelings about it. Some women remember it, see it as having no significant impact on their lives, but feel uncomfortable because they are given the message that there is something wrong with them if they do not feel traumatized and upset and hateful toward the person who assaulted them.

If sexual molestation is part of your history, the first step is to examine your current pattern of problems and see if there could be a connection to earlier experiences. There is no specific pathway leading from sexual molestation to later personal difficulties, but there are several frequent patterns that may be related. Examples include sexual problems; depression; self-injury; dependence on or abuse of drugs and alcohol; inability to maintain any enduring relationships with men or women; severe eating disorders such as anorexia, bulimia, and obesity; a lot of physical complaints; and certain specific fears such as agoraphobia. Of course, you can have any of these problems without having been sexually molested. The point is if you have these problems and a history of molestation, it may be worthwhile to examine what happened. On the other hand, if you are able to manage your daily life, work, and carry on relationships fairly well, you may not need to explore the effects and meanings of the molestation. Some women are able to put the earlier experiences aside easily or, for a variety of reasons, are less bothered by sexual molestation. While we do not know exactly why this is easier for some women than others, we do know that women who have trouble dealing with the assault years after it has occurred include those who:

- Were severely beaten or physically injured during the assault
- Were threatened with loss of their own life, with harm to someone else's life, by retribution from authority (the nonparticipating parent, God's punishment, the abuser), or by the withdrawal of love by the abusing person
- Had a relationship of implicit trust and protection with the offender (as any child should expect from family adults)
- Were involved in abuse over a period of time from which there was no reasonable escape (as in a family)
- Loved the person who abused them or felt loved by them
- Were molested in the place where they lived rather than in a less intimate location
- Desired contact with the person and became sexually aroused during the contact
- Felt extremely deprived of care and love while growing up
- Were unable to tell anyone about it or, if they did, were not supported but ignored or accused of lying or exaggeration

In other words, the most difficult incidents for a person to resolve emotionally are those that are most terrifying, most invasive, most secret, least escapable, and involved with a person who was loved and trusted. A woman's own perception of the event is critical—to one person, molestation including "only" touching of the genitals and breasts while clothed could be extremely upsetting and have long-term consequences, even though to someone else it would seem like a rather mild incident.

Was it sexual abuse? There are two perspectives that define abuse—the view of the victim and society's view (the law has other specific definitions). If an activity felt abusive to you, then that is a valid starting point for discussion. Society may have a different idea about what abuse is, but that does not automatically mean that the person involved is incorrect. For example, until recently most states in the United States regarded forced intercourse as rape only if the people were not married; if they were married, rape could not be charged, regardless of the force used. On the other hand, several women we have seen tell of an adult friend of the family or a much older brother who engaged in sexual activity (including ejaculation) with them, but the women absolutely do not regard this activity as sexual abuse. In fact, one woman said, "It was the only time I really felt loved and safe with anyone; the rest of the time they [family members] were yelling, criticizing, or hitting." While society may still call this abuse, it is important to acknowledge how differently the activity was experienced by the particular woman involved.

Reshaping the effects of the past. Our pasts are part of us. There is nothing we can do to change what happened. What we have the power to do is change our reactions to what happened. Perhaps you recall a time as a teenager when you felt your father was too strict about your free time and schoolwork, and you were certain it was because he didn't want you to enjoy yourself. Years later, in thinking back you may have reconsidered and decided that it was his way of showing that he cared.

If a sexually traumatic event has happened very recently, you may want to let at least three months go by until you try the following suggestions, since you may feel better without any exploration of the incident at first. If you are currently being sexually abused, we recommend you go directly to a therapist or call a crisis hot line for safe locations in your area. If you go to a therapist, they are required by law to report the ongoing activity if you are under eighteen. They will report it to a government agency that will then investigate and recommend treatment and legal action for those involved.

The following suggestions apply if the abuse is at least three months behind you. If the abuse is more recent, if you are very distressed, or if you have had a series of losses and changes in the last few years, you might benefit from seeking out a therapist to explore these issues with you.

One step toward recovering from sexual abuse is to try to relive

it in your mind. Think about what happened in detail, from beginning to end. Let yourself feel, touch, hear, see, and smell as much of the setting and action as you can. Write it down if you want to. Repeat the detailed account at least ten times, start to finish, without taking a break. You may want to ask a close friend to listen to your story. That person does not have to help make you feel better—no one can really do that—they just have to listen.

There are several reasons for this exercise. One may be obvious—to relive it and survive. In addition, some of your emotions may become more intense; others may recede. It is likely, for example, that you will notice a bit less fear and more anger. Emotions in themselves are neither good nor bad. Your emotions can be very useful signals about what you need to address in your life. Anger and resentment and fear are understandable reactions to sexual abuse. If you can relocate them back in the abuse, and examine closely the actions and the persons who elicit those feelings, it may help to reorganize the emotions you've felt during the time since the abuse. For example, instead of being enraged and mistrustful of all men, you need to recognize your anger and mistrust of the man or men who abused you. Your fears, instead of covering all strange or social situations, are actually related to being taken advantage of and threatened in this earlier set of circumstances. Acknowledging feelings is sometimes difficult because they conflict with each other. For instance, if your father abused you, it may be hard for you to recognize your rage against him and against your mother, if you also loved them. Recognizing anger is important, however. It can help connect feelings to appropriate actions and people and can begin to free you from the grips of general fears and vague unidentified anger toward yourself and others.

A misdirected sense of responsibility for what happened is a common reaction to abusive experiences (not unlike people's reactions after being involved in accidents, injuries, and other misfortunes). You may feel that you could have avoided it or even that you actively encouraged it. In fact, *you were not responsible and could not have done more.* At the time, you did whatever you could to survive. What you did not do is make the other person act sexual toward you. He or she made that choice. If the event was a rape and you were by chance in a dangerous part of town when it happened, it would be good to avoid that area in the future if you can, but that may not be possible. *Women don't make men rape them.*

What was it about the situation that made you feel responsible?

Did someone call you "bad" or tell you it was your fault? Whose voice is that?

In incest situations especially, a sense of guilt and responsibility can be caused by having looked forward to the contact. Some women who have been abused in their families wanted the physical contact because it was the only time they got attention or the feeling of being cared for. The combination of love and sexual abuse in families is extremely confusing to children. A number of these women, especially those who felt deprived of more appropriate parental affection, may to their astonishment find that this pattern of abuse repeats when they have children. The exposure to abuse combined with love gives children the sense that these emotions are automatically connected—that showing love involves, or allows, sexual abuse. They may not be aware they are learning this connection, just as most of us are unaware of other patterns of interaction we pick up from our families.

Another guilt-ridden aspect of childhood sexual abuse is sexual arousal. A number of women, when asked, will acknowledge that they were sexually aroused, even orgasmic, making them feel almost "perverted" when they look back as adults on this response. Nevertheless, it certainly makes sense that a child would become sexually aroused if a person who has been loving and caring starts kissing and caressing her. The acts and responses are normal—it is the roles of the actors and the context that are not acceptable.

Ways of helping yourself. Some of these ideas will be more useful to you than others. We will begin with childhood molestation memories:

• We have already discussed thinking about what happened and sorting out where your feelings of fear, anger, sadness, or helplessness come from. If it occurred in your family, examine your feelings *now* toward all the people involved *then:* parents, stepparents, brothers, sisters, and other relatives. Try to imagine them sitting in the room with you now. Knowing what you know, what would you like to have said to each of them? What do you wish they had said or done then? And now?

You may want to write down your reactions so that you can take a look at them. It will help clarify the predominant feelings attached to each person and the longings and hopes buried in your relationships with them. For example, you may find that your anger toward your mother is greater than toward your father, even if he had the sexual contact with you. It's important to recognize and separate your feelings as a starting point toward reexploring your past.

• Try to imagine yourself at the age when the sexual activity was occurring: Picture where you lived, the touch of your favorite toys, the smell of food cooking, and the sounds in the house at dinner. If you have a photo of yourself at that age, get it out and look at it. If you don't, just imagine yourself as a child in a place where you spent a lot of time, and pretend that this child is sitting beside you. What are your feelings toward this child? Can you comfort her? How? If she feels responsible for what happened or for not acting differently, can you forgive her? Before you put your image of the child away, try to leave her some wisdom from your experiences over the years.

This imaginary journey is sometimes quite revealing. It will point to some issues about your struggle with yourself, your willingness to suspend self-judgment, and your readiness to separate the present you from the past child.

• Depending on the way you prefer to express yourself, try writing down what happened or drawing a series of sketches of the scenes that stick in your mind. Discuss it with someone you know well, asking her just to listen. If you're asked to listen to someone else's story, just try to understand what they are saying and feeling rather than attempt to give advice.

• If the abuse was secret, you may want to tell family members now. The major caution here is that you not expect your family to sympathize, support you, or even to take sides. Some families even get angry at the child to whom this happened. Some families split up over this news, depending on the circumstances; others do not. Consider taking this step while in counseling of some type or even seeking a therapist for a few sessions of family therapy to help you to break the news.

• If the abuse was recent, you may need to take some action to feel more safe: changing your phone number, putting a security system on your house, buying a dog, or taking self-defense classes. If you choose to buy a weapon, be sure to take lessons first to get comfortable using it.

• If you were raped and did not go to a doctor, do so. It is important to be tested for sexually transmitted diseases and, if there was ejaculation, pregnancy. You do not have to report the incident to the police. Usually the hospital or physician will. However, if you know anything about the assailant or could identify him, your report may help police locate him.

• Watch out for self-blame, feelings of helplessness, and excessive

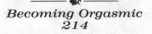

anger or fear. Comfort yourself if you notice you often think "I could have . . ." or "If only I hadn't gone out . . ." You may have asked for love and attention, but you did not ask to be molested and you did not "deserve" it. Feeling helpless is dangerous, and excessive fear or anger (being unable to control these feelings at least part of the time) becomes destructive to the rest of your life. For example, you may begin to dislike all men or be unable to enjoy any sex. Beyond what we said earlier about trying to separate the sources and the true targets of these feelings, these are problems best dealt with by thoughtful friends along with some therapeutic assistance.

• Consider different types of therapy, depending on what you can accommodate: an individual therapist for you alone, a couples therapist if your relationship has become strained, or a family therapist if your family needs to be involved. Alternatively, consider a support group made up of and for women who have been sexually molested.

The point of taking any action with respect to earlier sexual trauma is to put it in perspective so that it does not dominate your current life. These suggestions may have stirred up some memories and feelings for you; when they settle, they should be in a slightly different, more livable pattern.

FINDING PARTNERS IN AN AIDS AGE

If you are single, divorced, or widowed and are looking for male sexual companionship, you have discovered a number of new complexities in a process that was never very simple in the first place.

AIDS is certainly affecting the selection of partners. Casual sex is clearly more dangerous than it was before, even though herpes and other sexually transmitted diseases have caused severe problems in the past, including infertility and illness, in both women and men. The current estimates (in mid-1987) are that 1 million Americans are thought to be infected with the AIDS virus, and more than 90 percent are unaware of it. Infection among heterosexuals is just under 4 percent of the current cases but is expected to pass 5 percent by 1991. Though the majority of cases are among males, an increasing number of AIDS carriers are women. For example, in New York City 10 percent of the AIDS cases are women.

What makes the problem of AIDS especially difficult is the nature of the disease. It can lie dormant, or incubate, for as long as seven to ten years, meaning that any sexual partners over a number of years may expose each other to AIDS if one is a carrier. That means if you had sex with four men in the past three years, and two years prior they each had sex with four others, and their partners each had four partners in the two years before them, you have been exposed to thirty-six different possible carriers of AIDS in the past seven years. In addition, one does not know one has the disease without a blood test for antibodies to the virus, and by then it may be too late to protect the most recent sexual partners. All in all, we are faced with an extremely serious, currently incurable, potentially plaguelike disease. People often have one of two extreme reactions to AIDS: terror, or denial that they could ever get the disease.

We all need to be concerned about AIDS and proceed with caution. The current health guidelines for safe sex, unless each person is certain not to have the AIDS virus, are primarily focused on no exchange of bodily fluids. Body fluids include saliva, blood, semen, and vaginal fluids. This means no coitus or anal sex without condoms; no fellatio or cunnilingus without a condom for the man and a shield for the woman's genitals (although the latter may not be sufficient protection); and no kissing where saliva can be exchanged.

THE AIDS EPIDEMIC

How can people safely conduct their sex lives in an AIDS world? As this is written in early 1987, approximately 40,000 diagnosed cases of acquired immune deficiency syndrome (AIDS) have been diagnosed in the United States, with about 22,000 deaths. There has been a great deal of legitimate concern about the spread of AIDS, and also a great deal of hysteria based on misinformation and misunderstanding of the nature of the AIDS virus. For women who are exploring their sexuality and beginning to grow in sexual responsiveness, here is some information to help you guide your decisions about sexual contact with others:

1. AIDS is not very contagious. If it were very contagious, like the common cold, we would have 40 million cases instead of 40,000 cases. The majority of AIDS cases involve male homosexuals or intravenous drug users who share infected needles, with only a small percentage being people infected through blood transfusions or heterosexual intercourse.
2. AIDS cannot be transmitted by casual contact. Indeed, there are no documented cases of AIDS among those who routinely care for AIDS patients, except for a very small number of cases among health-care workers who accidentally came into contact with a patient's blood or saliva through

direct openings (such as the mouth or surface cuts) on their own bodies. It is apparently impossible to contract AIDS from hugging, kissing, sharing food, and so forth.

3.   While it is possible to transmit AIDS during heterosexual sexual activity, the odds of this occurring are not high. For transmission to occur, the AIDS virus is most readily transmitted by direct access to the bloodstream through a cut or other lesion. However, because the vagina has a rich network of small blood vessels, if the AIDS virus is present in male semen, it could be transmitted to the woman during sexual intercourse.

4.   Since the AIDS virus can be transmitted to the vagina through semen, having a male partner use a latex rubber condom is an excellent idea. To date, research indicates that a condom is an effective safety measure. However, do not use natural or lambskin condoms. Recent research indicates these condoms do not prevent transmission of the virus.

5.   The majority of cases of AIDS in women have been reported in women who are intravenous drug users, who often also engage in prostitution. Obviously, the more men one has sex with, the higher the risks for contracting a virus like AIDS. The majority of cases of AIDS in women who are not prostitutes or drug addicts have occurred in women who have sexual contact with bisexual men.

6.   If you and your sexual partner are monogamous and neither of you has had sex with anyone else in the last eight to ten years, the chances of your contracting AIDS if you remain monogamous are almost zero. If you are not in a monogamous relationship, you should avoid any sexual contact with men who have had large numbers of sexual partners, who are intravenous drug users, or who are also engaging in homosexual activity. You should insist that your male partner wear a condom, and you should avoid unsafe sexual practices that involve exchange of body fluids.

SAFE SEX GUIDELINES

The following list outlines sexual activities that the medical profession currently believes to carry various degrees of safety. Given the rapid changes in scientific knowledge of AIDS, these recommendations are likely to change within the next year. You need to keep informed through your local AIDS hotline. The guidelines were developed by the Scientific Affairs Committee of the Bay Area Physicians for Human Rights and the Scientific Advisory Committee of the San Francisco AIDS Foundation. They appear in a booklet called *Medical Evaluation of Persons at Risk for AIDS* by J.M. Campbell, published by the San Francisco AIDS Foundation in 1987.

NO RISK

Social kissing (dry)
Body massage, hugging
Body-to-body rubbing (frottage)

Using one's own sex toys (vibrators, dildoes, etc.)
Mutual masturbation

LOW RISK (DEPENDS ON BARRIER OR SPECIAL PRECAUTIONS)

Anal or vaginal intercourse with rubber condom (not natural or lambskin condoms)
Fellatio interruptus (stopping before climax)
Fellatio with condom
Mouth-to-mouth kissing (wet kissing)
Oral-vaginal or oral-anal contact with protective barrier
Manual-anal contact with glove
Manual-vaginal contact (internal) with glove

MODERATE RISK (TRANSMISSION POSSIBLE BUT NOT PROVEN)

Fellatio (to climax)
Oral-anal contact
Cunnilingus
Manual-rectal contact
Sharing sex toys
Ingestion of urine

HIGH RISK (TRANSMISSION PROVEN)

Receptive anal intercourse without condom
Insertive anal intercourse without condom (risk less than in receptive partner)
Vaginal intercourse without condom (both partners)

What does this mean for you as you begin a new relationship? There is no foolproof way to be certain about the other person. And, unless you have never had any sexual contact, you can't be certain about yourself. Two negative AIDS HTLV-III or HIV tests over six months, with no intervening sexual partners, would be close to certain, but it is difficult to arrange this. If you are interested in someone sexually, we recommend you follow these guidelines:

1. Get to know the person first rather than rushing into sex. Old-fashioned advice, perhaps, but wise. See if you feel he is generally trustworthy or rather deceptive. Find out if he is concerned about AIDS; if he's not, that's a worry. Let him know that you are. If he pushes for sex without precautions, be careful since he may have been indiscriminate with partners in the past.

2. Ask some direct questions; offer some direct information. Yes, this part is awkward, but if you know the person a bit, you can

simply admit you feel awkward and stumble ahead. AIDS is deadly, and we will gradually begin to make allowances for each other's worries. You may want to lead with an admission of your own worries about AIDS. You don't have to discuss details of past partners, but you do need to know whether there were bisexual, needle-using, drug-abusing, or AIDS or AIDS-related complex (ARC) partners in your backgrounds. If either partner received blood transfusions prior to 1983, he or she may also be at risk. The test for the AIDS antibody became available in 1983, so blood has been screened since then.

3. Spend more time in sexual foreplay and sexual activities that do not include sharing of bodily fluids.

4. Practice safe sex; use condoms carefully so that ejaculate does not spill out during withdrawal.

Of course, there are other issues involved with finding a sexual partner, but the AIDS issues will probably influence sexual pairings most heavily until the disease is brought under control. These issues may be hardest on nonmarried people who do not want a committed sexual relationship but rather a casual one. One cannot realistically act casual about the AIDS threat, and it is especially the people who prefer casual sex who are more at risk.

LIVING IN LONG-TERM RELATIONSHIPS

The culture: The more it changes, the more it stays the same. When we live in a culture, it's impossible to be objective about it or even describe it very well. It's difficult to see something from the inside. We all have impressions about what we think the culture expects from us—but do those impressions reflect our culture or do they just describe our own perceptions and sensitivities? When people call the 1980s "superficial" and "materialistic," could they also be revealing that they are missing a sense of meaning and connectedness?

Therefore, when we discuss cultural issues what we really mean is our impressions of social messages about what we should be doing and thinking, and why it may be difficult to change.

Too much is never enough: Having it all. Somehow, in the attempt to broaden women's options to include areas beyond home life, many women have simply come to feel saddled with more burdens. It appears that it is no longer sufficient to be competent at work or at home. Now many women feel that unless they marry, raise

children, *and* have careers, they are not complete or valued members of society. Women who try to perform well in any of these areas, not to mention all of them, are often exhausted from trying and feel that they are getting nowhere, or they work at an ever-more-frantic pace hoping to find satisfaction somewhere ahead. If you are one of these women and you want to change, there is a straightforward, though difficult, antidote. It is essential to rethink what's most important to you—not to your parents, your partner, your children (these considerations can be made later), but to you. Talk to yourself, and talk to others (saying it out loud can make it seem more real). Then examine what kind of effort you have to put into the less important areas to feel satisfied. Let your partner know; discuss it with him. Figure out where you feel you will and won't compromise with family members. Then design your commitments, schedule, and free time with these priorities in mind. Try it for six months, and review the problems and mistakes and gains. Revise what needs to be changed. Come back again, because the answer can change, to the question of what's important to you. Keep repeating (it usually takes a long time) the process until you have some sense of balance and equilibrium about how your various roles feel.

Feminine and masculine mystiques. Many women still want to feel feminine—the problem is that no one quite knows what *feminine* means. Working women are especially aware of the difference between what they may have learned to connect with femininity— being demure, subservient, cooperative, and supporting a man who takes risks and makes decisions—and the requirements of work— assertiveness, decisiveness, competitiveness, and independent thinking. A number of career women we have seen report feeling somewhat defeminized at work, and it takes some time to emerge from the rather strict social roles required at the workplace. Another factor we have already mentioned is that both women and men are often exhausted when they come home, feeling as if they have nothing left to give. Yet many women still have to cook dinner, talk, and solve family problems. As one woman said, "I don't feel masculine or feminine. At night I feel like a cross between a machine and a zombie."

We notice that when women complain about not feeling feminine enough, they are missing something in themselves and something in how they would like to be treated by others. A similar situation occurs for men who feel some pressure, in general or from their partners, to be more emotionally expressive. Many couples come to us with this complaint. Yet with rare exceptions, the male does have clear ways of expressing emotion—perhaps through anger, perhaps through practical tasks for the family, perhaps through sex—but it is not the immediate affectionate and emotional expression that the woman wants. It is direct emotional expression that is stereotypically connected to women but that for many men—in spite of how emotional they may feel—remains foreign. It feels uncomfortable, awkward, and artificial.

If you would like your partner to be more emotionally expressive, we encourage you to try the following. First, tell your partner why you want this change, why it is important to you (for example, because it would make you feel good, more loved, more appreciated). Make sure that he understands that this is something *you* are missing, rather than his problem. Second, we encourage both of you to let the other know what kinds of ways you already use to express care and affection. It is important to appreciate the effort the other is *already* making. It's much easier to alter style if you feel you are in an atmosphere of appreciation rather than one of criticism. Third, it's important to recognize that you each need to have a way of expressing that's your own, not orchestrated and controlled by the other. This means a period of first noticing feelings before expressing them, so that it begins to feel more natural to be aware of feelings. Fourth, pick several specific events or times when emotional expression is most important for you. Expect irregular and uneven attempts; be responsive and appreciative whenever possible.

This difference in emotional expression is not just linked to gender—many men register the same complaint about their partners. A common historical contributor to our styles of emotional expression is the pattern we witnessed in our families—and we don't just copy what we saw, we may continue the balance that was established. For example, your mother may be cool and withdrawn and your father warm and effusive. You may be either, but you are likely to pick a partner who is different from you in style, because one of the internal rules you learned was that "couples have different emotional styles."

Another angle on the topic of sex roles is how children are regarded in our society. Although there is a lot of talk about the importance of family and children, we in the United States continue to be a society that regards the raising of children as less important work. This is reflected in decreasing funds available to support nutrition and education for children, as well as in the lack of paid maternity and paternity leave in almost every business and work setting in the country. As a society we give a clear message that work is more important than child care, that one only has children if one of the parents is willing to give up working and the associated income temporarily, and that we are not willing to pay for every working establishment to grant mothers and fathers a partially paid leave to begin to raise a newborn. Many parents are therefore forced to rely on child-care facilities within six to eight weeks after childbirth, or to assign one member—almost always the woman—the role of primary child rearer.

If a man desires to participate in child care by staying home when the child is sick, taking a self-assigned paternity leave, or not staying late at the office in order to spend more time with his children, he may be doing so at the risk of a promotion and nonacceptance by his male colleagues. In fact, he may wonder if child-care involvement makes him less masculine. Like the career woman, the man committed to child-care has to struggle first of all against his own stereotypes about "real men," and secondly he must accept the mixed reactions he may get from other people.

Religion and spirituality. Religion has always played an important role in directing the evaluations people make of themselves, their lives, and the meaning of the happiness and misery they face. Most religions have something to say about sex—especially about when, with whom, and what activities are right or wrong for sex. For many of the major religions, there is a subset of people within the religious order for whom celibacy is a chosen path because of the conflict between family life and religious devotion. For some people who are devoutly religious, it appears that their religious doctrine states that sex and religion are in conflict, and all sexual behavior in some way compromises religious ideals. As a result, they may be less sexual or more guilty about being sexual.

Nonetheless, there are many people who consider themselves very religious and who are also satisfied and comfortable with their sexuality. One of the things that seem to make a difference is whether or not emotional bonds are seen to be a way of expressing faith and belief in God's teachings. If human connections are seen as important, religious beliefs permit expression and satisfaction in sexuality; if the only correct way of expressing faith is through contemplation and prayer, then sexuality will be difficult to reconcile.

If you feel your religion is in conflict with your sexuality, you may need to talk to several people who are knowledgeable about your church teachings. We suggest several people because, in our experience, different people will interpret the same religion in different ways. In Catholicism, for example, each pope has varied his interpretation of the Bible and Catholic dogma.

If talking to others within your church does not help or in fact makes your own conflict worse, you may benefit from talking to a counselor or therapist outside your church, since your conflict may be more than a religious one. It may extend into all aspects of your self-esteem and your relationships with others.

Some people eventually work out this conflict by revising their perspective of what proper sex is; some people broaden their ideas of sexuality; others decide on some form of celibacy, engaging in all sexual activities except intercourse or engaging in no sexual activity at all. Couples can be happy with these choices if they both agree on the decision. Still other people revise their commitment to spiritual values, which may mean choosing a different formal religion or practicing spirituality without the help of formal doctrine. Whatever direction a person or couple decide on, it is often a difficult, emotional, and important transition. This is especially true for couples, where one partner may reach a different decision from the other, in which case a resolution is needed. This usually takes time, patience, and a low-pressure environment.

Sex in long-term relationships. People who have long-term relationships usually begin them with the hope, if not the conviction, that the relationship will not end. For people who marry, nearly 50 percent of them can expect to divorce. However, the *other* 50 percent will stay married—in fact, over 35 percent of Americans who do marry will stay married longer than twenty years.

What happens to a couple's sex life over the years of a relationship? We would like to focus on a few areas that seem to be common concerns for people.

EMOTIONAL AND SEXUAL GRATIFICATION IN LONG-TERM RELATIONSHIPS

In 1983, Philip Blumstein and Pepper Schwartz, two sociologists at the University of Washington, published a book called, *American Couples: Money, Work, and Sex.* Their book is based on a study of 12,000 couples and gives us some very valuable insights into what works—and doesn't work—in maintaining a gratifying emotional and sexual relationship over the years. The couples that were studied are a very diverse group, including heterosexuals and homosexuals, drawn from all occupations, educational levels, and different parts of the country, so we can have some confidence about the validity of the information that is presented. Here are some highlights on their conclusions about marital and sexual happiness in heterosexual couples:

• The nature of American marriages is changing. One major change is that both husband and wife work full-time in the majority of current marriages, even when they also have small children. Marriages occur later in people's lives now. Couples marrying for the first time are an average of about five years older now than was the case in the 1960s. Marriages are also less permanent, as the current divorce rate is three times higher than it was in the 1960s.

• The major negative influence on sexual satisfaction for happily married couples is simply fatigue. With both partners working, raising children, and running a household, it requires scheduling of "quality time" to have a good sexual relationship.

• There is some decrease in sexual frequency the longer a couple remains together. Nevertheless, only 15 percent of couples have sex less than once a month after ten or more years of marriage (while 63 percent of this group reported sex once a week or more).

• An automatic loss in sexual gratification or frequency of sex with aging is a myth. Such losses, when they occur, represent the effect of life stresses, relationship dissatisfaction, poor health, or other factors, rather than the effects of age per se.

• Sexual gratification suffers when the emotional relationship isn't going well. Sex doesn't occur in a vacuum, and when you are not feeling good about your relationship, your sexual interest and arousability decline. This is a little more true for women, but it also applies to men.

• Sex works best in relationships in which the man and the woman are equal initiators of making love. Similarly, both partners feeling free to say no occasionally is also related to good sexual adjustment.

• Men, more than women, find that their children inhibit their sex life. Again, some planning for opportunities to have unrestrained, spontaneous, or noisy sex (instead of quietly, at night, in the bedroom) is a good idea for keeping the sexual sparks alive in relationships.

• Women value intercourse itself as a part of lovemaking a bit more than men do. Intercourse itself seems to mean something special. It is one of the few sexual activities that requires equal participation for both partners to enjoy it. It is also an opportunity to be emotionally expressive together without talking.

• Women, including sexually satisfied women, tend to want more kissing, hugging, and cuddling than is currently part of their sex life.

• The occurrence of oral sex (both male to female and female to male) is related both to marital happiness and to sexual satisfaction. This is more true for men than for women; women who give or receive oral sex are only slightly happier than women who do not.

• How you feel about your partner's physical attractiveness (weight, health, body hygiene) strongly influences your sexual satisfaction. However, very attractive couples resent one partner getting more attention from others.

• More women than men have needed to be in love in order to have sex. When this need is combined with the fact that women are more financially dependent on their spouses than the reverse, it may make women more possessive. This seems to have less to do with being female than with being in a less powerful position and being afraid of living on one's own.

• The partner who needs the other less or is less in love has more power to do what he or she chooses because the more powerful person has less to lose.

• Despite the so-called sexual revolution, most couples strongly value monogamy and fidelity. Secret affairs or "open marriage" tend to be associated with eventual breakup of the relationship. However, one act of infidelity does not mean that a person is beginning a series of affairs.

• Nonmonogamous couples are about as happy with their sex lives as monogamous couples. The major difference is that nonmonogamous couples are not as sure that their relationships will last—they have less commitment.

The underlying messages of *American Couples* are that it's the pressures and fatigue of daily life that are the major threat to sexual satisfaction, and that more open communication about sex would overcome many of the other issues that negatively influence sexual satisfaction.

Long-term relationships go through phases and adjustments. The sexual relationship also changes. A common, almost universal, pattern is a decrease in sexual frequency and some decrease in desire. It decreases for many reasons. Sexual interest is unusually high in the beginning, falling-in-love stage of a relationship. Then competing factors interfere, such as work, children, and returning to school. Strains such as illness and financial problems can also compete with sex for a couple's energy and attention. Sex can then become a low-priority activity and can become rather boring, because no one takes the time or energy to nurture it and help it evolve with the relationship.

In other words, sometimes sex becomes infrequent because the participants are expecting it to "take care of itself." After all, some couples have told us, it seemed to do just that in the beginning of the relationship. Everything was pretty good then.

The major task for most couples is to continue to develop and nurture their sexual relationship, given who the individuals are and what kind of changes they experience. This may mean trying new activities, using somewhat different ways of touching, trying to fantasize from time to time, and acting out some fantasies as a couple. In addition, each person may have to reconsider what is important about their partner and sex. Most frequently we ask, in one way or another, whether partners can:

- Let go of ideals about sex and live with what it is now.
- Let go of the past—and all the mistakes and irritations the partner has made.
- Decrease their tendencies constantly to evaluate themselves, one another, and the relationship.
- Permit themselves and their partners to change.
- List the rituals they now engage in and see if more seduction and intimacy could be built into these rituals. By *rituals,* we mean such things as eating together, spending certain times together, doing a specific activity each week, blocking out some time to be alone, or always kissing when greeting one another.

While this is not the place to go into these points in depth, if sex is losing its freshness for you, or if you and your partner currently seem to be "out of step," perhaps these themes will get you started.

Alcohol (and other drugs as well) can take its toll in long-term relationships. Alcohol, in small quantities, can make you *feel* more sexual, but in fact it decreases your physical arousal or vasocongestion. With increasing amounts of alcohol, arousal will be slower, and it will take longer to have an orgasm. We are taught to expect that alcohol increases sexual responsiveness; in fact, it primarily increases the willingness to acknowledge sexual feelings. Occasional alcohol use is rarely a problem. But if a person drinks regularly over time (two to three hard drinks or the equivalent on most days), there may be a gradually increasing chance of physical consequences, including sexual dysfunction from vascular, neural, or hormonal problems. An additional consequence of alcohol abuse for some couples is a greater likelihood of arguing, even to the point of intense rage or violence. Alcohol can apparently serve to remove barriers to feelings that are normally contained and controlled or of minor intensity. Why it can work in this way is not known, but it is probably some combination of its physical effect and people's expectations about what it is supposed to do. If you think you or your partner has problems related to the use of alcohol, call your local alcohol treatment center to see if

there is someone who could give you an opinion and information on where to get help if you need to do so.

And finally (perhaps the most obvious point), most people, at certain times in a relationship, need to be by themselves. This is not abnormal or suspect, but people often do not recognize, or feel guilty about having, such needs. They may even blame their partners and see them as uncaring. What can happen with these individuals is that they attempt to get distance in other ways—irritability, withdrawal, or even lack of interest in affection or sex. If you think this may be happening to you, try to see if you can recognize the signals of your need to be alone and let your partner know. It does not have to be a rejection if you mention briefly why you need some time and would like his help in protecting it. He may need the same from you at some point. Try to find supportive ways of letting one another know.

13
Enhancement

When we say "enhancement," we are talking about the expansion of your sexuality to include new dimensions. For some people, enhancement may mean trying new intercourse positions, exploring different, nonintercourse activities, acting out some fantasies, or having sex at a different place and time. For other people, new partners, group sex, renting X-rated movies, or swapping partners may be the directions they choose for enhancing their sexuality. What we would like to do in this chapter is mention a few basic guidelines for expanding your sexuality in ways that are not hurtful or destructive. We will also mention specific activities that many couples are curious about but which they may find difficult or upsetting to actually try.

One general guideline is that usually new sexual activities that directly involve two people should not be tried at the expense of one person's fear or discomfort. Coercion or force—in the form of a demand, a complaint, or even a sarcastic or joking remark—generally has a negative effect on a person's overall enjoyment. This is not true under certain circumstances, such as both partners agreeing that a certain amount of force is part of sex play.

If it does turn out that one partner is uncomfortable about trying a particular activity, try to figure out what is upsetting about it. Then, and this may be thought of as another guideline, think of and talk over ways that might gradually help the person learn to enjoy trying this new area of exploration. For instance, a woman may be afraid of having oral-genital sex with her partner because she does not want him to ejaculate into her mouth. This concern is a common one, and there are several ways to deal with it. One is to talk over and agree on some kind of signal for the man to let the woman know when he feels orgasm starting. The signal can be a touch, a sound, or anything that's comfortable, natural, and clear enough to understand.

Another guideline to keep in mind is that you don't have to enjoy every kind of sexual activity in order to be a sexually healthy person. If some activity completely turns you off, no matter how much you think and talk about it, or how gingerly you try it, that's okay, as long as your feelings are not preventing you from freely expressing yourself in other sexual ways. Usually the more sexually hesitant person in a relationship feels a greater pressure to become less "inhibited." When there are many discrepancies between partners in their desires for sexual activities, problems may result. But if there are just a few areas of mismatched tastes, and there usually are a few for most couples, mutual consideration and respect seem to work best.

Perhaps the most important thing to remember is to try to change those areas that seem to be changeable and important to both of you, and not to blame yourself or resent your partner for not being able to get past his or her discomfort. Keep in mind that attitudes and interests sometimes evolve slowly, and you may find it amazingly easy to try an activity next year that you would not think of trying now.

Even in the best of relationships, suggesting something new to do sexually can feel risky. "Will he [she] think that our sex is terrible or dull because I want to try something different?" Both partners need to feel that *they* won't be rejected (even though a particular idea might be), and that at least they can feel free enough to bring something up and talk about it. This goes back to our earlier discussion of the general support and trust that are necessary when someone initiates and when someone chooses to refuse a sexual activity.

ORAL-GENITAL AND ANAL LOVEMAKING

But what about specifics? One way to enhance sexual relationships is to explore oral-genital sex. When done to the female, oral-genital sex is called *cunnilingus;* when done to the male it is called *fellatio.*

A frequent concern of both men and women about oral-genital activity is cleanliness. We have mentioned how most of us grow up with the idea that the genital area is dirty. Even though you may now realize that genitals are as clean as any other parts of your body, you may still feel uncomfortable about touching them with your mouth.

One way that we have found helps couples to deal with this concern is to take a shower together and to spend some time washing each other's genitals. This not only helps assure clean and fresh-smelling genitals, but gently lathering the genital area with soap and warm water can provide a great deal of sensual pleasure.

Naturally, if one of you has a cut or sore on your genitals, a sexually transmitted disease, or herpes, you should not engage in oral or other sexual contact until the condition is cleared. In addition, oral sex should not be done if one partner has tested positive for the AIDS virus or has good reason to suspect exposure to AIDS from prior sexual contact, drug use, or an untested blood transfusion.

Another worry that couples often have is exactly how to provide good oral stimulation to their partner. If this is true for you, let your partner guide you with some suggestions on what feels best. One pattern that you might try is to begin with fondling genitals and gently nuzzling *around* the genitals—the stomach, thighs, and pubic hair. During fellatio, the woman can hold the penis and take the tip of it into her mouth, or run her tongue around the coronal ridge of the penis. The coronal area, especially on the underneath side of the penis (the side closest to the scrotum) is especially sensitive. It's important that the woman do only as much stimulation as she feels comfortable providing. At first, a little genital touching and kissing may be the extent of fellatio. Later, perhaps after many experiences like this, she may feel comfortable providing more direct stimulation to the penis. At this time, try varying the pressure and rhythm on the penis. Many women find it difficult to encompass the length of the erect penis in their mouth. It is not necessary to move your mouth back and forth over the entire length in order to provide good stimulation; instead you might try using your hand to stimulate the lower part of the penis (near his body) and your mouth in a similar rhythm across the upper part of the penis. A good way to discover the best tempo is to follow your partner's movements and responses.

During oral stimulation to the woman, the same progression can be used. Begin slowly and gradually around the genitals, and then provide more direct stimulation to the clitoral area. Some women like very slow tongue movements, others like a very rapid flicking movement across the clitoris, or a sucking motion applied to the clitoris. Start slowly, and build tempo and pressure according to what the particular woman enjoys. Some communication is helpful. It's important that you *both* enjoy what is going on. One cautionary note: Although oral stimulation to the vagina is a pleasurable source of stimulation for women, the male should *never* blow air into the vagina, since air can enter the bloodstream directly and be extremely dangerous.

During oral stimulation, many couples enjoy touching other areas of the body. The male might fondle the woman's breasts or thighs while stimulating her genitals; the woman might stroke her partner's scrotal area during fellatio. Sometimes touching or holding

a part of your partner's body while he or she is orally stimulating you is a nice way to feel closer and more mutually involved.

There are several different positions in which oral-genital stimulation is possible. The one who is being stimulated can stand while the partner is kneeling or sitting, both can lie down curled on their sides with faces near each other's genitals, one person can lie between the other person's legs, or one person can kneel to stimulate the other who is sitting on the edge of a bed or comfortable chair. The one being stimulated can also sit on the upper chest of the partner who is lying down. In this position, the partner who is being stimulated is almost kneeling above the other's face. The one who is doing the pleasuring is free to stroke the other partner's buttocks or breasts, and the person being stimulated is free to fondle the partner's genitals. Try experimenting to find which positions you most prefer. During this exploration, at first the man should be relatively still—let the woman explore and experiment as she becomes accustomed to oral stimulation. It's a good idea for her to have as much free movement of her head as possible, so that if the penis inadvertently goes a bit too deep, she can withdraw quickly, rather than have a choking sensation. This means that at least initially, it's not a good idea to use a position in which the man's weight restricts free movement of the woman's head.

Oral-genital stimulation does not always have to result in orgasm. It can be used during foreplay to pleasure each other. It can last just a short while before or after intercourse, or you can continue it for as long as you like. As we discussed earlier, many women do not like the idea of taking ejaculate into their mouths. If this is true for you, you should work out some convenient signal so this doesn't happen.

On the other hand, you may prefer to allow the male to go ahead and ejaculate in your mouth. Some women do not mind the taste and consistency of this fluid and so they usually swallow it; other women can't stand to swallow it. Of course, there is no danger of becoming pregnant, and swallowing the ejaculate is not harmful. However, if you do not wish to swallow the ejaculate, it is possible to position your mouth in such a way that when your partner ejaculates, you merely hold the fluid in your mouth and rinse it out or dispose of it into a tissue. As a couple, you need to work out a pattern that is satisfying to both of you.

Mutual oral-genital stimulation, known also as "sixty-nine," is something you might want to try if you are both comfortable with fellatio and cunnilingus. Although many couples enjoy mutual stimulation, it is sometimes difficult to enjoy giving and receiving oral

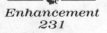

Enhancement
231

pleasure at the same time. Positions can also be a problem, and you will have to experiment to find one that suits you best. Having the woman on top allows her to control the depth of the penis better, although this is also possible with a side-to-side position.

Anal stimulation is also very arousing for some couples. You can manually stimulate this area during intercourse or foreplay. If you do try anal intercourse (inserting the penis into the anus), it's important to proceed very slowly and gradually. The anal muscles are much tighter than the vaginal muscles, and physical damage plus a good deal of pain may result if this is done too roughly. A lubricant such as K-Y jelly is necessary, and a comfortable position has the woman lying on her back with her legs slightly bent at the knees, and her hands free to guide her partner if necessary. Some couples like to use pillows under the woman's buttocks as well. If you have never tried anal intercourse, it is best to start out by inserting a finger, slowly and gently. Over several sessions, you should be able to insert two fingers. It is especially important to make certain that the woman is not experiencing any discomfort. One way to ensure this is to let the woman guide the man as to how fast and how hard to thrust. Being sexually aroused also helps. If any discomfort does occur, try again some other time.

After the woman has become used to the insertion of two fingers, you can try penile stimulation. Again, go slowly—trying one, two, or three fingers first before trying to insert the penis. Make sure that the penis is well lubricated with K-Y or Astroglide or that you use a lubricated condom.

It's very important that you not go on to vaginal intercourse immediately after you have tried anal intercourse. The reason is that some of the natural bacteria in the rectum may cause vaginal infections if they are transmitted from the anus to the vagina. If you do want to have vaginal intercourse right after anal intercourse, the man should wear a condom during anal intercourse and then remove it before going on to vaginal stimulation; or if anal intercourse without a condom takes place, the man should wash his penis well with soap and water before going on.

Anal intercourse does not *cause* AIDS, but it is a way in which the virus is transmitted. AIDS is more common among male homosexuals, but this is because of the tendency for gay men to have many sexual partners. Multiple partners means increased risk of transmission of the AIDS virus between people, no matter what their sexual

preference. If neither sexual partner in any monogamous relationship has the AIDS virus, you can't get AIDS from each other no matter what you do sexually.

OTHER FORMS OF ENHANCEMENT

There are as many variations to sexual activity as you care to take advantage of—enhancement depends on you and your partner. You can try having sex at a different time of the day, waking up your partner during the night, or finding a private place out-of-doors. If you usually like to be freshly showered for sex, you might try making love after some sweaty activity on a warm summer day. Or if you generally like to spend a long time making love, try a "quickie"—some frantic lovemaking before you have to be somewhere. Try to think of ways that would expand your particular sexual experiences. Some books, like Alex Comfort's *The Joy of Sex*, will give you some basic ideas from which to begin.

From time to time, newspapers or magazines mention aphrodisiacs—various substances that might increase sexual desire. Alcohol is often thought to increase sexual desire by decreasing a person's inhibitions. In small amounts, alcohol does tend to relax people, which may or may not make sexual arousal easier. In larger amounts, alcohol has a negative effect on sexual desire, and it frequently can interfere with the male's ability to have or to maintain an erection. For many women, alcohol inhibits orgasm.

Marijuana may also act to decrease inhibitions, but it does not necessarily act as a sexual stimulant. Some people report feeling more sexual pleasure and others report less sexual pleasure after smoking marijuana. Other drugs such as amphetamines, amyl nitrate ("poppers"), and cantharides ("Spanish fly") may cause temporary increases in sexual desire, but they can all have dangerous and even deadly side effects. Poppers and Spanish fly cause dilation of the blood vessels, with the latter also causing severe inflammation of the urinary tract. Cocaine is also described by its users as an enhancer of sex. Of course, even if this were true, cocaine is an extremely addictive, lethal drug, and no one should ever consider using it for sexual enhancement.

Perhaps the best physical aphrodisiacs are feeling healthy and being physically active. Both help you to feel better about yourself and more energetic. If your physical condition concerns you, and you would like to make some changes along these lines, there are some books in the bibliography that will give you a start.

Delaying Ejaculation

Increasing the pleasure you get from sex often involves giving yourselves more time for a relaxed sensuous experience. Often, however, what a couple does sexually is determined by when the male partner ejaculates. Orgasm does not have to signal the end of a sexual encounter. Although at times you may want to continue pleasuring after the male has ejaculated, you may also, at times, desire to delay ejaculation for a while. It is possible to do this through techniques that seem to inhibit this reflex. A technique was originally developed by Dr. James Semans in 1959 in order to teach men to extend the time to ejaculation. Later, the Semans procedure was modified by Masters and Johnson and has become known as the "squeeze" technique.

The idea behind both techniques (the pause and the squeeze) is that the man learns to control the timing of ejaculation without decreasing the amount of stimulation or the erotic pleasure of arousal and orgasm. He learns to delay ejaculation either by pausing and stopping all sexual stimulation or by squeezing at a certain place on the penis.

It's important for the male to learn to determine when he's going to ejaculate. Most men are aware of a special sensation that signals that ejaculation is about to occur. This is sometimes called the feeling of "inevitability," because the reflex has been triggered and will occur automatically whether or not stimulation is continued. This response seems to be unique to men; among women, discontinuing stimulation will almost always prevent orgasm from occurring.

The pause. If the pause technique is used, stimulation and movement must stop well before the feeling of inevitability occurs. The male then waits until his high level of arousal subsides and he feels that stimulation can be resumed. Some men will experience a partial loss of erection, but renewed stimulation will bring this back. The advantage to the pause technique is that it is relatively simple. If the pause is used during intercourse, the man doesn't need to withdraw but can simply stop all movement. Couples often enjoy using these brief moments to experience feelings of closeness and gentle caressing.

A possible disadvantage is that pauses during intercourse may

interfere with the woman's buildup of arousal and her orgasmic response. One way to deal with this would be for the man to stimulate his partner manually until movement can be resumed.

It's important that the male receive a lot of stimulation rather than a little. This will allow him to get accustomed to prolonged arousal without interfering with the enjoyment of sexual stimulation. We also suggest that the male partner *not* try to control his ejaculation by thinking about something else (work, an unpleasant scene, and so on)—not only does this work poorly but it also decreases the pleasurable erotic quality of the sexual experience. The pause technique takes practice—probably several weeks—but the more it is used, the more effective it will become. For this reason, the male may choose to practice ejaculatory control on his own. This can be done by masturbating and using the pause two or three times a week. Usually the man will find that after a while he can continue ten to fifteen minutes of active stimulation with as many as three pauses. These individual masturbation sessions are helpful for a number of reasons.

1. They allow him to learn when to pause. It's useful to learn when it is too late as well as too early to pause. There will be times when this is misjudged and ejaculation happens anyway. Don't worry if this happens; missing the moment is another way of learning to identify it better the next time.

2. The man is free to experiment with varying the length of time he pauses. It's important to learn how long the pause needs to be in order to allow stimulation to be continued for another period of time. At first, the male may find he needs to pause up to five minutes. After practice, the pause may be reduced to one minute or less. Keeping a written record is often helpful in order to see the progression of shorter pauses, fewer pauses, and increasing amounts of sexual stimulation. Of course, control during masturbation is likely to be a lot easier than control during foreplay or intercourse. It's a good idea to use lubricant, fantasy, and erotic material such as pictures or stories during masturbation to help the physical experience seem more stimulating.

The squeeze. The squeeze technique is an alternative that some couples prefer. During the squeeze procedure, the man or the woman applies pressure to a certain area on the penis just before the moment at which ejaculation seems inevitable. This will inhibit the ejaculatory reflex and enable the couple to resume sexual stimulation. Often, the man will lose some of his erection until stimulation is resumed.

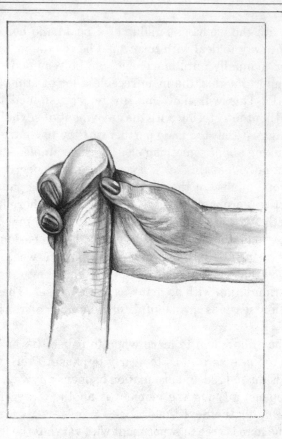

The squeeze can be applied either by the male or the female, and as with the pause, practice improves control. Probably the best way to begin learning this skill is for the man to use the squeeze during masturbation. He can then learn when, how hard, and how long to squeeze. Squeeze using the thumb and next two fingers. The thumb is placed just under the coronal ridge with the other two fingers directly opposite on the other side of the penile shaft.

Sufficient pressure must be applied to stop ejaculation. Often men (and more often women) are surprised at the amount of pressure that can be applied to the erect penis without causing discomfort. This is because the erect penis is filled with blood and because it contains a lot of spongy tissue that helps absorb the pressure that is applied.

Some men find that positioning their fingers in the way described does not lessen their arousal level but rather triggers ejaculation. This is usually because *(a)* the man continued stimulation too long, and ejaculation had already begun; or *(b)* the position of the fingers on the head of the penis creates extra stimulation. If this happens, try

applying the squeeze just under the coronal ridge, without touching the head of the penis.

If the squeeze is practiced during masturbation, the man should provide plenty of vigorous stimulation before squeezing. Often, fantasy or the use of erotic material such as pictures or stories helps to increase arousal and the sexual quality of the experience. As with the pause, over time, the man will probably be able to engage in fifteen minutes of stimulation with zero to three squeezes, and the length of time he needs to squeeze should become briefer.

Practicing these techniques during masturbation is not absolutely necessary if strong feelings against masturbation make this difficult. However, we would encourage men to reevaluate any negative feelings in light of the benefits to be gained. Possibly some of the ideas expressed in chapter 3 will be useful. Should you still decide to practice these techniques without masturbation, it will, as we said earlier, take time and patience to find the best mutually acceptable way to learn to control ejaculation.

More details about self-help programs for male sexual problems and enhancement of male sexual pleasure are provided in books on male sexuality listed in the bibliography.

AGING AND SEXUALITY

You may be surprised to find a discussion on sex and aging in a chapter on enhancement. Often, however, the changes that take place in the sexual cycle of older men and women enable a couple to explore new avenues of sensual pleasure. Several good books on sex and aging are listed in the bibliography.

There are some obvious changes that both men and women will notice as they grow older. It will take longer for the man to achieve an erection and for the woman to begin lubricating. There may also be less total lubrication produced. The older male has greater ejaculatory control and can maintain an erection for a longer period than a younger man. However, the feeling of "inevitability" that signals ejaculation is often not experienced by the older male. Occasionally ejaculation will not occur at all.

After orgasm, the physical changes that have occurred during sexual arousal will return very rapidly to the unaroused state—this is true for both men and women.

Knowing what to expect as you age enables you to take advantage of some of these natural changes. For example, since it usually takes longer for erection to occur in older men, foreplay often becomes a more relaxed, sensuous experience for couples. Also, the longer time before ejaculation allows for extended foreplay and longer intercourse, an experience that may have previously been rare or nonexistent.

The fact that the older male may not ejaculate during sex often causes great concern. Unless a couple accepts this as a normal aspect of aging in the male, they are likely to experience anxiety and frustration in their attempts for orgasm. Sometimes, switching stimulation—for example, from intercourse to oral-genital or manual pleasuring—will enable the male to ejaculate. At other times, however, a feeling of pleasure and enjoyment from sexual closeness is possible even though ejaculation does not occur.

Other changes, both physical and emotional, add to the enhancement of sex in later life. Skin texture often changes, becoming softer and smoother, and feelings of trust and comfort between partners in a long-term relationship add to the enjoyment of sex. For many couples, menopause, which signals the end of the woman's childbearing years, often means a new freedom from worries about contraception and allows sexual expression to become more spontaneous.

For the older female, as we have already discussed, intercourse may bring some discomfort because of a normal thinning of the lining of the vaginal walls. This can be eliminated, however, through the use of lubricating creams or hormone treatment. See chapter 8 for more details.

Although changes do occur, sexual responsiveness and the desire for sex do not disappear with age. Studies have shown that men and women often continue to be sexually active through and beyond their seventies. Two important factors in continued sexual interest and functioning seem to be a fairly active sex life with regular sexual contact, and the availability of a sexual partner. Rather than indicating the end of sexuality, aging permits expansion, enhancement, and continued sexual growth.

CONCLUSION

There are many other important areas of sexuality that we have not considered here. Premarital and extramarital sex, the problems of sexual partners for divorced or widowed women, the value of homo-

sexual relationships, and many other facets of sexual expression are topics that deserve a good deal of special consideration. The unique problems and emotions in these areas go beyond what we can adequately deal with in one book. We suggest that if you are interested in, or living in, any of these situations, you check the bibliography for books that deal with these specific areas. We hope that the basic ideas and feelings we've discussed in the previous chapters with regard to the development of your own sexuality with and without a partner are a good beginning for you, whatever your particular set of circumstances at the present moment.

14
What Next?

It may be that even after trying the ideas and suggestions we have offered, you are still dissatisfied with your own sexuality or your sexual relationship with your partner. So what, if anything, can you do next?

There are a number of approaches you might consider. First, try to specify exactly what it is that you are dissatisfied about. Are your concerns reasonable, in light of what you have learned about female sexuality and the couple relationship? Or are you aiming for unrealistic goals? The most obvious realistic concern would be if you have not had an orgasm, either by yourself or with your partner, by this time. Some unrealistic goals include having an orgasm each time you have intercourse, having simultaneous orgasms, and having multiple orgasms. Although all these may be goals you would like to experience at some point, it is perhaps a little too much to expect them right now. Remember, you have been making some big changes in yourself and your sexuality as you followed this program, and it may take some time for these changes to stabilize and make further growth possible.

If, however, you do feel dissatisfied with the results of this program, or if you are reasonably happy with the results so far but would like to make further gains, there is a variety of approaches to consider. You should think over each of the following alternatives carefully and discuss them with your partner, if you have one. Which alternative fits best for your current concerns and which approach is likely to be productive for you are judgments that only you can make.

Let nature take its course. If you have attained your most immediate goals but still feel you would like to continue to change, you might consider just relaxing and enjoying your new sexuality at this point. As you continue to have pleasurable self- and partner sessions, you will more or less automatically find that your attitudes continue to become more positive: Your sexual arousal will increase, you will gain skill at arousing yourself, and your orgasmic capacity will grow. Additionally, as you and your partner continue to learn about each other and to communicate with each other, sex between the two of you will also become more pleasurable. This process is one we have seen in our patients after we finish active therapy with them. By follow-up time (three to six months after the end of therapy), most women and couples report further positive changes.

Do some more work on your own. If you have not reached some of your important goals but feel that you are changing and that you have seen some progress during this program, you (and your partner) may want to continue to try together on your own.

If there are specific areas of your own sexuality or your relationship that concern you, you could reread the relevant sections of this book and repeat the prescribed exercises. A second try often produces results though the first attempt did not. Like any experience you repeat, it is always different the second time—you are a bit different, for one thing, and therefore you pay attention to different details and messages.

Additionally, you may want to read some other books that can be helpful. The bibliography at the end of this book is intended as a guide. It has a brief note on what each book is about to help you choose the most relevant book for your particular concerns.

Other sources of information may also be helpful to you. Does your local college or adult education program have courses on sexuality, marriage, personal health, exercise, and so forth that would benefit you? Does your local church, women's club, or other community organization sponsor lectures, workshops, or retreats on these topics? Are there X-rated movie theaters or adult bookstores near you that can provide some additional fantasy material? You may be surprised to discover just how much is available if you start pursuing these different sources of new information.

Work with a therapist. This option is one you may consider if this program has not really produced any significant results for you. You may feel that you want individual therapy for your personal concerns (such as your self-esteem, some moods, and so on), marital or relationship therapy if your general relationship with your partner is troubling you, or specific sex therapy if your primary concern is your sexuality or sexual relationship with your partner. Again, you must think about, discuss, and decide which of these modes of therapy is most likely to meet your needs now.

We have previously mentioned that there are two sexual issues that often require working with a therapist: a low level of sexual desire and an aversion to sexual activity following childhood sexual abuse or adult rape. If these issues apply to you, work with a therapist is suggested.

Whichever mode of therapy you choose, you will next be faced with the difficult process of choosing a therapist. There are two major components in making this choice, and unfortunately, there are no clear-cut, easy rules for making such a decision.

The first issue in making your choice concerns the competence of the therapist. Psychotherapy is offered by a number of different professional specialists—psychologists, psychiatrists, social workers, marriage and family therapists, and pastoral counselors, to name just a few. It's important that you have a lot of information about any therapist's training, qualifications, and ability. Since it may prove difficult to obtain direct information about various therapists' qualifications, you may want to concentrate your selection on the clinical psychologists (with Ph.D. or Psy.D. degrees) or psychiatrists (with M.D. degrees) in your area. The reason for this is that both the professional training and the state licensing or certification laws are usually more rigorous for these disciplines than for the others. This is not to say that all other specialists are not competent (or that all psychologists and psychiatrists *are* competent); but in the absence of direct knowledge of a particular therapist's ability, this rule is a helpful first screening of possible alternatives.

In choosing a clinical psychologist or psychiatrist, be sure that he or she is licensed as such in your state. This ensures that the therapist is formally qualified, by training and experience, to conduct psychotherapy. Additionally, certification by the American Board of Psychiatry and Neurology, the American Board of Professional Psychology, the American Board of Family Psychology, or the National Register of Health Service Providers in Psychology, over and above state licensure or certification, provides another safeguard for you. Don't be embarrassed to ask about these certifications and licensures. No responsible professional is anything but pleased to work with a client who has reassured herself about the therapist's formal qualifications.

Of course, there are also many highly competent clinical social workers. Again, make sure that the social worker you are considering is a state-licensed *clinical* social worker and also that he or she is certified by the relevant national specialty board. Some states (California, for example) also license a category of professionals called *marriage and family counselors*, and this form of state licensure also helps to ensure that the therapist is properly trained and state regulated in his or her practice of psychotherapy. Other specialties—

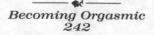

psychiatric and psychosocial nursing—offer degrees and special licensing requirements. These specialties do not currently have required training in sexual or marriage problems, and thus decisions about them will depend more on an individual's credentials.

As a next step in ensuring therapist competence, you might try to get some personal opinions about your prospective therapists. While therapists do not provide letters of reference from satisfied customers, such information can often be found. Your family doctor, clergy, and friends can often recommend a therapist on the basis of direct personal knowledge of the therapist's ability.

How does one locate a therapist? There are a number of alternatives. Your county medical society can provide you with the names of psychiatrists, and your county or state psychological association can provide a list of licensed clinical psychologists. If there is a city, county, or state mental health clinic near you, you may also contact their outpatient clinic for therapy or a referral. Similarly, the state or county social work association or association of licensed marriage and family counselors can provide a referral. If you live near a university or medical school, try contacting the departments of psychiatry, psychology, or social work. Training programs in psychiatry and clinical psychology usually run outpatient clinics where you can obtain qualified therapy, often at a reduced fee compared to private practitioners. Do not be afraid of a training program because you may get student therapists. If they are well supervised, they are often highly motivated, very concerned, good therapists. And university sites try to offer and be aware of innovative treatment approaches that have been or are being evaluated. Do ask about their experience (they should have some prior experience) and the nature of their supervision. If you feel you must have a nonstudent, ask the training clinic about the availability and cost of faculty-trainer therapy.

Once you have located some therapists who meet the qualifications discussed above, you must then make a second and more difficult choice: Among several qualified therapists, which one is likely to be best for you?

As a first step in making this decision, try to match the therapist's specialty with your concern. If you are concerned about yourself, seek someone who does primarily individual psychotherapy. If your relationship concerns you, seek someone who specializes in marital therapy. We recommend that you find a state-licensed mental health professional who meets the criteria listed above and who specializes in marriage, rather than going to a "marriage counselor" or "psychotherapist." The reason for this is that state laws vary—in some states, literally anyone can represent him- or herself as a marriage counselor or psychotherapist.

A similar situation exists in regard to "sex therapy." If your concerns are primarily sexual, seek a licensed and certified clinical psychologist, psychiatrist, or social worker who has had additional training in sex therapy and now specializes in this area. We do not recommend that you go to a "sex therapist" because again, there are no state licensure laws to regulate who can use that title, and indeed there is no professional discipline to ensure adequate training of such people. Once again, your county medical society, state psychological association, or department of psychology or psychiatry at the nearest university or medical school should be able to provide the name of someone who specializes in sexual therapy.

Having found a therapist who is formally qualified and who specializes in your area of concern, the decision about this therapist's ability to help you now becomes a personal matter. Therapists differ in their theoretical orientation, of course, and while there is no clear-cut evidence that any one particular approach is more effective than another, some types of therapy work best for particular problems and for particular types of people. Decide what you want out of therapy, and have a frank and open discussion with your prospective therapist in the first session. Does he or she agree that your goals are reasonable? Ask for a brief description of the type of therapy he or she conducts: Does it seem to address your concerns? If not, discuss with the therapist what you would like to work on and how. The therapist may convince you to try things in a different way than you had originally planned, which can be quite valid. Alternatively, the therapist may provide you with a referral to a colleague who is a better match for your expectations. Once in therapy with someone, realize that therapy is a difficult and demanding process. Don't quit early, or "doctor-shop"—don't jump from therapist to therapist looking for someone who will "cure" you without any effort or difficulty on your part. At the same time, if you are dissatisfied with your therapy, discuss this with the therapist rather than just quitting. You may decide that this therapist is not for you, but talk about this with the therapist and mutually decide what to do (continue, quit, or get a referral to another therapist) rather than just dropping out.

One final word of caution: The code of ethics of all the mental health professions forbids any direct sexual contact between patient and therapist. If a therapist initiates any direct sexual contact between the two of you, this should be reported immediately to both the state licensure board for the person's profession and to the profession's national organization. In addition, therapy and dating do not mix. If your therapist begins to ask you to go out for dinner or other social contact with him or her, even without a direct sexual overture, you should stop therapy with that person (and decide for yourself if it is a friendship you want instead). Dating without sex is not necessarily technically unethical, but it is poor therapeutic judgment and not considered in the client's best interest. The reason is that the essence of the therapeutic relationship is to help the client decide on and change in the directions that he or she needs. To become involved directly in a client's life destroys the therapist's ability to remain neutral and may make the client suffer more. In short, the therapist becomes part of the problems rather than a consultant for solutions.

If you feel a need for further growth, do pursue one of these pathways to additional change. With the passage of time, further work on your own, or psychotherapy, you can make progress. You have the capacity for change and growth, if you give yourself a chance.

Here are some addresses for locating and verifying the credentials of therapists.

PSYCHOLOGISTS
American Psychological Association
National Register of Health Services
Providers in Psychology
1200 17th Street NW
Washington, DC 20036

American Board of Family Psychology (Diplomate psychologists in family and marital as well as marital and sex therapy)
6501 Sanger, Suite 15
PO Box 7977
Waco, TX 76714

PSYCHIATRISTS
American Psychiatric Association
1700 13th Street NW
Washington, DC 20036

SOCIAL WORKERS
National Association of Social Workers
7891 Eastern Avenue
Silver Spring, MD 20910

MARRIAGE AND FAMILY THERAPISTS
American Association of Marriage and Family Therapy
1717 K Street NW, Room 407
Washington, DC 20006

SEX THERAPISTS
There are several certifying organizations; this one is perhaps the largest.
American Association of Sex Educators, Counselors, and Therapists
11 Dupont Circle NW, Suite 220
Washington, DC 20036

Note to Professionals

Originally, most of our work with women in therapy was done in the context of weekly, short-term sex therapy with couples. However, in more recent years, we have used the program outlined in this book in several other ways. We have worked with women who do not have regular sexual partners, in both individual and group therapy. We have also worked with couples in couples group therapy. As part of larger research studies on therapy format, we have used this program in an intensive daily treatment mode. We have also conducted a study of the effectiveness of dual sex cotherapy teams compared to a single therapist. In all of these various types of therapy, we have found that the effectiveness of the program remains unchanged. This is a strongly structured program, then, that can be used in many different types of therapeutic settings. In addition, we recently contributed to a study of the effectiveness of this program in which some women saw a therapist only three times and otherwise worked on their own. These women used this book and an accompanying film, also called *Becoming Orgasmic*, which is discussed below. This study showed that the women treated with this minimal therapist contact or guided self-help were just as successful in reaching orgasm as women who saw a therapist every week for fifteen weeks.* The other research studies mentioned above are listed in the annotated bibliography.

Considering all these studies together, combined with our other clinical cases, we have worked with over 150 nonorgasmic women, using this program. Our overall results indicate that over 90 percent of women who follow this program learn to have orgasms regularly during masturbation. Around 80 percent of women become orgasmic in partner-related activity, such as manual or oral caressing of the woman's genitals, and about 35 percent of our women regularly experience orgasm during intercourse. These results approximate orgasm

*P. J. Morokoff and J. LoPiccolo, "A Comparative Evaluation of Minimal Therapist Contact and Fifteen-Session Treatment for Female Orgasmic Dysfunction," *Journal of Consulting and Clinical Psychology*, 54:3 (1986), 295–300.

—— ✦ ——

rates found in sociological studies of healthy, normal women, so the effectiveness of this approach is very strong. In addition, over 95 percent of the women (and their partners for women with partners) report greatly increased overall satisfaction with their sexuality.

Some women—especially more traditional, religious, older women—have some objection to the masturbation component of this program. These women often ask if they couldn't simply begin with the couple-focused work and omit the first several chapters of this book. Indeed, some sex therapists do not routinely include the self-exploration, body work, and masturbation-training components of our program. However, there are now several published research studies, done by other sex researchers, comparing couple-only treatment with our type of program.* All these studies showed the greater effectiveness of a program that includes the self-exploration and masturbation elements, so there is good reason to help clients work through initially negative feelings rather than just agreeing with them.

Briefly, we would like to mention how several different therapeutic approaches might make use both of this program and three fifteen-minute films that are specifically designed to enhance the ease of trying each step. As mentioned above, the films have the unit title *Becoming Orgasmic: A Sexual Growth Program for Women* and are available from Focus International, Inc., 14 Oregon Drive, Huntington Station, New York, NY 11746, (516) 549-5320. The first two films, subtitled "Discovery" and "Self-Pleasuring," can be shown to women with or without a sexual partner, thus complementing the material in chapters 2–7. The final film, subtitled "Sharing," is for women who do have a sexual partner, and it follows the content of chapters 8–10. All three films show one woman's exploration of her body, the pleasure it can provide for her, and her growing sexual response through orgasm. Some of the common reactions, doubts, and uncertainties that accompany each stage of growth are also expressed. We believe that the films are useful as models for overcoming some of the uncertainties of progressing through the program. The films may be of particular benefit to male therapists, since they provide a female model who discloses her fears and concerns.

For a woman involved in individual or couple therapy, the actual exercises are outlined clearly in the preceding chapters. Although some discussion of them may be necessary, more therapy time should

---

*For a review of studies on treatment of orgasmic problems see B. L. Andersen, "Primary Orgasmic Dysfunction: Diagnostic Considerations and Review of Treatment," *Psychological Bulletin*, 93:1 (1983), 105–136.

probably be spent on the particular woman's feelings about each step, both before and after she tries to do them. We recommend that the therapist have the woman write down her reactions to each exercise (What was difficult? Easy? How did she feel? How pleasurable was it?) as soon as possible after each attempt to do a specific part. These written records should be brought to the therapy session. We have found that they are efficient and effective means toward understanding any difficulties the woman may be having. The questions presented within the chapters themselves might form an additional basis for discussion.

If the films are also used, the therapist might show each step before a woman tries it herself. A preliminary viewing of the film would be particularly useful to explain how to go about each exercise, or at those points that seem particularly emotion-laden for the individual woman. It would allow a chance for her to react and to ask questions. However, some parts of the film may be better used after the woman has tried on her own, in case she might tend to form a particular "set" on how she should respond. The decision of when to show the films should be based on the material involved and on the particular woman's strengths and sensitivities.

Women involved in group therapy may also use the book and films in a format similar to that for individual or couple therapy. Group therapy also provides a unique opportunity for women to gain perspective on their sexual growth and, when handled well, a group can offer additional support beyond the individual therapy experience. Care should be taken in forming a group—one of the most important variables is that of a current sexual partner. Groups seem to work better if they are homogeneous as, for example, if each woman involved is in a permanent, long-term relationship with someone. In addition, it may be helpful to separate women who have never had orgasm from those who are infrequently orgasmic.

In any case, it is important for the therapist to encourage mutual support among the group members and to discourage any tendencies for comparison among their different rates of progress. To emphasize from the beginning the expectation that each woman will have an individual rate of progress should be useful.

For those women who do have sexual partners, the third film and chapters 9–11 are intended for the couple to use together. Although the partner's participation in the group may be extremely helpful, it is not a requirement. It is possible for the woman to transmit the information she has gained to her partner on her own, as long as they have a very good and cooperative relationship. If the partner wants to be part of the actual therapy, he can be included in several ways. One possibility is to have part of each of the later group sessions include the male partners. Another possibility is to have an additional meeting set aside for the males only, with less time spent in combined male-female sessions.

Regardless of the therapeutic format, a few guiding principles should be kept in mind. First, the woman should be aware that learning to have an orgasm is only one part of sexual growth and that it will involve more than just learning a series of techniques. Second, the woman's feelings and thoughts are extremely important to the ease or difficulty she may have at various points. Feelings should not be seen as secondary to the actual "doing" of the various steps. Third, orgasm is likely to be different from what the woman expected, and some time should be spent discussing how it differs from her expectations and what that difference means to her. Fourth, as women become more sexually responsive, some of their permanent partners may be ambivalent about accepting her changes. Time should be spent both with the woman and her partner to deal with any covert or overt problems that may accompany the woman's sexual growth.

A Selected Annotated Bibliography

The following books discuss a variety of aspects of personal and sexual growth. They vary in style from very personal information-sharing to more technical, academic presentations. Obviously the list is a selective one, and we view it as a good starting point. The starred (*) titles are for those readers who want only a representative selection from a particular category.

GENERAL SEX INFORMATION

This group of books offers an overview of general information on sexual behavior, sexual attitudes, and the treatment of male and female sexual problems.

*BLUMSTEIN, P., and SCHWARTZ, P. (1983). *American Couples: Money, Work, and Sex.* New York: William Morrow & Co.
> This book describes large scale studies of sexual behavior and relationships in contemporary America.

*CARRERA, M. (1981). *Sex: The Facts, the Acts, and Your Feelings.* New York: Crown Publishers.
> A very complete, easy-to-read book with a nice emphasis on overcoming misinformation and sexual myths.

*CROOKS, R., and BAUR, K. (1986). *Our Sexuality* (3rd ed.). Menlo Park, Calif.: Benjamin Cummings Publishing Co.
> This is probably the most widely used college human sexuality textbook. It is especially good in that it focuses strongly on personal growth issues.

HITE, S. (1976). *The Hite Report.* New York: Macmillan Publishing Co.
> A collection of sex histories from 3,000 women.

HUNT, M. (1974). *Sexual Behavior in the 1970s.* Chicago: Playboy Press.

KILMANN, P. R., and MILLS, K. H. (1983). *All About Sex Therapy.* New York: Plenum Press.
> Written for the general public, this book describes the work of Masters and Johnson, Kaplan, and other well-known sex therapists.

———— ❧ ————

TAVRIS, C., and SADD, S. (1977). *The Redbook Report on Female Sexuality.* New York: Dell.

SPECIAL TOPICS
Sexual Fantasy Guides

BARBACH, L. (1984). *Pleasures: Women Write Erotica.* Garden City, N.Y.: Doubleday & Co.

*FRIDAY, N. (1974). *My Secret Garden.* New York: Pocket Books.

—— (1975). *Forbidden Flowers: More Women's Sexual Fantasies.* New York: Simon & Schuster.

Menstruation, Premenstrual Syndrome (PMS), and Pregnancy

ASSO, D. (1983). *The Real Menstrual Cycle.* New York: John Wiley & Sons. A summary and critique of the research on the menstrual cycle, variables influencing it, and menopause.

BROWN, W. A. (1979). *Psychological Care During Pregnancy and the Postpartum Period.* New York: Raven Press. A summary of the psychological aspects of pregnancy, designed for health-care professionals (especially primary physicians). Very readable and clinically oriented.

*BUDOFF, P. W. (1980). *No More Menstrual Cramps and Other Good News.* New York: Penguin Books. An informative book by an obstetrician and gynecologist. Reviews PMS, dysmenorrhea, breast cancer, and hysterectomies, and how to decide on the best course of prevention and treatment.

GANNON, L. R. (1985). *Menstrual Disorders and Menopause: Biological, Psychological and Cultural Research.* New York: Praeger Publishers. A systematic review of the research literature on menstrual disorders and menopause from a multidisciplinary perspective.

SANDERS, D. (1985). *Coping with Periods.* New York: Mutual Books. Describes means of managing menstrual difficulties.

Sex, Menopause, and Aging

*CUTLER, W. B., Garcia, C. R., and Edward, D. A. (1983). *Menopause: A Guide for Women and Men Who Love Them.* New York: W. W. Norton & Co. A careful review of research on menopause and its treatment. Quite detailed and with clear explanations, sketches, and useful guidelines.

GREENWOOD, S. (1984). *Menopause Naturally: Preparing for the Second Half of Life.* San Francisco: Volcano Press.

———— ❧ ————

A Selected Annotated Bibliography

This is an interesting book about menopause symptoms and their treatment. It also considers the context of women's lives during these changes.

REITZ, R. (1977; 1979) *Menopause: A Positive Approach.* London: Univan Paperbacks; New York: Penguin Books.

SARREL, L. J., and SARREL, P. (1984). *Sexual Turning Points.* New York: Macmillan Publishing Co.
Covers what the authors identify as seven stages of adult sexual development.

*SCHOVER, L. (1984). *Prime Time: Sexual Health for Men Over Fifty.* New York: Holt, Rinehart & Winston.
An informative, readable book for men who are middle-aged or beyond. It also has good information for women, and for coping with aging in male partners.

STARR, B. D., and WEINER, M. B. (1981). *Sex and Sexuality in the Mature Years.* New York: Stein & Day Publishers.
A study of sexual adjustment in 800 older Americans, with good suggestions for adjusting to aging.

Incest

MALTZ, W., and HOLMAN, B. (1987). *Incest and Sexuality: A Guide to Understanding and Healing.* Lexington, Mass.: D. C. Heath & Co.
A self-help book to assist women who have experienced incest and may still be having repercussions.

BODY WORK

COOPER, K. H. (1985). *The New Aerobics.* New York: M. Evans.
A useful exercise guide designed to develop general and cardiovascular functioning and help maintain it throughout life.

*DOWNING, G. (1972). *The Massage Book.* New York: Random House.
Illustrated, complete guide to massage, including couple and self-massage and mention of meditation techniques.

MONTAGUE, A. (1971). *Touching: The Human Significance of the Skin.* New York: Columbia University Press.
Explores the mystery of the sense of touch.

STUART, R. B., and DAVIS, B. (1972). *Slim Chance in a Fat World: Behavioral Control of Obesity* (condensed ed.). Champaign, Ill.: Research Press.
A weight reduction program that concentrates on changing eating patterns rather than just cutting calories.

YOUNG, C. (1973). *Self-Massage.* New York: Bantam Books.
Techniques for relaxation and renewal through self-massage.

———— ❦ ————

RELIGION AND SEXUALITY

The books in this section deal with sexuality in relation to morality, Christianity, and Judaism.

BIRD, J., and BIRD, L. (1970). *The Freedom of Sexual Love*. Garden City, N.Y.: Doubleday & Co.
> For Catholics; carries the nihil obstat and imprimatur, indicating that the book is "free of doctrinal or moral error." Contains material helpful for those with concerns about sexuality and Catholic doctrine.

FELDMAN, D. (1975). *Marital Relations, Birth Control, and Abortion in Jewish Law*. New York: Schocken Books.

KOSNIK, A., CARROL, W., CUNNINGHAM, A., MODRAS, R., and SCHULTE, J. (1977). *Human Sexuality: New Directions in American Catholic Thought*. New York: Paulist Press.

NELSON, J. B. (1979). *Embodiment: An Approach to Sexuality and Christian Theology*. Minneapolis, Minn.: Augsburg.

STEINMETZ, U. G. (1972). *The Sexual Christian*. St. Meinrad, Ind.: Abbey Press.
> Discusses the man-woman relationship, marriage, and sexuality. Proposes that antisexual prohibitions are not a true part of Christian thought.

PERSONAL GROWTH

The following books address areas of self-esteem, confidence, and personal awareness. All make specific suggestions on how to go about understanding where you are and how to change.

BACH, G. R., and WYDEN, P. (1981). *The Intimate Enemy: How to Fight Fair in Love and Marriage*. New York: Avon Books.
> For those women with partners, this book discusses the value of fighting, how to benefit from fighting in constructive ways, and problems of intimacy.

*BOSTON WOMEN'S HEALTH COLLECTIVE. (1984). *The New Our Bodies, Ourselves*. New York: Simon & Schuster.
> Very informative book about the experience of being a woman. Includes anatomy and physiology, sexuality, relationships, lesbianism, rape, nutrition, birth control, pregnancy, menopause, and self-help health care.

BURNS, D. D. (1980). *Feeling Good: The New Mood Therapy*. New York: Signet.
> A useful and clear self-help book for readers with depression and low self-esteem.

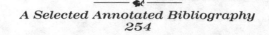

A Selected Annotated Bibliography

CAILLIET, R., and GROSS, L. (1987). *The Rejuvenation Strategy.* Garden City, N.Y.: Doubleday & Co.

    A health book discussing a wide range of resources for developing a vital life-style.

ELLIS, A., and HARPER, R. A. (1975). *A New Guide to Rational Living.* North Hollywood, Calif.: Wilshire.

    A book whose goal is the development of a rational approach to dealing with problems.

GOLEMAN, D., and BENNETT-GOLEMAN, T. (1986). *The Relaxed Body Book.* Garden City, N.Y.: Doubleday & Co.

    Discusses means of relaxation and living with a variety of modern stresses.

HALPERN, H. M. (1975). *Cutting Loose: An Adult Guide to Coming to Terms With Your Parents.* New York: Bantam Books.

    This book may help readers to reexamining which of their beliefs and values are really their own, and which they no longer need.

O'NEILL, N., and O'NEILL, G. (1974). *Shifting Gears.* New York: Avon Books.

    Deals with life crises usually associated with the middle years, such as divorce, death, job loss, changing life-styles.

*RUSH, A.K. (1973). *Getting Clear.* New York: Random House.

    A book for women on becoming more physically, emotionally, and intellectually self-aware. Written in a warm, personal style, with numerous exercises. Topics covered include body awareness, massage, sex roles, communication, abortion, childbirth, meditation, and consciousness-raising.

WITKIN-LANOIL, G. (1984). *The Female Stress Syndrome: How to Recognize and Live with It.* New York: New Market Press.

    A guide for identifying and dealing with stress and psychological strain in daily lives of modern women.

OTHER SEXUAL GROWTH AND SELF-HELP BOOKS

These books are more personal than the books listed above under "General Sex Information" or "Personal Growth." As such, they may be useful for further exploration of attitude change, sexual technique, and special problems.

BERGER, R., and BERGER, D. (1987). *Biopotency: A Guide to Sexual Success.* Emmaus, Pa.: Rodale.

    A self-help book for men with erection problems and an evaluation of treatment alternatives.

CAMERON-BANDLER, L. (1985). *Solutions: Practical and Effective Antidotes for Sexual and Relationship Problems.* San Rafael, Calif.: Future Pace.

A self-help book that uses a new system of psychotherapy called "neuro-linguistic programming."

*COMFORT, A. (1972). *The Joy of Sex.* New York: Crown Publishers.

COMFORT, A. (1974). *More Joy.* New York: Crown Publishers.

These best-sellers are an "advanced course" in lovemaking techniques.

GILLESPIE, L. (1986). *You Don't Have to Live With Cystitis.* New York: Rawson.

Written by a physician, this book offers a lot of practical information on managing cystitis and related problems.

*HASTINGS, D. W. (1972). *A Doctor Speaks on Sexual Expression in Marriage.* (2nd ed.) New York: Bantam Books.

Covers both anatomy and physiology as well as sexual techniques, dysfunctions, and so forth.

*McCARTHY, B., and McCARTHY, E. (1984). *Sexual Awareness: Enhancing Sexual Pleasure.* New York: Carrol and Graf.

A good book on sexual growth for both men and women.

MESHORER, M., and MESHORER, J. (1986). *Ultimate Pleasure: The Secrets of Easily Orgasmic Women.* New York: St. Martins Press.

A study of sixty women with exceptionally good sex lives.

*ZILBERGELD, B. (1978). *Male Sexuality.* New York: Bantam Books.

Self-help for common men's problems and a good section on sexual myths and fallacies.

BOOKS FOR PROFESSIONALS

These books are recommended for therapists and other professionals who work with clients who have sexual problems or concerns.

ARENTEWICZ, G., and SCHMIDT, G. (Eds.). (1983). *The Treatment of Sexual Disorders: Concepts and Techniques of Couple Therapy.* New York: Basic Books.

From Europe, a thorough and thoughtful perspective on the theory, meanings, and treatment of sexual problems.

CUTLER, W. B., and GARCIA, C. R. (1984). *The Medical Management of Menopause and Premenopause: Their Endocrinological Basis.* Philadelphia: J. B. Lippincott Co.

Review of literature on menopausal transition and treatment. Popular summary available in Cutler, Garcia, and Edwards' book listed under sex, menopause, and aging.

MASTERS, W. H., and JOHNSON, V. E. (1966). *Human Sexual Response.* Boston: Little, Brown & Co.

The classic work on the anatomy and physiology of the sexual response cycle.

———. (1970). *Human Sexual Inadequacy.* Boston: Little, Brown & Co.
  Describes the basic treatment approach for sexual dysfunctions in
  males and females.
KAPLAN, H. S. (1974). *The New Sex Therapy.* New York: Brunner/Mazel.
  Kaplan's therapy program adds some modifications to the Masters-
  Johnson format, including a discussion of psychoanalytic concepts in
  relation to sex therapy.
OFFIT, A. (1981). *Night Thoughts: Reflections of a Sex Therapist.* New York:
  Congdon and Lattes.
  An interesting critique and commentary on practicing and understand-
  ing therapy for sexual problems.

The following five books are general scholarly readings on sexuality
and sex therapy:

BANCROFT, J. (1983). *Human Sexuality and Its Problems.* New York:
  Churchill-Livingston.
GEER, J., HEIMAN, J., and LEITENBERG, H. (1984). *Human Sexuality.* Engle-
  wood Cliffs, N.J.: Prentice-Hall.
KAPLAN, H. S. *The Evaluation of Sexual Disorders.* (1983). New York:
  Brunner/Mazel.
LEIBLUM, S., and PERVIN, L. (Eds.). (1980). *Principles and Practice of Sex
  Therapy.* New York: Plenum Press.
LOPICCOLO, J., and LOPICCOLO, L. (Eds.). (1978). *Handbook of Sex Therapy.*
  New York: Plenum Press.

Professionals who work in the area of sexuality may also wish to
subscribe to these professional journals:

Archives of Sexual Behavior (bimonthly), Plenum Press, New York.
Journal of Sex and Marital Therapy (quarterly), Brunner/Mazel, New
  York.
Journal of Sex Research (quarterly), Society for Scientific Study of Sex,
  Philadelphia.

The following journal articles and book chapters are relevant to the
particular program described in this book:

HEIMAN, J. R., and LOPICCOLO, J. (1983). "Clinical Outcome of Sex Therapy:
  Effectiveness of Daily versus Weekly Treatment." *Archives of General
  Psychiatry, 40,* pp. 443–449.
LOBITZ, C., and LOPICCOLO, J. (1972). "New Methods in Behavioral Treatment
  of Sexual Dysfunction." *Journal of Behavior Therapy and Experimen-
  tal Psychiatry, 3,* pp. 265–271.
LOPICCOLO, J., and FRIEDMAN, J. M. (1985). "Sex Therapy: An Integrative
  Model." In S. J. Lynn and J.P. Garske (Eds.), *Contemporary Psychother-
  apies: Models and Methods.* New York: Charles E. Merrill Co.

LOPICCOLO, J., HEIMAN, J. R., HOGAN, D. R., and ROBERTS, C. W. (1985). "Effectiveness of Single Therapist versus Co-Therapy Teams in Sex Therapy." *Journal of Consulting and Clinical Psychology, 53*(3), pp. 287–294.

LOPICCOLO, J., and LOBITZ, C. (1972). "The Role of Masturbation in the Treatment of Sexual Dysfunction." *Archives of Sexual Behavior, 2*, pp. 163–171.

MOROKOFF, P. J., and LOPICCOLO, J. (1982). "Self-Management in the Treatment of Sexual Dysfunction." In P. Karoly and F. Kanfer (Eds.), *Self-Management and Behavior Change.* New York: Pergamon Press.

———. (1986). "A Comparative Evaluation of Minimal Therapist Contact and Fifteen-Session Treatment for Female Orgasmic Dysfunction." *Journal of Consulting and Clinical Psychology, 54*(3), pp. 295–300.

There is a film series (three films), also titled *Becoming Orgasmic,* designed for women using this book. The film is available from Focus International, Inc., 14 Oregon Drive, Huntington Station, New York, NY 11746, (516) 549–5320. The films are also available in videotape for office or at-home use.

Index

Menopause, 138–144
  complexity of, 138
  cultural meaning of, 141
  decrease in estrogen in, 139
  freedom from contraception in,
      238
  keeping healthy in, 142–144
  psychological changes and, 141
  reproductive system changes
      during, 138–139
  sexual activity after, 139
Menstrual cramps, *see*
      Dysmenorrhea
Menstrual cycle
  changes in sexual desire and, 154
  important changes during, 120
  sexuality and, 123
  and woman's sexual response,
      99–100
Menstrual flow, 120
Menstruation, 18, 118–130; *see also*
      Premenstrual syndrome
      (PMS)
  beginning months of, 118–120
  irregular cycles, 121–122
  monthly cycle, 120–121
  sexual response and medication
      for, 130
  sexuality and menstrual cycle,
      123
Monogamy, 225
Mons, 34
Multiple orgasm, 99
Muscle control exercises, 48–50
My Secret Garden, 78, 80, 185

Nutrition
  in menopause, 143–144
  and PMS, 124–125

Open marriage, 225
Oral contraceptives, 161, 162
  sexual desire and, 154
  in sexual response, 100
Oral sex, 224, 228, 229–232
Oral stimulation
  mutual or "sixty-nine," 231
  positions for, 231
  resulting in orgasm, 231
  to women, 230
Orgasm, 98–99
  changes in body during, 90
  changing positions to achieve,
      107
  clitoris in, 98

fears about, 90–92
ideas and expectations about, 115
inability to experience, 3
during intercourse, 196–201
  "fading" procedure for,
      198–199
  incidence of, 197
  pressure to have, 188–189
  rapid switching technique for,
      199–201
  techniques for, 198–201
lack of need for, 97
from masturbation, 56
multiple orgasm, 99
as part of sexual growth, 1–2
penis in, role of, 98
physical responses in, 92–99
simultaneous orgasm, 196
"triggers" for, 106–108, 194–195
worry about, 93
vaginal stimulation in, 98
vibrators in, 110
Osteoporosis, 105, 140, 143, 144
Ovariectomies, 105
Ovulation, 120
Ovum, 120

Pap smear, 7
Partner, *see* Sexual partner
Pelvic inflammatory disease (PID),
      129
Penis
  insertion of, 193, 201
  role of, in orgasm, 98
  size of, 192, 193
Perineum, 36
Personal sex history, 18, 19–26
  self-inquiry, 19–22
  self-reflection, 22–25
Physicians, selecting, 130–131
Pleasure, discovering, 58–60
Pleasuring each other, 167–186
  accepting each other's sexual
      desires and needs, 186
  expectations, 167–168
  fears and worries about, 182–184
  how to begin, 170–184
  positions, 171–172
  things to think about and talk
      over, 172–184
  verbal and nonverbal
      communication, 168–170
PMS, *see* Premenstrual syndrome
Pornography, as term, 81; *see also*
      Erotic literature, Erotica

About the Authors

JULIA R. HEIMAN, Ph.D., is currently associate professor of psychiatry and behavioral sciences at the University of Washington Medical School in Seattle. She is also director of the Interpersonal Psychotherapy Clinic and the Reproductive and Sexual Medicine Clinic. Dr. Heiman has published a wide variety of research and clinical articles on sexual issues, including a textbook, *Human Sexuality* (coauthored with J. Geer and H. Leitenberg). She is particularly known for her work on sexual arousal patterns and female sexuality. Dr. Heiman is past president of the International Academy of Sex Research and the American Board of Family Psychology, where she is a diplomat in marital and sex therapy.

JOSEPH LoPICCOLO, Ph.D., is currently professor and chairman of the department of psychology at the University of Missouri. He has a distinguished career in the field of sex therapy and sex research, including numerous chapters and articles as well as the *Handbook of Sex Therapy* (coedited with L. LoPiccolo), widely acclaimed as one of the standard references in the field. He founded and directed the Sex Therapy Center at the State University of New York at Stony Brook, where he and Dr. Heiman originally worked together. He is a fellow of the American Psychological Association and past president of the Society for the Scientific Study of Sex and continues to give lectures and workshops throughout the international community.

Let Us Know

We would like to hear from you regarding your opinion of this book and whether or not you found it of value. You do not need to identify yourself by name, so please be as frank as possible.

General questions

1. Your age _____
2. Your sex _____
3. State you live in _____
4. City or town _____
5. Income of your household _____
6. Are you married now? No Yes   (no. of years married _____)
7. Are you living with a sexual partner now?   No   Yes
   (no. of years together _____)
8. Have you been married previously?   No   Yes
   (total no. of years previously married _____)
9. Do you have children?   No   Yes
   (no. biological children _____   no. adopted/step-children _____)
10. What kind of work do you do (include homemaking)? _____
11. How many hours/week do you work? _____
12. Are you paid for your work? _____

How satisfied are you currently with the following areas of your life?
(Circle the answer that best describes you.)

	Not at all	Somewhat	Very	Extremely
13. Relationship/marriage	1	2	3	4
14. Work	1	2	3	4
15. Family	1	2	3	4
16. Friends	1	2	3	4
17. Other (specify) _____	1	2	3	4

About this book (circle the appropriate answers)

18. Did you read this book? No 10% 25% 50% 75% over 90%
19. Did you try some of the
    suggestions?   No 10% 25% 50% 75% over 90%

20. Did you find the book useful?

	Not at all	Somewhat	Very	Extremely
	1	2	3	4

Why or why not? _____

_____

21. Have you seen a therapist or doctor about a sexual problem or concern?   Yes   No

22. Have you ever become sexually involved with someone outside your marital or committed relationship?   Yes   No

About your sexuality, please answer each question twice, once for before you read this book and once for afterward. Please respond, even if you only read part of the book or if you did not change as much as you wished. Circle a B for BEFORE reading the book and an A for AFTER reading the book next to the answer that best describes you.

23. How frequently do you and your mate have sexual intercourse or activity?

    (1)   B   A   Once a day or more
    (2)   B   A   2 to 4 times a week
    (3)   B   A   Once a week to once every 2 weeks
    (4)   B   A   Once a month or less
    (5)   B   A   Not at all

24. How frequently would you like to have sexual intercourse or activity?

    (1)   B   A   Once a day or more
    (2)   B   A   2 to 4 times a week
    (3)   B   A   Once a week to once every 2 weeks
    (4)   B   A   Once a month or less
    (5)   B   A   Not at all

25. How frequently do you feel sexual desire? This feeling may include wanting to have sex, planning to have sex, feeling frustrated due to a lack of sex, etc.

    (1)   B   A   Once a day or more
    (2)   B   A   2 to 4 times a week
    (3)   B   A   Once a week to once every 2 weeks
    (4)   B   A   Once a month or less
    (5)   B   A   Not at all

26. How often do you masturbate?

    (1)   B   A   Once a day or more
    (2)   B   A   2 to 4 times a week
    (3)   B   A   Once a week to once every 2 weeks
    (4)   B   A   Once a month or less
    (5)   B   A   Not at all

27. How long does intercourse usually last, from entry of the penis until the male reaches orgasm (climax)?

(1)	B	A	Less than 1 minute
(2)	B	A	1 to 2 minutes
(3)	B	A	2 to 4 minutes
(4)	B	A	4 to 7 minutes
(5)	B	A	7 to 10 minutes
(6)	B	A	11 to 15 minutes
(7)	B	A	15 to 20 minutes
(8)	B	A	20 to 30 minutes
(9)	B	A	More than 30 minutes

28. Overall, how satisfactory to you is your sexual relationship with your mate?

(1)	B	A	Extremely unsatisfactory
(2)	B	A	Moderately unsatisfactory
(3)	B	A	Slightly unsatisfactory
(4)	B	A	Somewhat satisfactory
(5)	B	A	Moderately satisfactory
(6)	B	A	Extremely satisfactory

29. Overall, how satisfactory do you think your sexual relationship is to your mate?

(1)	B	A	Extremely unsatisfactory
(2)	B	A	Moderately unsatisfactory
(3)	B	A	Slightly unsatisfactory
(4)	B	A	Somewhat satisfactory
(5)	B	A	Moderately satisfactory
(6)	B	A	Extremely satisfactory

30. Who usually initiates sexual intercourse or activity?

(1)	B	A	I always do
(2)	B	A	I usually do
(3)	B	A	My mate and I each initiate about equally often
(4)	B	A	My mate usually does
(5)	B	A	My mate always does

31. When your mate makes sexual advances, how do you usually respond?

(1)	B	A	Usually accept with pleasure
(2)	B	A	Accept reluctantly
(3)	B	A	Often refuse
(4)	B	A	Usually refuse

32. If you try, is it possible to reach orgasm through masturbation?
    - (1)   B   A   Nearly always, over 90% of the time
    - (2)   B   A   Usually, about 75% of the time
    - (3)   B   A   Sometimes, about 50% of the time
    - (4)   B   A   Seldom, about 25% of the time
    - (5)   B   A   Never
    - (6)   B   A   Have never tried

33. If you try, is it possible to reach orgasm through having your genitals caressed by your mate?
    - (1)   B   A   Nearly always, over 90% of the time
    - (2)   B   A   Usually, about 75% of the time
    - (3)   B   A   Sometimes, about 50% of the time
    - (4)   B   A   Seldom, about 25% of the time
    - (5)   B   A   Never
    - (6)   B   A   Have never tried

34. If you try, is it possible to reach orgasm through sexual intercourse?
    - (1)   B   A   Nearly always, over 90% of the time
    - (2)   B   A   Usually, about 75% of the time
    - (3)   B   A   Sometimes, about 50% of the time
    - (4)   B   A   Seldom, about 25% of the time
    - (5)   B   A   Never
    - (6)   B   A   Have never tried

35. Can you reach orgasm through stimulation of your genitals by an electric vibrator or any other means such as running water, rubbing with some object, and so on?
    - (1)   B   A   Nearly always, over 90% of the time
    - (2)   B   A   Usually, about 75% of the time
    - (3)   B   A   Sometimes, about 50% of the time
    - (4)   B   A   Seldom, about 25% of the time
    - (5)   B   A   Never
    - (6)   B   A   Have never tried

36. Can you reach orgasm during sexual intercourse if at the same time your genitals are being caressed (by yourself or your mate or with a vibrator, etc.)?
    - (1)   B   A   Nearly always, over 90% of the time
    - (2)   B   A   Usually, about 75% of the time
    - (3)   B   A   Sometimes, about 50% of the time
    - (4)   B   A   Seldom, about 25% of the time
    - (5)   B   A   Never
    - (6)   B   A   Have never tried

37. When you have sex with your mate, including foreplay and intercourse, do you notice some of these things happening: Your breathing and pulse speeding up, wetness in your vagina, pleasurable sensations in your breasts and genitals?

    (1)   B   A   Nearly always, over 90% of the time
    (2)   B   A   Usually, about 75% of the time
    (3)   B   A   Sometimes, about 50% of the time
    (4)   B   A   Seldom, about 25% of the time
    (5)   B   A   Never

38. Is your vagina so "dry" or "tight" that intercourse cannot occur?

    (1)   B   A   Never
    (2)   B   A   Rarely, less than 10% of the time
    (3)   B   A   Seldom, less than 25% of the time
    (4)   B   A   Sometimes, 50% of the time
    (5)   B   A   Usually, 75% of the time
    (6)   B   A   Nearly always, over 90% of the time

39. Do you feel pain in your genitals during sexual intercourse?

    (1)   B   A   Never
    (2)   B   A   Rarely, less than 10% of the time
    (3)   B   A   Seldom, less than 25% of the time
    (4)   B   A   Sometimes, 50% of the time
    (5)   B   A   Usually, 75% of the time
    (6)   B   A   Nearly always, over 90% of the time

40. When you have sex with your mate, do you feel sexually aroused?

    (1)   B   A   Nearly always, over 90% of the time
    (2)   D   A   Usually, about 75% of the time
    (3)   B   A   Sometimes, about 50% of the time
    (4)   B   A   Seldom, about 25% of the time
    (5)   B   A   Never

41. Does the male have any trouble getting an erection before intercourse begins?

    (1)   B   A   Never
    (2)   B   A   Rarely, less than 10% of the time
    (3)   B   A   Seldom, less than 25% of the time
    (4)   B   A   Sometimes, 50% of the time
    (5)   B   A   Usually, 75% of the time
    (6)   B   A   Nearly always, over 90% of the time

42. Does the male have any trouble keeping an erection, once intercourse has begun?

(1)	B	A	Never
(2)	B	A	Rarely, less than 10% of the time
(3)	B	A	Seldom, less than 25% of the time
(4)	B	A	Sometimes, 50% of the time
(5)	B	A	Usually, 75% of the time
(6)	B	A	Nearly always, over 90% of the time

43. Do you have any other comments, or is there anything else you think is important for us to know?

_____

_____

_____

_____

Please tear out this questionnaire and mail it to:

Julia R. Heiman, Ph.D.
University of Washington Medical School
Harborview CMHC
326 Ninth Avenue
Seattle, WA 98104